Elephant Gold

Elephant Gold

P. D. STRACEY

NATRAJ PUBLISHERS

DEHRA DUN

FIRST PUBLISHED 1963
FIRST INDIAN EDITION 1991

© *P.D. STRACEY*

To the memory of

A. J. W. MILROY, I.F.S.

Published by Upendra Arora for Natraj Publishers, Dehra Dun
& Printed at Gayatri Offset Press, New Delhi

CONTENTS

ILLUSTRATIONS

Map showing distribution of Asiatic Elephants

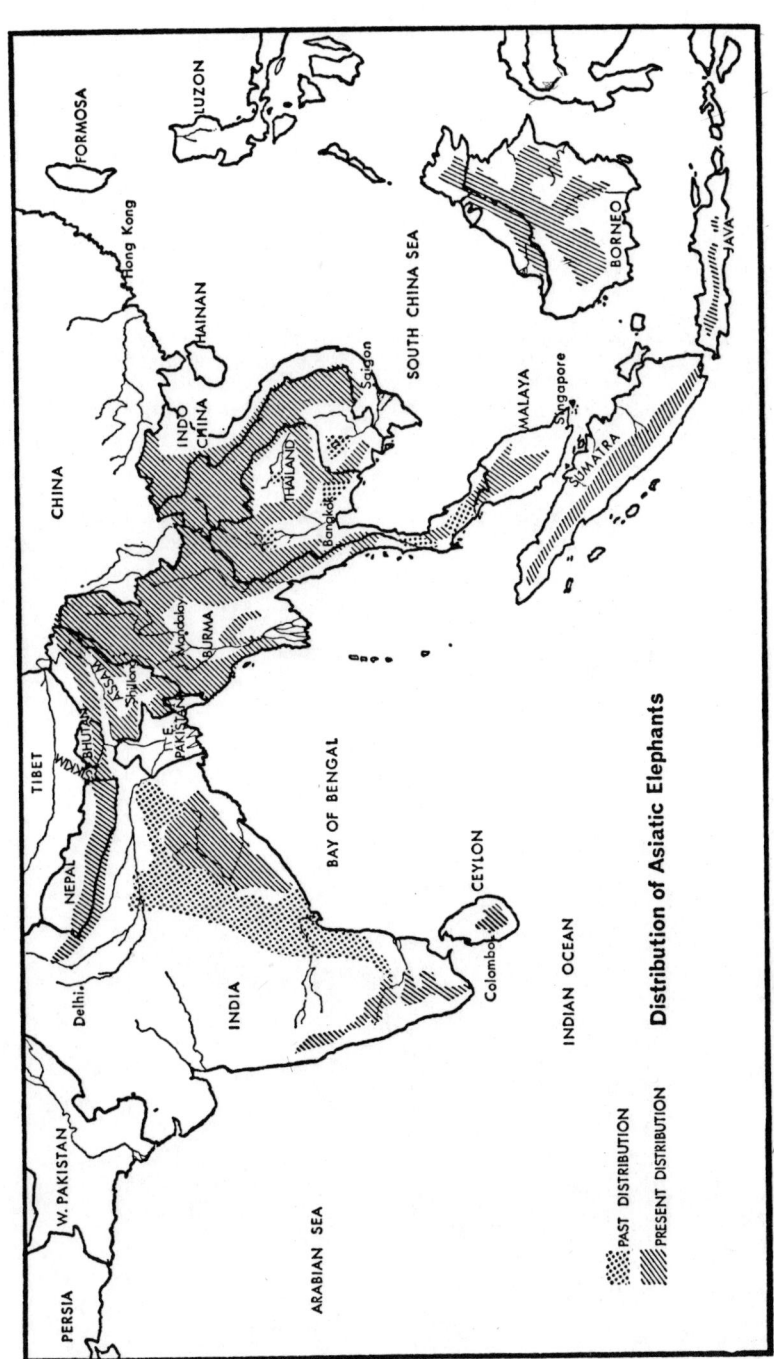

Distribution of Asiatic Elephants

PAST DISTRIBUTION

PRESENT DISTRIBUTION

CHAPTER 1

A STOCKADE OFFICER'S LIFE

I began my career as an elephant catcher for the Assam Forest Department in the North Cachar Hills; but it was during my brief spell at the training depot that I first became intimately acquainted with elephants and it was there that I got the feel of my new assignment.

The depot was conveniently situated at railhead to receive captures brought out of the hills along the three or four marching routes. Always there was a fascinating and ever-changing kaleidoscope of elephants: elephants domesticated and wild, elephants fresh from the forest and elephants worn out with the strain of capture and training; elephants young, brisk and impetuous; elephants old, ponderous and bored. Everywhere there were elephants, forming a moving frieze and background to the groups of puny men who went about their tasks among them, beating and scolding, cajoling and caressing, bathing and feeding, in the inescapable daily routine of training.

Carts loaded with rice straw or firewood rattled along the dusty tracks, passed by silently padding elephants carrying loads of fodder. Side by side with elephants being bathed in the river, shapely girls discreetly manipulated their single thin cotton cloth to hide their bodies from the sly glances of the men. The whole countryside seemed to be alive with elephants and elephant men and the villagers had come to recognize them as a temporary part of their lives and to accept them as an unavoidable necessity during the cold weather season.

After a month of this idyllic life, I received my orders of transfer to the current khedda operations – the driving of elephants into stockades. The country of the North Cachar Hills is rugged, with bamboo forests full of elephants and buffalo. The hilltops were inhabited by the Dimasa Cacharis and there were a few isolated villages of those virile people the Kukis, the scourge of other tribes and feared even by their warlike neighbours the Nagas. I soon settled down in a grass hut near the railway station of Hathikhali, gateway to the stockade country.

The railway linking the Brahmaputra and the Surma valleys had been built at the turn of the century at great cost and toll of human life; today it holds the passenger spellbound with its succession of spectacular bridges, tunnels and curves. By tradition, the khedda staff were permitted to take a free ride on any goods train passing over the route, which happened twice a day. This privilege was greatly valued in an area devoïd of roads, where the only paths were the narrow village trails and the broad elephant tracks. Just before I arrived, a train had run into a herd of elephants in a narrow cutting and was derailed. Even more harrowing for the guard who told me the story, he was penned in the brake van into which an elephant's trunk kept intruding: the animal could go neither forward nor backward nor turn about, pinned as it was between the toppled wagon and the steep side of the cutting!

On my visits to the stockades, I used to walk along the well-trodden paths used by elephant catchers, but made originally by the herds they were trying to trap. At first one or two men used to accompany me, but as soon as I learnt the geography of the country and got my bearings I preferred to go alone with a bottle of beer and some sandwiches, walking the eight or ten miles which separated my camp from the stockades. When I had to sleep the night out my orderly, a Mikir who knew a few words of Hindi, would walk behind me with his conical basket on his back containing my bedding and a change of clothes, with a few tins of food and cooking utensils. Sometimes I had to depend on the stockade men for a bed and I soon got used to sitting with them round the fires, eating rice with my fingers. Later I would turn in under the lean-to shelters, with the front open wide to the night dew and only a raw silk sheet to cover me. I got used to sleeping in my clothes and having a sketchy wash in a stream before setting out with the men in the early mornings, examining tracks for signs of elephants and casting round for the noises which generally betray their presence.

I suppose my early wanderings on elephant back, and the earnestness with which I pursued the search for knowledge of everything elephantine, laid the foundations of the association with the government elephants and their mahouts, my 'koonkis' or trained elephants and their attendants, which was to prove so valuable to me. I was told early on that any self-respecting shikari should be able to get on and off an elephant's back without making it sit down and I soon learnt to climb up with the aid of the ears and trunk, and to slide off assisted by the front foot or down the tail. I could drive an elephant as well as any mahout, with my stockinged feet behind the ears. I learnt the signs an elephant gives and so was always prepared for their reactions to different situations and different animals. And of course I learnt Assamese as it is spoken by elephant men, with all the slang and colourful idiom of which they are capable.

Khedda days and nights were always pervaded with an expectancy that kept one on the alert. Many a night I was disturbed by a stockade man or messenger bringing news of a catch with the words 'Hathi porise!', the elephants have fallen. Sleep would be forgotten and the man closely questioned as to the number of the catch and the sizes of the elephants, after which plans would be made for sending reinforcements of koonkis if necessary. The news of a catch would soon spread in the camp – in fact there was always talk of herds or of impending catches in the neighbourhood of stockades. The Assamese catchers simply could not keep a secret of this nature to themselves and sometimes just before an auction a man would let slip the news that there was another catch in the stockade or on the way to the depot and bang would go our chances of getting decent prices for the elephants on hand. Although we took great trouble to conceal the news of a catch until its arrival at the training depot, invariably the information would leak out somehow.

Our usual time for auctions was the late afternoon, and if a catch arrived in the morning, we would try to keep the koonkis with their charges in some convenient patch of jungle at a distance from the camp until it was time to sell. We found that quick selling, starting immediately after the elephants had been brought into the depot, was the best procedure to circumvent the ringing of auctions. There was always the trouble-maker in our midst; everything would be plain sailing when suddenly pretended indifference and sluggish bidding would indicate his presence. At the worst we would suspend the auction and revert to sale by private negotiation. In those days we were practically giving large elephants away, mainly to local Assamese purchasers. Big tuskless males were fetching the ridiculously low price of three to four hundred rupees (thirty pounds) and even the most sought-after kind of elephant, a young female, fetched only about fifteen hundred rupees (a hundred and twenty pounds).

I went to Assam as a keen and impetuous young man with an open mind, eager to absorb all that I met with in a part of India which, even in 1930, was not yet fully opened up. Assam was a wonderful country for one who was not keen on city life and I took readily to the rather free and adventurous atmosphere of a little-known frontier province. When I had to retire after thirty years with the Indian Forest Service, I never regretted having chosen my profession or the country in which I worked.

I was a typical product of British-Indian stock and Western upbringing – an Anglo-Indian or Eurasian, as a person of mixed descent is known in India and farther east. On both my father's and mother's side I came from 'John Company' times and my blood was compounded of many strains – British, French, Portuguese, Dutch and Indian. My community had evolved as a distinct entity among the many races of India and came to occupy a particular little niche, in which traditions and respectability of a smug British pattern kept us aloof from the country in which we lived and earned our bread. We had once been of great service to the conquerors of India in building up the various strata of administration, at a time when it was impossible to find enough people for the jobs which called for toughness and enterprise; but latterly we had fallen on evil days. Still, we were the second line of British power, always at call to suppress civil disorder and to prop up authority during the period of India's struggle for independence. We were 'little Britishers', largely unconscious of the anomaly of our position and completely unaware of the indifference with which we were treated by the European on the one side and the Indian on the other, although no doubt in the eyes of the world a tragic product of British rule in India.

Our family had a long and proud record of service with the Government and we would have continued to be Government employees of a secondary status if we had not been fortunate enough to have a father and mother both blessed with some vision of the future. They made great sacrifices to secure higher education for their children and I think we justified their selflessness. I had set my heart on becoming a Forest Officer like my father and dared to aspire to the Indian Forest Service; I competed in the all-India competitive examination and was successful. After two years training at Dehra Dun, I was posted to Assam – one of the least-known parts of India until the Second World War brought it into prominence. Physically and temperamentally I was probably more suited to this wild and difficult country than some of the others who went to serve there and I never regretted it except from the domestic point of view.

Admittedly I was lonely in the early years and missed the 'flock' safety of my community, of whom there were very few in that part of India. But my natural receptiveness and candour prevented me from making the mistake of remaining aloof from both British and Indians. In my adolescent years I always tried to bridge the gulf between my people and Indians; although I was woefully ignorant of Indian history and culture, and completely outside the stream of politics and national aspirations that tinged the average Indian's outlook, I instinctively took my place as an Indian and a product of that country. At the same time I had no reservations with Europeans. I got on well with most people, perhaps mainly because I saw the other person's point of view and made allowances for it and I could be a dispassionate critic of all communities, including my own. I think that what helped me most in the early days in Assam was the feeling that I was an ambassador for my race.

All along it was a process of growing up, of shedding many of the inherited and imposed psychoses of a person of mixed blood in a British overseas possession where the sons are denied the places of their fathers, until finally I became free in a free India. In the midst of an active personal life I was only dimly aware of the political and social changes which were going on around me, a process which was accelerated by the war that ended when I was half way through my service. British rule in India came to an end when I was at an age which still allowed for adjustment of outlook and, although it gave me an unexpected advancement in my career, it also provided the sternest test I had yet had to meet. My experiences as a hunter were confined to that golden period of a man's life when his muscles and reflexes are still perfect and his thirst for experience unquenchable; it was lucky for me that it coincided with the twilight period of British rule in India, for after that we were far too busy.

There were still comparatively few Indian officers in the higher ranks of service when I first went to Assam and hardly any Indian tea planters with the British companies except a few who had been promoted. The gulf between Indians and Europeans was great and few of the former were ever seen in the social milieus where they now predominate. The different clubs saw to that. People like me moved mostly in closed circles of their own or 'got by'. I did neither. I was saved by my natural liking for the outdoors and my sporting reputation, while the state of my finances always kept me on a tight rein where social life was concerned. Yet my outlook was almost entirely Western and my heart exclusively British. The abdication of King Edward VIII, or the Prince of Wales as we continued to call him, shook my little world of English thought and tradition. I married someone who, though Indian in origin like myself, was entirely British in outlook and if she had survived the war, I might today be one of the many expatriates which India sent to England.

Soon after arriving from the Forestry Training Institute at Dehra Dun I met A. J. W. Milroy, head of the Forest Department; it was a meeting which influenced my whole career. His reputation as a keen forester and strict disciplinarian had seeped through to the division at the bottom of the Brahmaputra valley adjoining Bengal to which I had been posted and it was with some trepidation that I watched the preparations to receive him. My immediate superior, the Divisional Forest Officer, was away somewhere on personal business and it fell to me to do the honours.

The day before the Conservator's arrival, I went out with the Ranger's gun to get something for the pot. After much stalking and dodging about on the edge of the villages I managed to bag a peafowl, which I sent proudly to the camp kitchen. Imagine my consternation when almost the first words Milroy greeted me with were 'Didn't you know that peahens are protected?' and he proceeded to lecture me on the inexcusability of even a new man being ignorant of the rules. The very next morning I was shocked to witness Milroy himself shooting a jungle fowl on the ground, to my mind an unthinkable thing to do – but jungle fowl were not protected. Nothing could have been a more effective demonstration of the combination of the idealistic and the practical in his nature with regard to wild life and I learnt the lesson.

But he was all geniality when, over dinner, he told me he was looking for a successor to the officer in charge of elephant catching and asked me if I would like to join kheddas. When the meal was cleared away, the old Forest Officer launched into a description of a khedda drive, using the salt cellars and sundry cutlery to demonstrate the position of the stockade, the wing walls, the elephants and the drivers. When I jumped at the offer I did not realize that I was embarking on a part of my career which was to give me many happy years and a knowledge of the Indian elephant which was to develop into a lifelong interest. By the time we said good night I was already fired with the exciting prospect of a khedda officer's life.

For the first five years of my service I remained on khedda duty which occupied my time for some nine months of the year during the cold weather and dry seasons. In the rains, I would be posted to a range or divisional headquarters to learn the routine duties of a Forest Officer and to pass my departmental exams. This period would be spent in considerable impatience waiting for the approach of the Durga Puja season which marked the virtual end of the monsoon in Assam, a festival which carried with it the magic promise of winter and the beginning of activities in the forest once again. Then I would be off to join yet another khedda operation with its free and exciting life in tents or grass huts, close to elephants and elephant men.

It was a life which suited my tastes and temperament to perfection and my occasional contacts with local society at a planters' club, or my visits to district headquarters to collect stocks of medicines for the depot, or gunpowder and caps for the stockade guns, merely made me appreciate the jungle more. One Christmas my brother brought my future wife to stay with me and two of my brothers were there as well; we had a wonderful time visiting the stockades to see captured elephants being removed, or shooting pigeon and jungle fowl. We had a fine set of huts, double walled with grass to keep out the cold and with an open verandah fitted with screens which could be lowered at night. Inside we sat round a fire burning on the earth floor, enjoying the noises and smells of the training depot adjoining our camp. Sometimes we would spend the nights out, sleeping in shelters vacated for us by the stockade men. Those were wonderful days, with the Assam winter at its best in the dry valley between the Naga and Nikir Hills where that particular khedda was being conducted.

One of the things I most enjoyed in my life as a stockade officer was walking back to camp in the dusk, when the forest was full of strange noises and imaginary encounters. On one such trip, soon after I joined my first khedda, I had taken the wrong route and had gone quite a distance into strange surroundings when I was frightened out of my wits by an eerie whooping sound. I had never heard anything like it and for a few seconds I stood on the path wondering what kind of strange and dangerous animal could be making this noise. Creeping forward cautiously, I traced the cries to the tops of some large trees; perched in the branches were some black and cinnamon-brown gibbons. I later made a closer acquaintance with these apes and found them to be the most friendly and delightful of pets. Another time I was thoroughly frightened by a tremendous stampeding in the undergrowth, the noise seeming to retreat and then come towards me. After a time I ventured slowly forward and made out the black and tan bodies of a large herd of gaur (*Bos frontalis gaurus*) which, after their first wild rush, were standing silent in an attempt to locate the danger. It was my first glimpse of these beautiful and impressive wild cattle, which have now been so ravaged by successive attacks of rinderpest that their numbers are sadly depleted in hills which were once teeming with them.

In my early years I was keen on shooting, no doubt encouraged by my experiences in the forests of southern India with my father who was a Forest Officer like myself. I liked nothing better than to pore over a gun merchant's catalogue before going to bed, ticking off and underlining the weapons which took my fancy but for which I never had the money. My first tiger was killed with a shotgun I borrowed from the local village headman. It was, of course, a piece of youthful foolishness, but in fact it was also a calculated risk. I decided that the tiger could only come out of the dense cane jungle by one path and it could not approach me from the rear because of an expanse of water. As there was no tree in which to tie a machan, I sat on the ground and waited. The tiger duly came out along the path and I shot it, though it nearly turned the tables on us through the inefficiency of my shooting and the unexpected reactions of my companion.

I suppose like any other hunter I had to slake my blood lust before settling down, but looking back it is surprising how little one shot in spite of much expenditure of energy. I passed many nights on borrowed elephants and I loved the magic of the ghostly moonlight, padding silently through cane breaks and trees, even though I brought little back. I was the only one of my generation of Forest Officers in Assam who did any real shooting, though in my senior age-group there was a man named Louis de la Nougerede who in his time had been the Nimrod of Assam. I was told amazing tales of his shooting abilities and I believe his must be the all-time record of five tigers bagged in fifteen minutes.

Early in my service I acquired a second-hand Chevrolet tourer, the ideal car for the Forest Officer and tea-planter. When the war broke out and petrol rationing was introduced it did not worry me too much, for I mixed kerosene oil with petrol and in spite of it the car used to go. By that time it was minus the hood and with a set of mudguards that flapped like wings. I used to keep it at my forest bungalow parked on a raised ramp and if going backwards down the ramp failed to start it, all I had to do was to send for one of my elephants and a long rope; the colony got quite used to see-ing me being towed by Mohan Prasad or John Bahadur.

One morning I was driving from Gauhati along the north bank to a meeting place where I was to register and issue licences to my trained koonkis before they started out on mela shikar, the method of noosing wild elephants from the backs of tame ones. I did not know it, but the road had been breached in places by late rains and floods. I had to fight my way over improvised crossings, shang-haiing the local villagers and PWD officials to get me through. If I had turned back I would have had to cross the Brahmaputra and recross it again farther up and it would have cost me two days and two hundred miles of motoring. At last I got through all the floods; it was well after dusk and I was haring along the last stretch of road when I suddenly shot off into the high grass at the side. It was impossible to get out unaided and, leaving my bearer with my dog Butcha, I set out along the road for help. After a time I met some road labourers returning from work who told me there was a planter in the neighbourhood. When I reached his house I was all out. Fortified by a drink and some tinned sausages, we returned to the spot where I had left the car. Here I found the bearer clutching a lantern and walking up and down the road with the dog on his shoulder because, he said, a leopard had been demonstrating in the jungle nearby. He was quite unconscious of the ridiculous spectacle he made.

We spent the night with the planter and next morning my elephants, which were not very far away, came and pulled the car back on to the road. This was the beginning of my friendship with this lonely planter, a man named Shanks, who was a shikari after my own heart. He said he had never met a man like me before, which was hardly surprising since the only people he dealt with were British planters like himself, labourers from the tea-gardens, and Indian clerks. I rewarded him with a shoot in the jungle, beating it with fourteen elephants. He invited a couple of neighbours, both veteran shikaris who had shot almost everything. One of them had shot 'the biggest bear in Asia', much to the chagrin of Shanks who had been waiting to meet up with just such a bear – preferably with its snout down an ant-hill, he said.

Shanks had some interesting stories to tell of the old days. Many years ago, he had brought the heavy boiler for his tea-garden machinery over forty miles of earth roads from the nearest river crossing with the aid of elephants. It was slung on large-rimmed wheels and pulled by two elephants tandem fashion. At one stage he had had to light fires under the animals' bellies to make them heave the tremendous weight out of a large pothole into which it had sunk. Elephants can exert their maximum strength only when pulling abreast, but the narrow earth roads in Assam at that time made such an arrangement impossible.

Some seventy-five years earlier, elephants had been used in an attempt to move the steam launch brought by the Nizam of Hyderabad from the railway station to the lake. In the language of those days 'the brutes did not pull together' and it was recommended that 'trained elephants of the Battery be used'. In such tasks, teamwork and training are needed as well as sheer strength. The only time I saw elephants working together abreast to pull a dead weight was when we were burying a big tuskless male elephant which I had had to destroy during my first khedda operations. By an ironical coincidence, the three koonkis which had captured him and brought him in had to move his dead body to the hole we dug on the river-bank. The hauling gear was improvised and a chain snapped frighteningly. Terrific effort was needed to move the four-ton body up the gently sloping bank and it must be admitted that 'the brutes did not pull together'.

The destroying of elephants was one of the few tasks I did not enjoy during my career as a stockade officer and fortunately it was seldom necessary. It was a lonely life at times, but I loved every part of it except for this and it was with reluctance that I went back to routine duties at the end of five years. My kheddas had created records which would never be beaten and I had captured more than a thousand elephants, more than any other catcher of the past could claim. Above all I had learnt a lot about elephants and came to love and admire them. For the rest of my life I was an elephant man.

CHAPTER 2

PIONEER ELEPHANT CATCHERS

India had always been a happy hunting ground for British adventurers and elephant catching did not escape their attentions. The most famous was Sanderson, who was born in India in 1850 and started his career in the Canal Engineering Department of Madras at the age of sixteen. He was the first to succeed in catching elephants in a stockade. The Muslim conqueror of Mysore, Hyder Ali, tried unsuccessfully to capture elephants by this method; and nearly a hundred years later, in 1867, Colonel Pearse also failed. Sanderson made his first khedda experiments in 1874 at Chamrajanager, some distance from the famous Kakankote stockade. He employed no less than eight hundred men for driving and captured about fifty-five elephants. A year later he went to Dacca in East Bengal, where he acted as superintendent of the Government khedda establishment for nine months. When he joined, there were fifty trained elephants and 159 under training. Each cold weather season, catching expeditions went out into the Garo and the Chittagong Hills and accounted for about seventy elephants each year. Only a slender staff of supervising officers or 'jemadars' and a few others were maintained permanently, the hundreds of men required for the work of stockade construction and driving being recruited locally on the spot.

After this experience, Sanderson returned to Mysore and perfected the khedda system there. The Muslim elephant men he took with him and their descendants were the mainstay of the catching operations and they still work as mahouts to this day, but the local Kurrabas and other castes soon learnt the art of driving elephants. There was no tradition of catching elephants anywhere in the south of India except by pitting and Sanderson had to perfect the stockade method by trial and error. In the seventeen years up to his death in 1892 at the early age of forty-two, Sanderson staged ten kheddas in which he captured 349 elephants in Mysore and 85 in Chittagong.

He was a remarkable man and possessed of boundless energy and great courage, as his accounts of adventures with wild animals show. They are well described in his *Thirteen Years among the Wild Beasts of India*, which will remain a classic for all time. He was a daring and imaginative person who refused to be overcome by difficulties. He wrote much about elephants and although he reveals himself as a keen observer, his general approach was one of 'debunking' the elephant and some of his conclusions seem to be almost perverse. His photograph shows a slim man with a bushy, walrus moustache, the fashion at that time, with a huge sola topee and the inevitable watch-chain. His weighty twelve-bore rifle is preserved by the Forest Department of Mysore at Bangalore, along with a few other khedda relics.

Sanderson was succeeded by a Mysore officer known as 'Khedda' Shamiengar, who also paid a visit to the Dacca elephant establishment to study the methods of catching in Bengal. The Mysore khedda department was closed down in 1890 since it proved unremunerative, but Sanderson's name will live for ever because of his association with one of the world's greatest showpieces, the Mysore kheddas. It is sad that owing to the submergence of the Kakankote site as a result of the construction of a dam, the 1960 khedda was the last one to be held there.

Away in the north-eastern corner of India there arose several famous catchers after the Government khedda organization at Dacca had closed down. The old elephant men used to speak of these operations, in which prefabricated stockade parts were carried on elephants. The catchers were accompanied by a large labour force and, as soon as enough elephants were located, the stockade would be assembled hurriedly and the herds driven in. Before Milroy's introduction of departmental kheddas early in the twenties, elephant catching was a free for all in which both European adventurers – mostly tea-planters – and Assamese catchers took part. Men like Errol Grey, whom I shall mention later, gave up tea altogether for this more lucrative business; but many others chanced their luck on the side by going into partnership with the local Assamese mahaldars (lease-holders of elephant-catching areas) while still holding positions in tea.

Dalrymple-Clarke, a police superintendent who had served as transport officer in the Manipur rebellion as well as superintendent of the Dacca khedda establishment for some time, went into partnership with some Assamese round about the years 1900–05. He bought elephants, which at that time were selling for as little as five hundred rupees, to sell them again to the great teak firms in Burma. The Bombay Burmah Trading Company had a contract with him for five thousand rupees per elephant delivered in Burma, an important condition of the agreement being that the animals should be free from foot-rot. The elephants used to be marched through the Naga Hills and Manipur in easy stages of ten miles a day and eventually delivered on the Sittang river. Part of the route was the same as the one traversed by 'Elephant Bill', though in the reverse direction, when he brought Bandoola and the Burma elephants over with refugees during the Japanese war. I remember in 1950 seeing a number of young elephants which were being brought to India for export to some foreign country; at the time Lower Burma and the port of Rangoon were cut off from Upper Burma by disturbances and the Shans thought nothing of marching their elephants over the famous Stilwell Road. I questioned the leader of the party, a Sadiya Khamti who knew Assamese, and we had a most interesting talk while the elephant babies frolicked in the Dehing river.

An interesting and probably highly-garbled story was told to me by old Badhal Jamadar, who as a young man had worked with Dalrymple-Clarke. Up to three hundred men would make the trip and after conveying the elephants into Burma, they would return by sea from Rangoon to Calcutta. It would appear that there was some trouble after one transaction, when a large number of elephants died mysteriously after payment for them had been made. Dalrymple-Clarke was brought out from England to give evidence in the case, as a result of which one of the elephant jemadars (supervising officers) got six years and an officer of the company was also punished. When called upon to produce the dead bodies as proof, Dalrymple-Clarke was equal to the occasion. Leading the party to a site on the river bank where he said the elephants had been taken ill – allegedly from anthrax which was a scourge at the time – he professed great astonishment that the river had changed its course, even washing away the graves of the buried elephants!

The most famous European catchers of those times were Errol Grey and his contemporary Fred Kingsley. Grey's name was well known among the elephant men when I first joined kheddas in 1930, and although he had long since retired, his reputation and his exploits were still fresh in their minds.. It was said that he would actually take part in the religious ceremony known as *puja* which precedes a stockade operation and involves the sacrifice of a white cockerel and other unpleasant rites; in such things he shared the life of his men and their elephants very closely. Grey caught elephants for nearly thirty years, mostly in North Lakhimpur where he 'cleaned up' the elephants, but he also went into Upper Burma and the Naga Hills.

When I went into the Naga Hills to build the stockade in the Bhagti Valley where I made my record catch of fifty-four elephants in 1936, I was thrilled to see 'Errol Grey, elephant catcher' over the date 1917 in the Sanis bungalow book and I proudly added my own name below it. During the war, a planter friend of mine known as 'Gertie' Millar was in the little known V-force used to stiffen the morale and resistance of the Nagas against the Japanese after the fall of Burma; he saw Grey's signature dated 1918 in the Fort Hertz bungalow book, along with other famous names such as that of the plant collector Kingdon Ward. Alas, both books with the names of well-known people, records of wild life and interesting happenings, must have been destroyed with the bungalows; one perished in the Japanese attack on India through Upper Burma and the other in the post-independence troubles with the Nagas.

Millar was amazed at Grey's feat of bringing elephants through the Chowkham Pass, nearly nine thousand feet high, over a series of knife-like ridges. When he traversed the same route during the war, he found elephant tracks worn deep in the soft sandstone rock; they must have been made by generations of wild elephants migrating to and fro across the Patkoi Ranges. The Khamtis, those great elephant owners of the Sadiya district of Upper Assam, still cross the mountains to exchange elephants and brides with their relatives in Upper Burma. Through this channel there must have been a constant flow of information on elephants, which has resulted in many similarities in the catching and training methods of Assam and Burma; and in these tracks, Errol Grey must have passed.

During my first independent kheddas in the winter of 1934-5, I was fortunate enough to meet this famous personality. I had a hundred-mile length of the foothills to stockade and for some of the lease areas there were no bidders. Somebody told me that Grey would soon be arriving on his annual cold weather visit to Assam and I spoke to Milroy about allotting him a lease area, but to my surprise he was rather lukewarm. 'You can ask him if you like', he said, 'but I must warn you that Grey does not like me. He thinks I put him out of business.'

I made inquiries from the local agents at Texpur and was told that the steamer on which Grey was travelling all the way from Calcutta would arrive the next morning. When it berthed, I went up the gangway and climbed the stairs to the little foredeck which adjoins the first-class cabins on the Brahmaputra side-paddle steamers. I was surprised to see a little man with a fresh face, grey haired, neatly dressed and holding a furled umbrella - so unlike the picture of the famous elephant catcher which I had been imagining that I was momentarily taken aback. Introducing myself, I had a brief conversation with him in his cabin. When I explained my mission, Grey was friendly but firm. 'I am sorry,' he said, 'there are no profits in the elephant-catching business of today to attract me. I have made my money and could not be satisfied with the small margin one gets nowadays.' I had to be satisfied with this and, after accompanying him to the dak bungalow where he used to spend a week making his arrangements to go farther up river to his camp, I said good-bye and left him.

In due course I visited Grey in his well-known camp on the Dikrong river, near the Harmatti tea estate. He received me courteously in his neatly constructed grass hut, with the hospitality for which he was famous. Apparently he spent his time growing vegetables and looking at the river. After tea, two or three elephants came up to be fed. 'These are all I have left from my elephant-catching days,' he said sadly. 'They made money for me and today they are my pensioners.' He used to maintain these elephants and refused all offers for their purchase.

Grey had the reputation of not welcoming women visitors to his camp, though he was always accessible to men. I was given an amusing account of how a rather jungly planter arrived to dine with Grey wearing a pair of slacks, to find his host dressed in a dinner-jacket, walking up and down swishing a little stick as if waiting for a naughty schoolboy to arrive. From the time of his retirement from elephant catching in the twenties until his death in the early years of the war, Grey lived surrounded by his faithful elephants and men, commuting every six months between a luxurious hotel in England and a grass hut on an Assam river. People used to say that these retired *koi-hais* or old-stagers, of whom there were several in Assam at the time, used to come out for various personal reasons. In some cases it was undoubtedly a feeling of nostalgia for the good times they had had in India. With Errol Grey, I am convinced the reason was his elephants. During the war I wrote to Grey for his notes on elephant catching and he replied from England, where he was seriously ill, that I could have them when he returned to India after the war; but alas his death robbed me of them. Other catchers, including Kingsley, were said to be jealous of Grey because he could always get a mahal or lease from government by private arrangement, which may well have been the case prior to the introduction in the late twenties of the departmental kheddas which killed off the private catchers. Grey's greatest successes were at mela shikar (noosing), just as Kingsley's were in stockades; but Grey built stockades as well and his men were invariably the north bank Khamtis led by Chowngion Gehain, their 'raja'.

Kingsley was the other notable tea-planter turned elephant catcher of those times. He first became interested in the business in 1897 when he went into partnership with his Assamese clerk's father. After that he was a sub-lessee of Errol Grey and other mahaldars for nearly fifteen years. His first big chance came when he purchased the Garo Hills mahal or lease area from 1911 to 1914 for half a lakh of rupees; he captured 255 elephants in three years, which was the period of the mahal lease in those days. Next Kingsley purchased the Goalpara (or 'Bhutan Mahal' as it is called, because that country has a half share in the elephant herds common to the north bank forests and the adjoining Bhutan Hills) for Rs. 66,000 with a royalty of a hundred rupees per elephant in addition. Prices of elephants were high at the time and this accounts for Kingsley's very big bid, which astonished the Deputy Commissioner who was conducting the auction. But although he captured 279 elephants in 1916 and 342 in 1917 (which were record catches until I came along with 392 and 437 twenty years later in my Sibsagar-Naga Hills kheddas of 1935 and 1936) he made no profit out of it, for various reasons. But on the whole Kingsley made so much money out of elephant-catching that the Assamese used to say 'he had eaten his belly full of gold.'

When I began to collect information about elephant catching I wrote to Kingsley, who had by then retired to Darjeeling where he and his brother had both been educated and where later they acquired much wealth and fame as tea-planters. To my pleasant surprise he promptly replied, and for a period of two months every week he sent me a bulletin, written in his own hand, in which he gave me a lot of information. Kingsley claimed that much of Milroy's reform of the khedda business was based on his suggestions and it might well have been so. But his greatest claim to fame (or notoriety, whichever way one looks at it) was his involvement in a sensational law-suit with the Assam Forest Department on the failure of his Goalpara lease area operations, which he put down to gross neglect and ignorance of the business by the local officers. The climax to a succession of alleged delays, one being the result of the rule that prohibits a European from entering Bhutan without a special permit, was the burning of the forests for regeneration purposes. This resulted in the loss of his depot with all its stores and, what was even worse, the scaring away of the wild elephant herds. His claim was for a lakh and a half, but he received a bare two thousand rupees from the court. Incidentally, the forest officer involved in the case, a rather intransigent individual, was later sacked, though for other reasons. After that Kingsley, as might have been expected, drifted out of Assam catching but he operated in the Bengal Duars and in Bhutan for some time. He is credited with being the first man to introduce stockades to the Garo Hills and to Bhutan and his name is perpetuated in a famous group of tea-gardens founded by his father.

Milroy, like me, was not a private elephant catcher but his influence on the business, in which he took part both as khedda officer and administrator, was far reaching indeed. He was first engaged in elephant catching as far back as 1909, when he had just joined the khedda service as a young officer, and it was while serving his time under the previous unreformed catching rules, that he first came to realize how much unnecessary cruelty there was in the business. With the support of his Conservator and the Governor of Assam, he drew up a revised set of rules which were enforced in 1922.

Milroy's greatest fight was to abolish the use of spears and cruelty in training operations and his aim was the rationalization and humanization of the elephant-catching industry. This he achieved, by personal influence and a policy of give and take. He introduced the departmental kheddas in which all parties stood to gain or lose on the results. Shares of koonkidars (owners of trained elephants or koonkis) were scaled according to the size and strength of the koonki in question. Phandis, that is professional elephant noosers, were severely controlled; but they were also cared for from a special phandis' fund from which were paid rewards for good work and compensation for accidental death or injuries. Stockade catching was made an operation of skill rather than force, with only four guns and twenty-five men; with the prohibition on carrying of guns, mela shikar or noosing became an art; while the training was conducted and controlled entirely with a view to reducing the heavy casualties and making it easier for the captured elephant to survive.

To a large extent Milroy's new system meant the death-knell of the European adventurer, whose main function had been to finance the Assamese catchers; no wonder Grey and others did not appreciate the changed conditions. Milroy was a strong man who did not hesitate to insist on having his own way, particularly where the fate of the elephant was concerned; but he was also fair and loyal to the Assamese catchers, who all respected and loved him.

In the course of his dealings with elephants and elephant men Milroy had, unavoidably, aroused a certain amount of bitterness. There was the case of the assistant to the chief mahout in my first kheddas, who used to carry about the medicine bucket for the doctor and do the syringing and cleaning out of the wounds of the sick elephants. He had been a *bor phandi* or 'great phandi' who had drowned his captive by swimming it upstream across the Brahmaputra and Milroy had promptly black-listed him. He was unforgiving in such matters and was a terror to blacklegs in the elephant-catching business. On the occasion of my first in-dependent khedda he had suddenly ordered out of the area a certain well-known koonkidar. I was bewildered but saw that the man left, though his koonki was allowed to stay behind and work. Before leaving the old man came to see me and with emotion narrated this story.

Fifteen years earlier Milroy had captured and purchased for the department a splendid young tusker which he called Jehangir. This elephant escaped soon afterwards and Milroy asked the koonkidar, a famous catcher, to go in search of the animal, promising to let him catch a wild elephant if he could recover Jehangir. After a fortnight in the jungle he came back without Jehangir but with a fine young captive. Milroy, suspicious, made inquiries and learnt that the koonkidar had spent all his time hunting elephants! He was infuriated and never let the man take any active part in kheddas again.

During my first season at khedda operations, I was often puzzled by the brief instructions I received from Milroy, but the lease-holders knew exactly what he meant. The old Conservator was held in great respect and no one ever questioned his orders. I was told stories of how, from some far away place in the interior, Milroy would send a runner with a message in Assamese scribbled on the inside of a cigarette packet, perhaps giving news of the movements of a herd and instructions on how to deal with it. When a big departmental khedda was on he would turn up frequently and unexpectedly, marching with his elephants led by Akbar and giving practical as well as moral support to his khedda officer and the lease-holders. In spite of his many duties as head of the Forest Department, he would always find time for his beloved elephants. His practical knowledge of them was derived from his early experiments with the departmental kheddas in Kulsi and the difficulties of coaxing elephants into stockades with the help of raw villagers recruited as drivers.

In 1936, Milroy died suddenly through overwork while still in harness. At the time I was on my last khedda and I heard the news when I was in the middle of his beloved North Cachar Hills inspecting stockades, some of which he had made famous in the twenties and to which I had been sent as a young beginner. They buried him in the local church at Shillong and his brother foresters erected as his memorial a brass tablet with the portrait of an elephant on it.

Before I close this section on famous catchers I must mention some of the Assamese catchers, of whom the Phookans of Charing in Sibsagar were the best known. Old Phookan, whom I never met, had worked with Milroy and after him the sons, led by the eldest brother Tilokanto. They had made their fortune out of elephant catching and were perhaps the only family to hold on to their earnings. Their record of association with elephant catching goes back over fifty years and although their heyday was the time of the single monopolist and later the large departmental khedda, they have still been holding their own.

When I first joined kheddas their name was famous and every

1. Painting an elephant of the Mysore royal stables for a religious ceremony

2. Elephant with the silver lotus flower howdah

3. The only white elephant known to be born in Burma in this century

one paid them great respect, for they were Milroy's favourite catchers. Tilokanto had stood by Milroy in his efforts at reforming the business when other mahaldars had viewed the new set-up with suspicion, if they had not actually refused to co-operate with him. The family of four brothers, of whom one had died early leaving his son to represent him, were a model of behaviour and were always to be relied upon to follow the khedda procedure and to observe its discipline. Their elephants, phandis and stockade men were all first class and the reputation of their depot was high. The sodagars or traders, who in the old days would ask for the departmental depot, now look for 'Phookan's depot'.

Simple living and hard working. Tilokanto was personally in the habit of coming out to the mahals each catching season until age and infirmity held him back. His influence in the kheddas was great and though Phookan's camp was always a little apart, he could be relied upon to help us whenever we needed it. He had remained in the business continuously, unlike the venerable Goramuriya Goswami, whose influence among Assamese elephant catchers was perhaps greater because of his high religious status and great moral weight, but who came and went because of his association with political and social movements. I shall have more to say about the Goswami later on.

Such men as Phookan were the real catchers and it is their records which should go down in the books; they were the backbone of the business. Another such was Chowngion Gohain, Errol Grey's chief stockade sirdar; when I knew him he was a tiny old Khamti in a coloured lungi and a large Shan turban. It was men like these who organized and conducted the catching and it was on their personal efforts that success or failure depended. Milroy used to say 'give me the Upper Assam mahaldar with the Lower Assam koonkidar, the Upper Assam koonki with the Lower Assam phandi'! I was indeed lucky to be able to combine them all in my record khedda of 1935-6 in Middle Assam. This was the last time that this formidable gathering of the greatest elephant catchers in Assam was to meet and the occasion was both my swan-song and my apogee in elephant catching.

It was also the exit, or very nearly so, of our veterinarian Dr

B

Pashupati Mukherjee, that remarkable man who will appear so often in my narrative as the 'Doctor Babu', a respected and affectionate title used by everyone who knew him or had to deal with him. A product of the old school, he was a typical example of the devotion to duty which one came to expect from such types. Early in service he had been transferred to the Forest from the Veterinary Department to look after our elephants and without him no khedda operation was complete. He could roar like a lion at some misdemeanour and coo like a dove when the need arose. I early learnt to rely on his counsel and help, whether in dealing with unwilling bidders or in extracting the purchase price of an elephant from a slippery customer; he was a tower of strength in such situations, for he had a wonderful memory for names and faces and every trader feared and respected him. On professional matters or on a point of khedda procedure his word was final. His sturdy independence and natural frankness was always set off by an engaging grin, while his refusal to compromise on matters of principle was known to everyone. He was a household word with every elephant man in Assam and with hundreds elsewhere and when he retired to his native Bengal soon after the departmental kheddas were closed down, his place as an elephant doctor was impossible to fill. Simple and unostentatious, he went home to devote himself to the marrying off of his many daughters, no doubt with the same assiduity which he used to display towards the saving of his elephants.

CHAPTER 3

MYTH AND HISTORY

Probably no other animal has been the subject of more myths and fanciful tales than the elephant. In the east it is a royal beast and part of the very foundations of India, land of tradition and symbolism, pageantry and glamour. Ever since the Vedic age, the elephant has figured largely in Indian mythology and religion. In the Rig-Veda, which marks the dawn of Aryan settlement some three thousand years ago, the elephant is known as *hastin* or 'the beast that hath an arm' and for a long time it was an object of awe and wonder. There was also a legend that elephants could fly, which may have had its origin in the resemblance of moving herds to fleeting masses of clouds; the miraculous transformation of clouds into elephants was said to be the result of the curse of an irate hermit, on whose head fell a branch of the gigantic banyan tree where the 'elephant clouds' had rested.

The myth that a certain super race of elephants possessed pearls in their skulls may also have had its origin in very ancient times. At least one case of something which primitive fancy might well have regarded as a 'pearl' has been reported in the present century. During the 1928 khedda operations in the Chittagong Hill Tracts, a Forest Officer who had to destroy a wild tusker found a small oval object, about as big as a man's little fingernail, in the fleshy pith of one of the tusks. It had the appearance and consistency of ivory, but was slightly rough and striated. The elephant men were very excited and claimed that it was a *gaja-mukta* or elephant pearl and extremely valuable.

Stories such as these have been handed down over countless generations, perhaps ever since Aryan times. The great northern plains, with their vanished forests, were the cradle of Aryan civilization, which spread into Bengal and Assam along the Ganges and Brahmaputra valleys. They were also the main range of the elephant from primeval times until fairly recently, when the forests have receded as a result of advancing desiccation. We find completely different traditions in the north and the south even to this day: the Aryans in the north, for instance, captured elephants in stockades, the Dravidians in the south by pitting; and these methods still survive in the two distinct areas. The traditional elephant language derived from the parent Sanskrit is common throughout India except in the distant south, Kerala and the Western Ghats. In the northern plains, too, Indian elephant lore was blended with that of the far eastern lands. In Assam especially, the traditions of northern India are mixed with those of Burma, Siam and Indo-China.

Then of course there are many fascinating stories associated with different religions in various parts of Asia. In Hindu mythology, the eight points of the compass are each guarded by an elephant and Indra, king of the gods, is said to have ridden on a great white four-tusked elephant named Airavata, which arose as a result of the churning of the sea of milk by the gods and demons to obtain ambrosia.

Buddhists believe that the Lord Buddha attained Buddhahood through good deeds done in previous lives. During all his lives except the final one he is known as Bodhisattava or Buddha-elect and the chronicle of his lives is known as the Jataka tales. One of his good deeds concerns his life as a white elephant named Chadanta, which had a silvery trunk and six tusks of different hues. He was the leader of a herd of eight hundred elephants which lived by the shores of a Himalayan lake, beyond seven mountains of which the Golden Mountain was the last and highest. Chadanta had two wives, one of whom he inadvertently offended and made her jealous. One day this wife entertained a holy man and prayed to him that she should be born into royalty. Her wish was fulfilled and in course of time she became the Rani of Benares. To please her king, she sent a party of hunters to bring back the six tusks of her former husband the white elephant. After an arduous journey lasting seven years, seven months and seven days, the leader of the hunters alone reached the lake. Here he dug a pit and Chadanta fell into it. The hunter tried to kill him with arrows, but failed. The elephant then asked his attacker why he was trying to kill him and was told that the Rani of Benares wanted his tusks. The elephant, understanding everything, asked the hunter to cut out his tusks. The man was unable to do so owing to the great height of the elephant; so Chadanta took the saw from the hunter's hands and fell dead as he was cutting off his own tusks. When the story was told to the queen, she died of a broken heart.

Thus it was that the Lord Buddha entered the womb of his mother Queen Maya as a white elephant for his final incarnation before emerging as a human being. In pre-Buddhist times, the white elephant was associated with the rain cloud, a symbol of life and prosperity and thus a fitting vehicle for the Buddha's incarnation. This is the reason why so-called white elephants are treated with so much respect and reverence in Buddhist countries such as Burma, Siam and Indo-China.

The white elephant myth is the most persistent and the most factual of these curious fables. Many light-coloured specimens have been called 'white' although they are not true albinos; but the real white elephant, like any other albino, has a pinkish skin and light-coloured hair and eyes. In 1943 I visited Agartala in Tripura State to see their famous white elephant and was very disappointed; the eyes were not those of a typical albino (they were light-coloured 'cat's eyes', as the local people put it) and the animal was off-white in colour, with light reddish-brown hair. I was allowed to photograph it and the difference in coloration when compared to a normal elephant stands out clearly. This is one of the very few photographs of a white elephant in existence; had such an animal been captured in countries farther east, such as Burma or Siam, it would have been venerated greatly because of its mythological association with the Buddha and it is unlikely that anyone would have been allowed to photograph it. This elephant had been bought by the Maharaja of Tripura for the ridiculously low sum of about £170, having been captured in the Chittagong Hill Tracts in 1939. It was a female, then about seven feet high and probably about ten years old. It remained in Tripura State until 1947, when it escaped one night from the jungle where it had been let loose to graze with the usual fetters on its legs. Although the Tripura family is Hindu by religion, it had been considered 'sacred' and was never ridden, being used only for leading processions.

It was perhaps only natural that Assam should have become the main source of ancient elephant lore because of its immense elephant population. Palakapya, a sage who lived in Assam in the fifth or sixth century BC, is generally regarded as the founder of elephant lore or Gaja-shastra as it is called in Sanskrit. He was supposed to have had a supernatural origin, having been born from an elephant. He lived and wandered with the wild elephants, eating only the food they ate; he learnt all about the ailments that afflicted them and is reputed to be the author of a treatise on their medical treatment. Palakapya was supposed to have had his hermitage 'where the Lohitya flows away towards the sea'. The Lohit is the present name for the Brahmaputra above its junction with the Dihang or Tsang-po – as the real Brahmaputra is called in Tibet – before it swings south towards Assam, cutting through the Himalayas in a series of mighty gorges. The modern Lohit is a tributary of the Brahmaputra, but it seems to have been the original name for the whole length of the river in ancient times. The reference to its flowing into the sea is, in fact, a correct rendering of the situation some hundred million years ago, when the waves of the Cretaceous sea lapped the Garo Hills, where the plains of East Pakistan lie today!

From the Ain-i-Akbari by Abul Fazl, a chronicle of the times of the Moghul emperor Akbar the Great, we find some fascinating glimpses of elephant lore. For instance, 'if in the rutting season an elephant is fighting with his match and a young one comes in his way, he very kindly sets him aside with the trunk and then renews the combat'. In fact when an elephant breaks loose in the rutting season nobody dares to go near him without being accompanied by a female elephant, when he will allow himself to be captured without offering any resistance.

Akbar had to overcome objections to allowing tame elephants to breed. The gestation period was then estimated to be eighteen lunar months and the young were supposed to suckle until they were five years old. This is interesting, as modern estimates of the elephant's gestation period allow twenty months for a female calf and twenty-two months for a male calf. In Akbar's time the natural life-span of the elephant was estimated to be one hundred and twenty years. There was also a belief that it was a good sign for elephants to have 'eyes of yellow and white mixed with red', which probably means light-coloured eyes. This belief is not shared by elephant men today, who consider such elephants to be dangerous and unreliable, often cowardly and potential killers when frightened or excited. White or yellow eyes, in fact, are anathema to the elephant connoisseur. I can remember at least two white-eyed elephants which were dangerous – one was a 'sakhni' (a female with tusks) which I had to destroy and the other was the last elephant I ever hunted, which nearly killed me.

The reading of various bodily signs and marks and their interpretation with different behaviour is highly developed in the Indian elephant trade. Our men recognized in the elephants we captured certain auspicious and inauspicious signs: the former would be welcome and would result in keen bidding for the particular animal, while the latter would have an unfailingly depressing effect on prices.

For instance, a black spot on the palate or on the tongue of the elephant meant bad luck to the owner and if such an animal was bought, the purchaser made sure that before it went to market the offending sign was removed. As with all other cruel practices, we used to frown on this one; but not very severely, as the operation was a comparatively mild one. The animal would be hog-tied and thrown and with everybody lending a hand to hold down the elephant, the mark would be rubbed with a corrosive 'blue-stone' (caustic sulphate) and then a little *ghee* or clarified butter would be applied over it to remove the soreness. During this process the elephant, which of course could only be so treated if it were a comparatively small one, would bawl lustily; but there was really nothing to it. The men used to say that the effacement of the mark was only temporary, though it would last long enough for them to effect a sale!

The elephant normally has five nails on each fore-foot and four on each hind-foot, making a total of eighteen in all and any animal with more or less than this was considered unlucky. A sixteen-nailed elephant was considered particularly unlucky and was almost unmarketable. I could never associate any abnormality of behaviour or lack of working qualities with the number of nails possessed by an elephant, but this was an important consideration in the owning or purchasing of an elephant, particularly for export.

The first thing that the men would do when a freshly captured elephant was brought into the depot would be to crowd around it and peer down at its feet to see the number of nails it possessed. The phandis who brought in abnormal animals would do their best to avoid showing the nails before the auctions, but the purchasers would insist on the elephants being brought forward on suitable ground for their examination. However, if there was no alternative to purchasing a sixteen-nailed elephant the traders used to carry out another subterfuge. I never actually saw this operation performed, but I was told that nails made from snail or mollusc shell were often fixed on the foot. No doubt they stayed on just long enough to deceive the purchaser.

Then there was the tail. A broom tail, one that was abnormally long and sweeping the ground, was considered very unlucky. A tail had to be just the right length, touching the hocks of the hind-legs. A tail at its best, moreover, should have glossy, crescent-shaped hairs, the one slightly overlapping the other. A stump tail would greatly reduce the price. I could point to at least one case of an elephant with a broom tail developing into a vicious man-killer, an animal called Shiv Dutt. The Doctor Babu always used to express astonishment that the Forest Officer, a senior man at that time, had purchased him.

There were other significant marks, such as the length of the trunk, the size of the ears and so on. Trunks had not to be too long or too short and the ears not too small. A thick, wrinkled skin, hanging rather loosely on the body and one that could be caught up in one's hand, a well-developed frontal bump and a hairy head were other good points. After all, most of these points are those which one associates with symmetry of form and can be appreciated. Naturally qualities of the spirit are also important: if an elephant puts up a good fight at the time of capture it denotes a noble temper and strangely enough such elephants gave us little trouble in training.

I have had experience of a very large number of koonkis – at one time I had a hundred of the best from all over Assam in my kheddas – and it was fascinating to hear the various stories about the more famous of them and to make the acquaintance of these elephants and their owners. Invariably the best animals from the point of view of docility, courage, endurance and freedom from vices had many, if not all, of the above good points. On the other hand it was common to find an elephant with some one or other of the bad points – particularly white eyes, sixteen nails and broom tail – prove unreliable on occasions.

In addition to these characteristics of individual elephants, the men concerned with the keeping of them also recognize a detailed caste system which was first described in the *Matanga-lila* or 'Sport of Elephants', the most readable and most instructive of the ancient Indian books on elephants. It shows clearly how interested people were in this curious animal and with what detail they recorded their observations and deductions.

The highest of the castes or *bandhs* is the *koomeriah* or thorough-bred, considered to be a royal animal and highly prized both for its qualities and its rarity. It has short hind-legs and a massive body, thick wrinkled skin like that of a crocodile, a thick trunk and noble head. It is dependable and courageous by nature and guaranteed not to lose condition easily. Then there is the *mreega* or deer-like type, named after the Sanskrit word *mrig* or deer, an animal with long legs, light weedy body and thin skin, certain to lose condition if not looked after properly and embracing the bulk of elephants. The *dwasala*, from the Persian word meaning mixed, is a type intermediate between the two.

Ancient Hindu literature classified elephants into eight classes according to build and temper, while the *Ain-i-Akbari* of Akbar's time recognizes four main types. The Ahoms of Assam in their *Hathiputhis*, which are written on strips of bark, associated different human qualities with the different elephant types and recognized a number of descriptive classes; but these minute delineations no longer interest any but the student of elephant lore.

When I visited the elephant stables of the Maharaja of Mysore in 1935, the *koomeriah* or royal *bandh* was represented by Chamundi Prasad, a magnificent animal with short, thick tusks turned sharply upwards. He was fat as a stud boar and had white patches on the face, ears and forequarters as a result of the painting he underwent from time to time for processions. Being a sacred elephant he could be given no work and I was not surprised to hear that he was always in musth – a condition in male elephants, of which I shall have more to say later, which is associated with the sexual urge. I have seen only one elephant with thicker tusks and a greater girth than Chamundi Prasad, a stupendous wild tusker which I came across a few years later in Goalpara. The *mreega* or 'deer' type in the royal stables included Airavatha, a very large elephant which later took the part of Kala Nag in Kipling's story *Toomai of the Elephants*, starring Sabu. At the time of my visit Sabu, unaware of his destiny as the 'Elephant Boy', was a little fellow shaping to become a mahout in the palace stables and his uncle, Bapu Sahib, was Chamundi Prasad's mahout.

The employment of the elephant in battle has given us many fascinating glimpses of the character of this noble animal. That it proved to be both a strength and a weakness to its masters was only to be expected, for its bulk could make it a threat to its own side when it stampeded. Once the original surprise and terror which the war elephant inspired in its opponents wore off, its value was largely lost, as the commanders in ancient times soon discovered. And of course once gunpowder was invented, the elephant vanished from the battlefield except as a carrier of baggage and dragger of cannon.

During the second millennium BC there was an epic quarrel between the Pandavas and the Kuruvas, who lived north of the Pandava stronghold at Hastinapur. This name means 'elephant town' and clearly indicates the use of elephants in the battles. The city is usually identified with a ruined site near Meerut in Uttar Pradesh; it lies in the bed of the Ganges, which must have washed the city away.

Cyrus the Great of Persia (558 to 530 BC) was killed in a battle with the Derbikes, who were equipped with elephants supplied by Indians fighting on their side. This was probably on the western borders of the sub-continent for, according to Meghasthenes, it is doubtful whether Cyrus ever exercised sovereignty over India proper.

The Greeks had heard strange and wonderful tales of the value of elephants in war and were eager to secure some. At the battle for a strong mountain fort called Aornus, a site which has been identified close to the modern town of Amb in the Swat valley, the defenders were pursued into the hills and turned loose their fifteen war elephants in the swampy country bordering the Indus. The animals were recaptured by Indians attached to the Macedonian army whose special business was elephants.

In 327 BC, at the decisive battle of the Hydaspes between Alexander the Great and Porus, the latter depended very largely on his elephants. The kingdom of Porus was between the Jhelum (Hydaspes) and the Chenab, in the Punjab of undivided India. His name probably represents the Indian 'Puru' of the famous Paruva clan. When Alexander started his invasion of India, many rulers submitted without a fight, including the king of Taxilla who ruled on the other side of the Jhelum. But Porus, when called upon by Alexander to give in, sent back a proud answer and a challenge. The subsequent battle of the Hydaspes was reckoned to be the stiffest opposition yet encountered by Alexander. Porus had two hundred war elephants with which he lined the high bank of the flooded river. He himself sat upon a huge elephant in the midst of his army. The army itself resembled a city: the elephants spaced at intervals of a hundred feet, in eight ranks, represented the towers of the city, with the infantry connecting them like walls.

It was the Macedonian cavalry, however, that was the decisive factor in the battle. Overcoming the terror of the horses at the sight, scent and sound of the strange beasts, they charged and the Indian soldiers 'fled for shelter to the elephants, as to a friendly wall'. The elephants, maddened by a ceaseless shower of darts from the Macedonian cavalry and confined in that crowded place, charged and wheeled, pushing and crushing friend and foe alike and the confusion was indescribable. Alexander's horsemen gave way when the elephants charged, only to turn and ply them with darts when they retreated, until the poor bewildered and exhausted beasts had to give way, trumpeting defiance. We are told that all the elephants were either captured or killed, a cruel and long-drawn-out business with only arrows and spears as weapons. Finally the Indian army was routed; but King Porus, who was wounded nine times, refused to flee and kept his seat on his huge elephant in the thick of the fight until all hope was gone. A brother of the treacherous Raja of Takshacita (Taxila) followed him on a horse with a message from Alexander, but Porus hurled a javelin with such force that it pierced the emissary right through his body. Porus then lost consciousness and fell from his elephant. Alexander was so filled with admiration for his courage that he spared his life and subsequently sought his friendship and alliance. Alexander sent all the elephants he captured to Macedonia via Kandahar and Seistan.

The battle of the Hydaspes proved that elephants could not face cavalry; but in spite of this they continued to be the mainstay of Indian armies for centuries to come. Chandra Gupta, the Mauryan emperor, with the great statesman Chanakya to guide him, consolidated his position after Alexander left India. He defeated Alexander's former general and successor to the throne, Sellucus Nikator, to whom he later gave five hundred elephants in exchange for his territory. Chandra Gupta had his capital at Pataliputra, where the modern cities of Patna and Bankipore stand today. His army included nine thousand fighting elephants and each animal carried three archers in addition to a mahout. According to

Megasthenes – the ambassador of Sellucus Nikator at Chandra Gupta's court – the king had a guard of twenty-four elephants and when he went forth to do justice, the first elephant was trained to make obeisance.

A thousand years later, when the conquering Arabs attempted to invade the north-western borders of India, the king of Sindh, whose name was Dahar, resisted stubbornly and a pitched battle took place near the capital, Raor. Elephants were used by the defenders and were routed by a strange weapon – naptha flares. One of the flares, carried by an arrow, set the howdah of Dahar's elephant ablaze and the maddened beast plunged into the water. Although Dahar managed to get ashore, he was hit by an arrow in the breast and, as he dismounted from his elephant, an Arab swordsman cut off his head. The death of the king resulted in the rout of the army and Dahar's queen, Rani Bai, took refuge in the fort of Raor, where the remains of the Indian forces were besieged. When further resistance was useless, the queen and her women burned themselves to death in the traditional style to avoid dishonour.

Another brave queen was the ruler of Gondwana, Queen Durgavati, who opposed Asaf Khan, general of the Moghul emperor Akbar who was engaged in the conquest of the Deccan in central India. She was descended from the famous Chandella rulers and was acting as regent for her young son. Durgavati was a great warrior and had a thousand elephants and twenty thousand cavalry. She was also a great hunter and, according to Abul Fazl, 'whenever a tiger made its appearance, she did not drink water until she had killed it'. When the vast Moghul army approached, the queen retired into the hills where she could collect five thousand fighting men. She put on armour and, mounted on an elephant, drove the invaders out of the hills. The tide was turned only when Asaf Khan brought up artillery. The queen fought to the last but, after being struck by two arrows, she fainted; when she came round and realized that the battle was lost, she asked her servant to put an end to her life. When he refused, she drew her dagger and did the deed herself.

After the death of the Afghan Sher Shah, who had driven

Babar's son Humayun from the throne at Delhi, the empire shrunk
to a small kingdom which was the subject of disputed succession.
King Adilshah had a Hindu minister named Hemu Bhargava, a
Gaur Brahmin, who in addition to being a highly efficient civil
administrator was the best military leader on the Afghan side.
Humayun returned from Persia to recapture Delhi and Agra but
died soon afterwards. His Governor at Agra fled to Delhi and
Hemu followed him to Tughlakabad, a few miles from Delhi,
where there was a great battle. Hemu had under him a thousand
elephants, five thousand horses and fifty-one cannons. In this
assault the Moghuls captured four hundred elephants and slew four
thousand men of the Afghan army but, thinking that they had won
the battle, they dispersed to plunder the enemy camp. All this time
Hemu was holding three hundred elephants in reserve and with
these and his cavalry he made a charge upon Tardi Begh, the Moghul
general. This was the turning point of the battle and Hemu
took possession of Delhi. Soon after 1556 at the second Battle of
Panipat, the Emperor Akbar, then a boy of thirteen, defeated the
Afghans. Hemu's five hundred war elephants, protected by armour
plate and with two hundred musketeers on their backs, made
repeated counter-charges, but their opponents on horses out-
flanked the elephants, slashing at their legs or shooting down their
drivers. Hemu was seated on the back of a lofty elephant when an
arrow pierced his eye. He pulled it out and bandaging his face
with a scarf ordered the fight to go on. But he fell in a faint in the
howdah on the elephant's back and the Afghan-Rajput army broke
and fled. A Moghul captain led the elephant to Akbar's camp,
where the half-conscious champion of the Afghan army was
beheaded.

Even up to the end of the fifteenth century elephant armies were
in existence. We read of the Raja of Vijayanagar having in his
army 551 elephants, while Hyder Ali of Mysore and the Pandya
kings of Madura used them in their campaigns. The elephant was
used much in the same way as a tank in modern warfare. It was
covered in armour plating and its duty was to push down fortress
gates, the doors of which were fitted with stout metal spikes at
close intervals to keep off the elephants. Some of these elephant

gates are still in existence in India. On the back of the elephant was a howdah or covered platform from which soldiers could discharge javelins and arrows. Elephants were also trained to swing heavy chains to mow down foot soldiers. After gunpowder came into use, huge cannons, the forerunners of the modern big guns, were in great favour as siege-trains and elephants were used to drag these ponderous weapons. Even the early British armies in India had special elephant batteries.

The art of domesticating and training elephants both for peace and war seems to have been developed originally in Asia. Carrington in his book, *Elephants*, gives a concise picture of the spread of elephant lore from India to Africa, beginning with the first contacts between Alexander the Great and the Indians at the time of the defeat of Porus and continuing after his death in 323 BC in the war fought between his successors who founded the Seleucid and Ptolemaic dynasties. It was during the time of the second Ptolemy in 280 BC that the first attempts to capture and domesticate the African elephant were made. This was the smaller forest elephant, *Loxodonta africana cyclotis,* whose range extended from the Red Sea coast to the Atlantic ocean, through Algeria, Tunisia and Morocco.

The Carthaginians first began the capture and training of African elephants about the year 277 BC and they were used by Hannibal in his campaigns against the Romans. Of the thirty seven elephants Hannibal took over the Pyrenees, the Alps and the Lesser Appenines, only one got farther than the Arno river. That Hannibal did not take Rome could well be attributed to the failure of the elephants over country quite unsuited to them. Although the Indian elephant is known to go up to ten thousand feet, it is essentially a lowlands animal and cannot survive without its normal foodstuffs. After Caesar's time the use of the war elephant died out and with the decline of the Roman empire the knowledge of the art of domesticating the African elephant was lost. It was extraordinarily revived, more than two thousand years later, by the efforts of King Leopold II of the Belgians in the Congo.

The development of Africa and India by European nations from the seventeenth century onwards resulted in a flood of information and stories about the wonderful wild life of those continents, in which the elephant took its full share. The exploitation of the African elephant for its ivory and the Indian elephant for its working capabilities has meant the recording of much observation, both accurate and inaccurate.

CHAPTER 4

THEORIES AND FACTS

The elephant is in many ways such an extraordinary beast that even today, after thousands of years of domestication, there are still certain things about it which are not fully understood. Around it has grown up a great edifice of lore and knowledge, including much that is still surmise and some that is based on misconceptions. Leaving aside the legends and myths, there are a number of stories and facts about the elephant which hold the imagination and are likely to do so forever, for they can never be entirely proved or disproved.

Pride of place must surely be accorded to the fascinating theory of the secret burial place of elephants. The picture of an old tusker tottering to a lonely place to die is too dramatic to be exploded once and for all and instances of dead elephants or their remains being found in Asia – or in Africa for that matter – are so few that it is no wonder that the legend has persisted. Sanderson has recorded that the Kurrabas of Mysore believe in elephant cemeteries and Sir Emerson Tennent in his book *Wild Elephant* wrote that the natives of Ceylon say there is a secret elephant burial place in a valley to the east of Adam's Peak, reached through a narrow pass of rock. During the last century, the Duke of Orleans organized an expedition in central Africa to try and find an elephants' graveyard; a very old man of the Bongo tribe told the party that many years before he had followed a tottering elephant for five days to a secret burial place guarded by sentinel elephants who attacked him.

Many men who have lived in the forests for long periods have not come across a single elephant skeleton, though others have found remains from time to time and the occasions are not so few and far between as is generally imagined. I myself found a dead elephant only once and significantly it was on the edge of a stream in a secluded part of the forest. A Burma Forest Officer more than fifty years ago recorded finding a dead tusker lying on his back at the head of a stream which was flowing in a sort of ravine; he could find nothing to indicate that it was anything except a natural death. A lady writing for the Indian papers several years ago described how she and her brother witnessed the death of an elephant in the Karnafuli river of the Chittagong Hill Tracts. The tusker emerged from the forest quite close to them, shaking his head as if in great pain, half walking and half dragging himself and almost falling at every step until he reached the water, into which he plunged with a hoarse noise never to come up again.

In Africa, Sir William Gowers described how he found, while travelling on a river steamer up the Nile, a large tuskless male elephant which must have died three or four days earlier. He attributed its death to heart failure as a result of its exertions in trying to climb the river bank. He was of the opinion that in eastern equatorial Africa the majority of elephants must die in the papyrus reed swamps. During the sinking of the cassions of the Blue Nile bridge at Khartoum, layers of elephant, hippopotamus and other animal bones were found some twenty feet below the bed of the river. Trader Horn speaks of old elephants repairing for death to special 'ozeys' or springs of clear water, near which it was possible to dig up green and discoloured ivory.

It has generally been concluded, and I think correctly, that most natural deaths of elephants occur in or near water. During our elephant-catching operations we invariably released dangerously sick animals as near as possible to water, preferably near a swamp, and we used to send out men each day to observe what happened. The stricken elephants would remain in the same spot for days, eating very little but drinking – or at least dipping the tips of their trunks in the water – before either moving away or collaps-ing and dying on the spot. Once they were dead, the body would be picked clean by vultures and other scavengers and the bones would disappear in the soft mud.

In tropical countries with their numerous agencies for breaking down and disposing of animal matter, from the white ant and dung beetle to the jackal and vulture, even the remains of such a large animal as the elephant can disappear in a few months. I once shot an elephant close to a forest tramway line and used to periodically visit the spot as I passed up and down in my trolley. It impressed me to see how quickly even the largest bones began to disintegrate and disappear. Porcupines and various carnivores, from the tiger to the jackal, lent their assistance to the removal and consuming of the bones and in two years' time I could not find the exact place without a long search, so luxuriant was the growth of the vegetation, assisted by the manurial value of the remains of the animal itself. This then is what happens to dead elephants.

Probably the most hackneyed topic after that of the secret elephant cemetery is the longevity of elephants. All the old theories regarding the age to which elephants live have received a severe setback from the publication of the findings of Major Stanley S. Flowers on the age of certain animals. Carl W. Neumann writing some thirty years ago in the *Illustrierte Zeitung* gave the elephant an age of one hundred and fifty to two hundred years. The ancient Indians believed that the elephant lived to three hundred years. The Moghuls believed that one hundred and twenty years was the average life-span. Sanderson was of the opinion that one hundred and fifty years was the least to which an elephant in the wild state would live. Flowers has brought down the figure to not more than seventy years at the most, the same as the life-span of man. His observations were made on animals in captivity and he was rigid in his specifications, demanding what would amount to a 'birth certificate' for the elephant. He refused to accept any uncorroborated statement of the age of an elephant – estimated, for instance, on how long it had remained in a circus, zoo or royal stables – and built his case only on validated histories.

His findings certainly came as a rude shock to most elephant men and personally I cannot accept them without reservations, although I am prepared to concede that there are a few well-authenticated instances of elephants living to a great age. There was the historic example of the Ceylon elephant Hurtala ('Pet') which was said to have served with the Dutch for one hundred and forty years of their occupation of the island and was the only animal not eaten during the siege of Colombo; it was believed to be one hundred and seventy years old when it died. There was also 'Princess Alice', who is said to have gone to Australia with an English circus in the early years of the century and to have died in Melbourne at the age of one hundred and fifty-two. These examples, however, must be regarded as 'not proven' and my case for a longer life-span for the elephant is built on other grounds.

The life-span of a generally hard-worked domesticated elephant, unable to enjoy its natural diet and either exercised inadequately or overworked grossly cannot be compared with that of an elephant in the wild state which, barring accidents and in the case of males death from fighting, would be expected to live to the very maximum of its life-span. One has only to compare the magnificent condition and appearance of a wild elephant, particularly the large male which has nothing to fear in the jungle except man, with the miserable appearance and condition of the average captive elephant to appreciate the advantages of natural environment, abundant and varied food and exercise which all wild animals enjoy in freedom.

Short of accurately recording the birth of an animal and following it up until its death – a possibility which is not always within the reach of the average keeper of an elephant since records become lost or are not maintained or because the elephant changes hands – how do elephant men judge the age of an elephant when it is first captured or acquired? The answer is purely by comparison and as a result of long experience. When a young animal is captured and brought to the depot for sale its sex, height and peculiarities, such as the number of nails on its feet and the length and appearance of its tail, are recorded and at the same time an approximate assessment of its age is made. To the old and experienced elephant men in the depot this is an easy matter, for they have seen elephants born and watched them grow up and to their professional eyes the size and appearance of the animal indicates a certain age, to within an accuracy of a few years. Such estimates can certainly be relied upon nearly as well as a birth certificate. It is true that as the maturity of an elephant progresses this assessment of its age is more difficult. In the growing stage the height is the safest indicator, but as the growth of an elephant generally ceases at about twenty-five years, after that the height is of no assistance.

But here comparisons with elephants of known age can be reliable guides, particularly on such points as the relative sunkenness of the temples, the turning over of the upper margin of the ear, the depigmentation of cheeks, base of trunk and tips of ears, the progressive thinning of the legs and trunk, the depth of the furrows on either side of the root of the tail, the speed and gait of the elephant, the appearance of the dung of an old animal with its undigested matter and stringy fibres, the condition of the teeth and the general shrunken condition of the frame. The accuracy may not be as great as in the case of a young and growing elephant where height is the main indicator, but several experienced elephant men will agree to within a few years of each other on the age of any elephant put before them.

It is mainly the teeth of the elephant which determine its lifespan. The surface of the grinders consists of a series of corrugations provided by the edges of biscuit-like plates which are, as it were, welded together to form the tooth. These plates grow forward and upwards from the back of the jaw, each plate having its origin in a sort of gelatinous-like white matter; each becomes progressively more solid in consistency the farther forward it is, while the corrugations become progressively more worn in relation to their position. When the front plate becomes so worn that it is useless, the end of the tooth wears away or breaks off and its place is taken by the plate behind it. After the twenty-fifth year, the elephant has to depend on two teeth in each jaw. And so the chewing value of an elephant's teeth, on which depends the digestion and assimilation of its food, depends on the number of fresh plates that are put forward to maintain the corrugations on the grinder. There must be a limit to this process, though I have always found several pulpy plates in tooth cases removed from the jaws of even the oldest elephants, giving every indication that they still had a lot of years in them.

About twenty years ago, the death took place of the famous Travancore elephant Chandrasekharan, which had taken part in processions for nearly sixty years and was estimated to be nearly one hundred years old. We had several old elephants in the Assam Forest establishment which were shown in their books as seventy years or more. These books are started when the elephant is first purchased for the department, generally when the animal is six feet or so in height and is thus still young enough for its age to be accurately assessed, even if there is no actual proof of the date of birth. Megh Mala was one such old cow who was shown as seventy-two years at the time of her death. Akbar, the famous tusker of Kaziranga, died in 1956 at the recorded age of seventy.

I have no hesitation in accepting these recorded ages as correct, for when Megh Mala and Akbar were acquired for the Forest Department many years ago as young animals, their initial ages must have been correctly assessed and recorded by experienced elephant men. If these two elephants, hard worked and only moderately well looked after during their service with us, could have lived to over seventy years, is there any doubt that if they had remained in the wild state they would, barring accidents, have lived longer? Although the elephant is susceptible to many diseases associated with man and livestock, which are its worst enemies, it is one of the healthiest animals existing and suffers from practically no ailments in its natural state except intestinal parasites. For these it has various natural remedies, in particular the mineral salt-impregnated earths and waters which are known as *pungs* and *mati kholas* or in general 'salt-licks'. The power of recovery of an elephant from illness and injury is also an indication of its great stamina and must count in any estimate of an individual's lifespan. The elephant is the king of the jungle and fears nothing once it has reached maturity. Certainly to come to conclusions, as Major Flowers has done, from elephants kept in captivity or under artificial conditions in zoos and circuses in temperate countries is,

to my way of thinking, unjustifiable. While I would not be prepared to agree with Sanderson when he says that 'it is by no means
improbable that elephants live to one hundred and fifty to two
hundred years', I would say that the life expectancy of the elephant
in the wild state is around a hundred years in favourable circumstances.

Next to the age of the Asian elephant, the most intriguing question is the maximum height which it attains. A lot of vagueness
exists on this question even among people who should be better
informed. The average person has an inherent tendency unconsciously to exaggerate an elephant's height, even in Assam
where the elephant is almost a breakfast-table topic along with
tigers and rhinos. I remember, as part of our efforts to entertain
the British troops during the war at Gauripur, parading a few
elephants before the boys in a height-guessing competition. It was
amusing to find the colossal heights they made them out to be
and the great divergence between individual estimates. Eventually
it was a man who had had some acquaintance with elephants in
Burma who came nearest to the correct heights. A useful formula
is that twice the circumference of the fore foot equals the shoulder
height, though for perfect accuracy an elephant should be measured in the standing position with all its weight on the feet, which
should be close together.

One hears and even reads, tall tales of eleven-foot and even
twelve-foot elephants. Sanderson at one time said that 'there is
little doubt that there is not an elephant ten feet at the shoulder
in India', and he offered a reward of a double-barrelled rifle to
anyone producing an eleven-foot-high elephant. He eventually
found one that was 10 ft. 7½ inches high. This belonged to the
Raja of Nahan-Sirmour in the Punjab, and he made a journey of
one hundred miles or so by palanquin from railhead to Nahan to
measure the animal with his own hands. Milroy was so keen on
this question that he made special inquiries about all the large,
domesticated elephants in Assam and used to send the Doctor
Babu, our forest veterinarian, to measure them. At that time the
biggest domesticated elephant in Assam was Jung Bahadur, a

magnificent tusker belonging to the Raja of Gauripur, which stood 10 feet 4½ inches at the shoulder. I knew this mighty tusker well, and I measured him personally more than once. During my visit to the Maharaja of Mysore's stables in 1935, I met Neelakanta Rao, a Forest Officer in charge of the Maharaja's shikar department, who had just returned from an expedition to Assam, Burma and Siam in search of the biggest elephants he could find for the royal stables. He had tried to buy Jung Bahadur, but the Raja of Gauripur refused to sell. His best bargain was in Siam and he told an amazing story of his efforts to get the elephant across to Burma along the route which later became notorious as the 'death railway' during the Japanese campaign. I saw this animal side by side with a large tusker from Assam, one from Malabar and several big elephants from the Mysore forests, but I could see no difference in their racial characteristics.

During the war, I measured a big tusker in the stables of the Maharaja of Gwalior and he was half an inch taller than Jung Bahadur. In 1957, I had measured for me the biggest elephant of the Maharaja of Nepal, Hari Prasad; he was 10 feet 9 inches at the shoulder. Many years ago when Subha Ghananath Pandey had come to Assam from Nepal to purchase elephants he assured me that there were some over eleven feet high in the country; but so far no eleven-foot elephant has ever been measured in the domestic state.

Turning to the available and reliable records of large wild elephants shot recently, we find there are several which are claimed to be eleven feet. The Maharaja of Talcher in 1953 killed a rogue tusker in Dhenkanal, Orissa, which was said to be eleven feet high. The Maharaja of Mysore during the last war shot an elephant in the Mysore jungle which was eleven feet in height. Mackrell shot a large elephant at Bismuri, also in the Goalpara division of Assam, in about 1938 which was measured with a long stick, from withers to the sole of the fore-foot, as 10 feet 11 inches. The circumference of each fore-foot was 64¾ inches, which doubled gives a height of 10 feet 9½ inches, thus almost tallying with the measured height. Lalji, Kumar of Gauripur, shot a huge *makhna* in the Garo Hills in 1945 during his elephant-catching operations;

the circumference of the fore-foot measured 66 inches, which would make the elephant eleven feet in height at the shoulder. Unfortunately the height could not be measured as the body of the animal was on the edge of a precipitous slope and threatened to roll over. Lalji, whose family has owned elephants for generations and who is a true elephant man, says that 'he was a specimen best of all that I have up till now surveyed'.

In 1946 a pair of very large tusks was collected from an old elephant which died near one of our upper forest camps in Goalpara under peculiar circumstances. The tusker was old and was either wounded or ill and he had obviously come for protection to the camp, near which he stayed for several days. Our men detected the presence of Nepali poachers from the nearby Bhutan border. They kept guard over the big fellow and after some days the poachers, finding they could not kill the tusker near our camp, withdrew and the elephant wandered away. A couple of days later a man, whose daily duty it was to collect milk from the Bhutan villages three or four miles north, came running in to say that the big tusker was standing near the road, looking very sick. The men redoubled their watching and the next night he collapsed and died. The tusks were a perfectly matched pair, each tusk weighing 82 pounds; they were collected immediately and I subsequently had them mounted and presented to the Assam Legislative Assembly. The foresters who collected the tusks measured the elephant's height as it lay, in a straight line from withers to the sole of the foot, and got a precise measurement of eleven feet. By a coincidence I arrived at the base forest settlement the very next day and was told about the incident. I immediately asked if the elephant had been measured and they said 'yes'. I then asked if the circumference of the fore-foot had been checked against the shoulder height but was told it had not been done. I at once sent men up to the spot to do this, but unfortunately when they reached the body they found some of the toenails had been eaten away, probably by porcupines, and so the measurement that was taken could not be compared with that obtained by the formula of twice the circumference of the fore-foot.

This formula does not work out with complete accuracy but is a useful check. Elephants, like human beings, are both big and small footed, while the age of the animal and the condition of the soles of the feet also influence the comparative degree of splay or spread. Then, allowance has to be made for the condition of the ground in which an elephant leaves its foot impression, for a comparatively small animal will appear to be a giant if it has left its mark in soft mud. On the whole, however, it is reasonable to assume the bigger the foot print the bigger the elephant. Often this is the only guide when proclaiming an elephant for destruction, but measurements of foot-impressions in soft earth or muddy places do not justify the announcement of twelve and thirteen-foot monsters which sometimes appear in gazette notifications of proclaimed elephants.

On the evidence of all these measurements, I think it is reasonably safe to conclude that the Asian elephant can reach a shoulder height of eleven feet, though such elephants must exist only in the wild state because ideal conditions are required for their uninterrupted growth. For obvious reasons, it will probably never be possible to measure a specimen alive. The African elephant is, of course, considerably larger; the record is twelve feet, measured by Sir William Gowers, Governor of Uganda in the thirties.

One of the most fascinating problems concerning elephant behaviour is the still rather obscure phenomenon known as 'musth'. As I said before in connection with the Maharaja of Mysore's royal elephant, this condition is caused by a period of psychological disturbance associated with sexual maturity and desire, associated with a discharge of fluid from the temporal glands. Although musth does not always have dangerous effects, elephants in this state are definitely unbalanced. The Indian term for any unexplainable behaviour on the part of a man or animal is 'pagla', meaning mad; and the Assamese elephant men always refer to musth elephants as pagla. I have never come across an elephant that was really mad and I do not think the term should be applied to animals, even in the case of a musth elephant, as the various forms of true insanity are confined to *Homo sapiens*. I believe, however, that all cases of assaults and sudden killings by domesticated elephants are either associated with the condition of musth or must be attributed to some provocation.

In the case of Hari Prasad, the great tusker of Nepal, one of the Forest Officers described him thus: 'During the rainy season every year he becomes mad. In 1955 he killed an elephant within a second during his madness. One bullet is still lying within his body through which pus still oozes out. He obeys orders, but not always, he walks according to his own will.' How delightfully does the last sentence sum up the behaviour of most big male elephants!

The most famous example in recent years of an elephant running amuck, presumably as the result of musth, was that of Udaigiri, the ceremonial elephant of the President of India. This young tusker was captured by us when he was about eight years old. I had him carefully trained and he was shaping to follow in Akbar's footsteps at Kaziranga when, much against my wishes, he was sent to Delhi in 1954 as the President's elephant. Udaigiri collapsed when leading a procession in 1956 and afterwards was seriously ill with pneumonia. The next year he suddenly killed his attendant who was trying to chain him, crushing the man under his feet; immediately afterwards he accepted food and became quite calm. Just before his death he had been confined for some time because he showed signs of musth and was considered dangerous, but later he appeared to be normal and was unchained. He was being taken for a walk up and down the courtyard when he suddenly ran amuck, attacking and smashing up a military truck that was passing and chasing a man into a doorway. His mahout bravely stayed on his back for nearly three hours trying to control him, but the man had to be rescued dramatically by lasso and hauled up on to the roof of a nearby building. All attempts to control the elephant having failed, he was shot dead.

When I got news of Udaigiri's tragic end I was greatly shocked and saddened. I knew him first, as I have said, as a young elephant under training, then as a growing tusker at Kaziranga and finally as the President's elephant. When I saw him in 1956 while he was summering in Dehra Dun he looked fat and overfed. I had advised the military officer in charge of him to keep him in the forests of

Dehra Dun during the summer and next year they were preparing
to send him there when the tragedy occurred.

Obviously Udaigiri had never adjusted himself to the change
from Assam to Delhi with its alternating great heat with extreme
aridity and severe cold, nor could he accustom himself to the lack
of a real 'elephant's life'. His illness was a result of this and almost
certainly a contributory factor to his tragic end, though it is
always possible that Udaigiri might have been a natural killer.

An elephant in musth acquires abnormal strength and ferocity
and other males will start and shiver with fright at the sight and
scent of a musth elephant. Many were the stories our men used
to tell in this connection. There was a beautiful single-tusked
elephant or 'gonesh' in my 1936 kheddas; he was not a large
animal but was immensely strong and his single, upturned tusk
gave him a menacing appearance. On one occasion when he was
in musth he was being taken down to the river and while still on
top of the bank he saw one of his rivals, with whom he had had a
tusking match on a previous occasion in which he had come off
second best. Rushing down the bank before his mahout could
stop him, he attacked his opponent, driving his single tusk through
his side at one blow and killing him within a few seconds.

The persistence of a large male elephant in musth is beyond
belief. Once when I had lost my elephant Sundarmala I searched
for her for weeks in the Dibru reserve and on one occasion we
met a very large makhna or tuskless elephant, his cheeks pouring
with musth fluid. He had in tow a small cow elephant which he
had abducted from a neighbouring garden; her leg chains were
still on and could be heard distinctly as she walked. As I was on a
male elephant, we gave the wild makhna a wide berth; but he persisted in following us, with his little companion trailing behind,
and in spite of our shouting he got closer and closer. I did not
know exactly what his intentions were, but it was obvious that he
resented the presence of our male elephant which he took to be a
rival. Eventually the mahout got so nervous that I had to fire my
gun. The No. 4 shot spattered the leaves of a tree above his head
and the dignified, but at the same time intimidating manner in
which he finally turned away was very impressive.

That was when I first came to admire the noble head carriage of a makhna as compared with a tusker which, unless he has up-turning tusks, always seems to hang his head a little. Except in a fight, an elephant is definitely handicapped by really long, heavy tusks, particularly when negotiating thick forest. This is one reason why tuskers are not used in the noosing of wild elephants in mela shikar, nor are they popular on shooting excursions, where a staunch female is hard to beat. But for me a makhna is the choice always.

I was once looking for a rogue makhna, which had attacked a party of Nepalis coming from a bazaar on the Bhutan border and which had lifted one of the men from his pony and carried him away into the jungle. It was a wild and solitary place, teeming with signs of elephants. Painstakingly we were following the tracks of a large makhna which had shown itself near a riverside camp in the early hours of the morning and which answered the description of the wanted elephant, which had a short tail ending in a knob. Suddenly we heard a distant and prolonged roaring; we stopped short in our tracks and then the noise came again. My mahouts whispered to me that the noise was made by a frightened elephant. We pushed on cautiously and presently caught sight of the backs of two elephants above the tops of the tall *tara* grass. Again came that angry roar and, by standing up carefully on Mohan Prasad's back, I could see what was going on.

One was a makhna, who was obviously in full musth, with the fluid pouring out of the orifices near his temples and down his cheeks. The cow was apparently disinclined for the sexual em-brace, for she kept on crossing her hind legs and moving forward whenever the bull attempted to mount her, her ears flat against her head in fright. When this happened the maddened bull would jab at her from behind, at the same time keeping her under restraint with his trunk; at this she would bellow with fright, her mouth wide open.

Suddenly we saw the trunk of the rogue go up into the still air two or three times and before I could resume my seat on the pad he had picked up Mohan Prasad's scent. He started to come towards us, hesitantly at first in short, wavering moves, his trunk questing and searching the air; then as he located us correctly, in a direct, swift walk which sent a shiver down my spine. All this while Mohan Prasad had been raising his trunk and lowering it as he took in the rank horse-like smell of the musth elephant, while my mahout Ontai alternately held my ankle and tapped the saddle near my feet as if telling me to sit down.

When I divined the makhna's intention I hurriedly resumed my seat. Although I could no longer see the approaching elephant for the tall grass, I tugged at Ontai's left sleeve to move him behind a small, bushy tree weighted down with climbers, partly to conceal ourselves and partly to intercept the oncoming elephant, who was coming on absolutely silently. But he immediately located our last position and shifted his course, as I could judge from the noise. I again tugged at Ontai to make him take Mohan Prasad to the right and we had just cleared the stuff that was concealing us when the rogue burst out on us. Not more than thirty feet away, he was shaking his head and coming on with swift, deliberate strides though not yet charging.

The almost head-on meeting was too much for Mohan Prasad. Could he have seen the musth elephant approaching from a distance it might have made a difference, but meeting him suddenly and headlong like this startled him and it was perhaps too much to ask him to face a musth elephant under such circumstances. With a hoarse bellow of fear, he turned and bolted. Once before he had done this when a wounded sambhar deer had suddenly charged towards him through thick undergrowth. Any elephant, no matter how staunch, will do this on occasions when startled.

As Mohan Prasad turned with a jerk, I just had time to half raise my rifle and to discharge it into the head of the oncoming elephant, which in another few paces would have been right on top of us. He went down in a flurry of dust and jungle, but I saw him pick himself up immediately and then, thank heavens, turn away and move off. Mohan Prasad took us into the jungle bellowing with fear, I holding on to the ropes having been swung round to face the tail, Ontai pulling and jabbing at the elephant's ear with the goad. We pulled him up at last and after we had recovered our breath and presence of mind at the sudden encounter, which might well have ended differently, we followed up the rogue. But apart from one distant glimpse of him moving through the forest, we never caught up with him and we soon lost his tracks among those of the many elephants which had been grazing in that spot.

On another occasion we were removing a small catch from the Rangapahar stockade not very far from the Naga Hills, the site of which is now covered by a forest plantation. I had a friend with his wife and little son staying with me and they came along to see the excitement. The roping operation had hardly commenced when the stockade men drew our attention to a big makhna which was moving about around the stockade some distance from it. He was in full musth and one could see the dark stain of the fluid down his cheeks. He kept on moving about restlessly, sometimes approaching the stockade quite close and this made the men shout at him. The spectators climbed to the top of the stockade wall, while some made for trees when he came too close for safety. He had obviously been consorting with one of the cows we had captured, but luckily for us he had escaped being driven into the stockade.

I had my camera with me at the time and decided to try and photograph him, especially as he was so boldly showing himself. At his next appearance I went forward to meet him. He was quite close to the stockade and I could approach him along a cleared path. He spotted me at once and stood quite still, his ears at full stretch, his trunk hanging straight in front of him, one foot a little ahead of the other. I knew the signs to be those preparatory to a charge but I had my plans worked out. Closer and closer I sidled up the path towards him, alternately looking into the view-finder and up at him. At last I felt I had got close enough for a picture and when I was about fifty feet from him I stopped to peer once more into the view-finder before clicking the lever – and at that very moment he charged. He started without a sound and I just had time to click and then to turn and run.

I raced madly down the path towards the wing wall of the stockade and when I reached it I took a dive through one of the large, square openings of the stout palisade, elbows first to protect my camera, only to plunge up to my knees and elbows into a small swamp full of sticky mud. When I extricated myself and turned there was the big makhna on the other side of the wing wall, squealing and kicking the ground with rage. His attention was attracted to something on one side, otherwise I think he would have tried to get through to me. I could hear shouts and laughter away to the left near the stockade gate. 'Fire a shot, someone!' I yelled, but it seemed an eternity before someone loosed off a shot over the head of the animal. He turned away then, with his short stump of a tail twisted in rage and giving out sounds like the squeaking of a child's toy, while I watched him with bated breath, not even stirring from where I was standing in the mud with my camera in my hand! It was a complete wreck of course and my precious picture was spoilt. They had to scrape the mud off me with a knife while we compared notes, laughing all the while. It transpired that while I had been stalking the makhna a number of the braver spectators had been on my tail. When the elephant charged they ran just as I did, but went away to the safety of the stockade wall itself – only to fall in a heap into the same swamp as I had. Some had lost their shoes in the mud while one had fallen flat and had been trodden on.

It is a wrong belief that only an elephant in musth demands or is capable of sexual congress. Musth is a sign of sexual maturity, but it is the female which comes into season and decides the matter. There are no obvious signs, except that the males will start paying attention to a particular cow, who makes little twittering noises and behaves in a rather peculiar manner which is revealing only to those who have experience of elephants. Presumably the cow exudes an attractive odour, otherwise it is impossible to explain how a bull elephant is led to her, sometimes from a long distance. Cow elephants when they are in season are irresistible to males; and males which are in musth behave as if they are drunk when attracted to a cow elephant of their choice. I have met people who say that a musth elephant is not capable during that period, but I refuse to believe it. On the other hand, although the musth con-

4. A 'royal' tusker, member of the highest elephant caste

5. A small herd of wild elephants

6 and 7. Newborn elephant calves

dition increases the desire for sex, it is not essential for the performance of the sexual act. The whole question of cohabitation between elephants would therefore appear to be still obscure.

Nilakanta Rao told me of how on one occasion in Mysore a wild tusker in musth concentrated his amorous attentions on a pregnant cow elephant of the Forest Department to the exclusion of another cow that was with it. When the pregnant cow would not yield to his intentions he was so rough with her, butting and pushing her about with his tusks, that eventually she died.

Cases of wild males trying to abduct tame cow elephants are not infrequent. One moonlight night I had climbed down from my elephant, a female accompanied by a calf, and started walking back along the path to camp. The elephant with her mahout turned back towards the village where she was stationed for timber dragging. She had hardly left me when I heard a terrific din, the roaring of the mother elephant punctuated by the bawling of the calf and the shouts of the mahout. I stopped still and listened, very frightened as I was at the time still new to the jungle (at first I had thought it was a tiger roaring). When I inquired next morning I was told that a wild tusker had come out of the jungle and attempted to make off with the cow elephant. The mahout gave a graphic description of how the tusker kept on circling his mount, while he could do nothing but shout and drive his elephant as hard as possible. The calf had added to the confusion by bellowing with fear and running under its mother's belly and between her legs. The mahout had nothing but his *dao*, a knife for cutting jungle, with which he tried to slash at the trunk of the wild elephant. His conduct was very gallant as he could easily have slipped off his elephant and left her to her fate instead of running the risk of being pulled off her neck.

One day when I was camped on the Gabhru river during my first kheddas a solitary elephant started visiting the camp; although he was not in musth, the phandis said he was attracted by a female koonki which had come into season. We often had the experience of solitary males penetrating right into camp and moving about among the captives. Generally they would not harm them, but many of our tame koonkis and departmental

c

elephants were badly injured by wild males when tied out in the jungle or even in a depot. It was as if wild elephants are impelled by curiosity to know what goes on in a training depot, or is it a natural sympathy for their captive brethren?

It was interesting to see the courting and mating of elephants in our camp, a process which is shrouded in so much speculation and mystery but which is really quite simple. It is no different from the mating of domestic cattle or any other quadruped for that matter, but there was no pushing or quarrelling as there is among cattle or dogs. The first time I witnessed such a scene the mating took place right in the open, in the middle of the depot, with all the men silent spectators but standing back in the shadow of the huts. This was surprising to me – the dignity with which the men witnessed the act, matching that of the animals which participated in it. The mating of dogs or horses or cattle invariably excites ribaldry and laughter among the spectators, but not this.

One by one the big koonkis attempted to mount the cow and it was only when one had failed that another took his place, again without any show of haste, violence or anger. It was surprising to see that some of the males in apparently good condition were unable to complete the act, whereas one of the Miri-owned koonkis, Kansira Goonda, who at all times was an animal of comparatively poor condition and looks, proved the most effective. On another occasion I witnessed the mating of two timber-dragging elephants. The male attempted to move the female away to a secluded spot with little pushes from the rear. Both the animals were hobbled and so it took him some time to move the cow away from the open space in which they were grazing. They were loose except for the tied front legs, but the shackled male elephant found no difficulty in performing the act.

It is surprising how the smaller cows, particularly those which had not had calves (*sarins* as the Assamese call them) are able to bear the great weight of the males. I have come across impressions in banks of earth and in hill sides, obviously made by copulating wild elephants and it would appear that the animals seek the assistance of some slope or undulation in the ground. Thom narrates how in Burma he once watched a large male pushing the female forward, holding her hind leg with his trunk, up a slope and then down again, mounting her as she came down the slope. I suspect that the female often leans against a bank of earth with her head so as to resist the weight of the large male on her hindquarters.

The fantastic stories one hears that the cow elephant lies on its back to receive the male, as in human beings, can definitely be discounted. Nevertheless the position of the organ of the male, as well as that of the female which faces vertically downwards to the ground, lends colour to these stories. The positions, in my opinion, call for the maximum virility on the part of the male elephant, as the arc of erection to be described by the male organ has to be seen to be believed. No wonder many apparently capable bulls are solitary wanderers, because of such inability to mate effectively. In this respect it is not age which decides the solitary state of male elephants, but their comparative virility – Nature's ruse to ensure the best sires.

CHAPTER 5

CAPTURING ELEPHANTS

The first records of elephant capturing and training date from the fifth century BC. The Greeks Megasthenes (200 BC), Strabo (AD 130) and Indicoplenstes (AD 600) all wrote on the subject, though their accounts are slightly contradictory and at times not very clear. The Chola kings of Tanjore, as well as the Ahoms of Assam, left a massive elephant literature.

For thousands of years the main demand for elephants has been for religious processions and marriage ceremonies. Most temples, particularly in the south, kept elephants and many wealthy men did so as a matter of course, loaning or hiring their elephants out for festivals. Maharaja Jung Bahadur of Nepal, founder of the Rana dynasty and the virtual maker of Nepal, owned a thousand elephants as recently as a hundred years ago and the princes all kept them according to their status. The landed aristocracy had always been the great patrons of professional elephant dealers, whose trade centres on the four annual melas or markets of north Bihar. Since time immemorial these melas were fed from the jungles of Assam and Bengal.

The most famous of these melas is the one at Sonepur near Purnea, known as the Harihar Chatra mela. It has always been held at the first full moon of November and the fair is visited by over five million people, who come to bathe in the Ganges on this auspicious occasion. At one time some six to eight hundred elephants would be up for sale at this mela. I was invited to attend the one in 1935 by the Raja, whose hereditary right to stage the function on his land was the excuse and the occasion for lavish hospitality. The huge fair, with elephants, horses, cattle, bright cloths and eatables and all manner of other goods, was a fascinating spectacle even for me who was used to Indian pageantry; it must have entranced the many European guests of the Raja. The numerous traders who had taken elephants from my kheddas for sale there had spread word of my absorbing interest in elephants; they were my best ambassadors and I was given a warm welcome. I spent my time wandering up and down the long lines of tethered elephants, in some cases recognizing animals we had taken out of the stockades. Certainly for an elephant man a visit to the Sonepur mela is an experience not to be missed; it is an elephant connoisseur's paradise and the visit did more to round off my education than anything else.

The next fair at which elephants are sold in Bihar is the Kharga mela which is held in January; then comes the Singeswar mela in February–March; and finally the Nak-mard mela in April. These four markets have served the Assam and Bengal elephant catchers for centuries. They must have been the main markets for the purchase of war elephants of Chandra Gupta Mauriya, whose capital was not far away at Pataliputra near the modern Patna, and they also served the princes farther west. The mind reels at the thought of the great elephant processions moving over the years from the lush jungles of the East into a slavery as great as that of humans in Africa and, in most cases, to early death. Thousands upon thousands of elephants must have changed hands at these four melas.

Coming to more recent times, the British army in India needed elephants for its guns and its commissariat and the horse did not entirely replace the ponderous elephant until the beginning of the present century. The military had a regular elephant-catching establishment in Dacca until 1900, when it was transferred to Burma because of the depletion of herds in the Garo Hills as a result of excessive catching.

Elephants were an indispensable necessity in that period of India's development when roads were still being built and the jungles were being explored and cleared for settlement, or surveyed for reservation. Tea-gardens maintained elephants for communication across rivers where bridges did not exist and planters' bungalows sometimes had a high elephant porch where the owner could mount and dismount in comfort during the rains. In regions like Assam and North Bengal, every district official had his complement of elephants for touring and baggage carrying. They were also used for shikar; right down to the thirties the annual Christmas camp and shoot was a regular feature. In Goalpura, still the best shooting area in Assam, the officials would have a friendly competition with the Raja of Gauripur, who could command twenty elephants of his own; with these added to the ten or more government elephants, bags of a dozen tigers a week were not uncommon. Finally, there was the timber industry which needed a great number of elephants to haul and stack its logs.

With all these demands, it is small wonder that elephant catching should have flourished in various parts of the sub-continent right up to the beginning of the twentieth century, after which it began to decline.

The Sanskrit texts laid down five methods of capturing elephants in the following order of desirability: in pens or stockades; by means of female decoys; by mela shikar or noosing from the backs of trained elephants; by nooses concealed on the ground; and finally by the pit method. These various systems developed and became peculiar to different topographical regions of India in the course of time.

Although the stockade method is the first to be described by ancient writers, it was probably of Aryan origin and the catching of elephants in pits was almost certainly practised earlier by the aboriginal inhabitants of southern India. In the north, there is no record of capturing in pits; whereas in the south the stockade method was unknown until introduced to the Mysore plateau by Sanderson, although the similar kraal system of Ceylon was practised from very early times. It may seem strange that the stockade was never used in southern India, situated as it is so close to Ceylon; but the main reason must be that it is unsuitable for hilly country, where the elephants of southern India are found.

Madras Forest Department as to the relative merits of shallower pits with straight sides and deeper pits with sloping sides and the latter won on merits. But whatever the merits or demerits of the system as a whole, nowhere have I seen elephants so well maintained and so well cared for as in the south. There the daily bath is something approaching a ritual and the dark, velvety appearance of the healthy skin is a result of prolonged scrubbing. The regular hours of work, the food and the attention given to it, make the keeping of elephants in the south a hobby only for those who can afford it, whereas in Assam and Burma even a village headman may presume to own an elephant.

In Ceylon, in addition to the kraal system, an interesting and very daring method of capturing elephants is practised by a class of Muslims called Panikkans, who are traditional elephant noosers. Ropes of rawhide made from long, thin strands of deerskin about twenty-five feet long are used to noose the legs of wild elephants. The nooses are spread on the ground, sunk an inch or two below the surface of the soil and camouflaged with eatables, the other end being anchored to a tree alongside an elephant path. Skilled men hide behind the trees and endeavour to secure the hind-legs of elephants as they pass. Surely the record for any elephant catcher must be that of Seeni Panikkan of Irakkaman in the Gal Oya valley who in 1959, at the age of seventy, was still vigorously employed in his trade; he had captured more than four hundred elephants in fifty years.

The Panikkans can train an elephant within three to six months and are said to be able to break in an animal within a week 'provided the trunk is first secured', a provision which demonstrates clearly the key nature of the trunk and head. In the Assam *hal* method the secret is constriction of the neck, which prevents the animal from using its trunk and enables trainers to approach it from the side; they can thus handle, stroke and feed it from the moment it is introduced into the stocks. To a lesser extent, this applies also to the kraal method of training in southern India.

Another description of the Panikkan method of capturing

elephants is as follows. About ten to fifteen men lie in ambush near an elephant path and when a herd comes along it is stampeded – if at night, by burning coconut leaf torches. A selected young animal is chased, the noose is quickly slipped over a hind-leg and the other end is wound round a tree or even a stout ant-hill. The elephant is pulled up short and falls on its face, when the other leg is similarly noosed. A neck rope is then applied and the animal is taken to the vicinity of the village, partly by force but mainly by stratagem. It is provoked into chasing men who tease it, shouting and dancing and waving cloths, and thus it is gradually made to go in the required direction. All this may sound easy, but to one who has seen how difficult it is to handle and tie even a small elephant when it is roped to a koonki, the controlling of a captured animal by human power alone is almost incredible. Yet it is done in the Congo, where young African elephants are chased by men who noose their legs and bring them under control.

In the Congo the use of enclosures to break in elephants is unknown, the animals being picketed out to stakes. One feature resembling methods used in India is the employment of trained elephants called 'monitors' in the training stage, though not for capturing. The success achieved with the long and patient experiments carried out by the Belgian authorities disprove the belief that the African elephant is incapable of being domesticated or taught to train its own kind. Sanderson says that Joseph Fayrer, who first conceived the possibility of capturing and domesticating the African elephant, at his suggestion imported four elephants from Bombay to Zanzibar under the care of two Europeans to see if they would withstand the tsetse fly. The Indian mahouts soon returned to their country and the two Europeans were killed. The elephants were not affected by the tsetse fly, but after some months two died and the expedition was abandoned. Apparently the difficulties of feeding and maintaining the elephants on the march with the available fodder were great. What a different story might have been written if the experiment had succeeded, or if the Belgian experiments to utilize the African elephant for domestic work on farms and for transport had been more generally applied.

Going farther east to Indo-China and Siam, we find the stockade and the lassoing methods employed and in addition a very interesting way of capturing elephants by harpooning. In Siam the stockade method, with hundreds of drivers, is something on the scale of the Ceylon kraal and the modern Mysore khedda. The gate is a sliding one, which is in itself a unique feature and along the top of the stockade wall runs a platform all round the enclosure from which men can observe the captured animals and keep them from breaking out by using long spears, fire and even gunshots. This type of stockade used to be constructed in Assam by our Shan catchers, there being no trench around the inside of the stockade wall as in the Assamese-built enclosure. This feature is an indication of the racial link with the countries farther east, which is so faithfully maintained in matters of dress and custom to this day by the Khamtis and Itonias, the Shan elephant catchers of Assam. In Indo-China the lassoing method is more a sport than an economic venture and was practised in recent times by the Emperor Bao Dai, principally in the Moi country. The ropes are of buffalo or ox-hide, long strips of moist leather being twisted together to form a rope as thick as a stout chain; this is fixed to the end of a ten-foot pole and fastened to a double cane band around the koonki's body, ending in a noose. The hind-leg of the wild elephant would be noosed in an action something like the swooping movement of a butterfly net. Here it is worth noting the contrast with the Assam lassoing or mela shikar method, where the rope is of jute fibre and is thrown over the head of the captive.

The third method is employed only in certain parts of Cambodia, particularly in Kompang-Thom, during the rainy season. It consists of harpooning the ears of swimming elephants from canoes. The elephant herds are prevented from returning to the hills at the end of the dry season, day and night watch being kept by men with trained elephants. When the floods are at their peak and the wild elephants have been penned in the lower levels by men on tame elephants, the canoes move into action. The helpless elephants are harpooned through the thickest part of the earflap, sometimes piercing both ears for greater control; the harpooned elephant is

then forcibly led and tied to the branch of a tree, in which a platform has been constructed for men whose duty is to watch over
the captive. The wretched elephant has to tread water or drown,
but when it is exhausted the men in the tree pass a noose under its
belly and support it. Finally when the water recedes, the captured
elephants are taken away to the training camp by tame elephants.
As can be imagined, the casualties in such a method must be heavy,
quite apart from the sufferings experienced by the captives.

A method of capturing elephants in Mysore which for sheer nerve
must rank with the most daring, particularly as it involves the
capture of large male elephants, necessitates the use of highly
trained female koonkis as decoys. Once a large solitary male is
located the decoy elephants, with mahouts concealed in blankets
on their necks, seek his company, grazing continuously alongside
and never leaving him. Sometimes the male will scent the men, in
which case he will lose no time in putting as great a distance as
possible between himself and the catchers; but if the whole business is skilfully done he remains unsuspicious to the end. In time
he becomes so enamoured of his treacherous companions, particularly if he is in a state of musth, as to be completely lost to everything else. Whenever he attempts to lie down for sleep the tame
Delilahs move away and he is compelled to follow them. In this
manner and with frequent relays of men and koonkis who are
changed about unobtrusively out of his sight and hearing, he is
reduced to such a state of drowsiness as to be unaware when his
hind-legs are tied, first with lengths of thin and later with thicker
ropes. The female elephants cleverly screen and shield the men
working on the ground during the whole process. Once his hind-
legs are securely roped, he is permitted to vent his rage and
exhaust his strength on nothingness, until he is ready for the neck-
rope or lasso, which is thrown from the back of a koonki. He is
then led away to his tying place and trained.

About twenty years ago, a large male tusker was captured like
this in Mysore while he was in musth and completely absorbed in
paying attentions to a female decoy elephant; but he was too
large and old and did not survive. In 1945 a tusker said to be

10 ft. 9½ inches in height was similarly captured in the Biligiriran-gan hills, happy hunting grounds of Sanderson and of so many other sportsmen after him.

I was also told of a magnificent tusker which was captured near Mymensingh in Bengal, on the southern borders of the Garo Hills of Assam, in the same summer. This animal was in the habit of visiting the koonkis and while he was in a state of musth it was decided to try to capture him. One morning he was surrounded by men on female koonkis and while he was paying attention to them, first his legs and then his neck were roped. He was said to have been in such a dazed condition that he was completely unaware of everything except the final roping; but on finding himself a cap-tive, his rage was indescribable. He remained tied in the same place for more than a month as it was impossible to handle him even with the biggest of koonkis. But when eventually he was sold to a neighbouring zamindar (large land-owner) for five thousand rupees, he had become so extremely weak and emaciated that he collapsed and died at the first stream he came to, after taking a few mouthfuls of water.

The Ahoms of Assam, a Shan race who ruled the country for nearly seven hundred years until the advent of the British, also used female decoys for capturing wild elephants. They main-tained a permanent trench, deep but only sufficiently wide to take one elephant at a time, running from the Naga Hills in a straight line to near their old capital, Rangpur, near Sibsagar. The trench had drop gates at intervals for cutting off and impounding the elephants one by one as they entered, following the decoys. The Ahoms used to feed these decoys on specially rich foods and native medicines until, according to the *Hathiputhi* – an ancient record of elephant lore written on sheets of bark from the *sassi* or *agar* tree – they emitted a peculiar and strong odour which could attract wild elephants, particularly the males, from great distances. The Ahoms were great owners of elephants as is to be expected of a warlike race living in a jungle-girt country such as Assam was in those days. In fact this animal was the only means of land communi-cation, along the high embanked roads built by their kings; now they are mostly abandoned but are still known as 'raj garhs'. It is said that the elephant for the king to ride upon was selected by placing a glass of water on its back, to see if it spilled over when the animal walked!

Large male elephants have been captured after being drugged with opium concealed in bananas, sugar-cane, elephant apples and other foodstuffs, though it is difficult to believe that an animal with such a well-developed sense of smell could be deceived by such methods. I was told by an old Forest Officer from Mysore that he once tried concealing opium in sugar-cane for the same purpose but with no success: although the 'loaded' pieces were hidden right in the middle of a heap of cane, the elephant's sensitive trunk enabled him to detect them and he discarded those pieces alone, eating the rest. I know how difficult it used to be to persuade sick elephants to eat the titbits in which we used to introduce medicines. The moment we put a powder into the ball of grass soaked in salt water with a few grains of rice – the standard hand-feeding titbit of the traders in our depots – the elephant would eject it from his mouth. I never actually saw opium or *bhang*, another opiate, being administered to an elephant, but I was told that molasses and even bananas are commonly used to conceal it.

CHAPTER 6

NOOSING ELEPHANTS

The most exciting method of catching elephants, and one calling for great skill and daring on the part of both koonki and rider, is undoubtedly mela shikar, in which wild elephants are chased and noosed by phandis from the backs of trained elephants. From time immemorial this method has been practised in Burma, Siam and Indo-China. On the Indian sub-continent it is now confined to the forests of the north-east including Chittagong and Bengal, but its main home is Assam and the Assamese are experts at it. In fact in pre-partition times, Assamese phandis as well as stockade men used to be taken over to Sylhet, now in East Pakistan.

Although kheddas, described in the next chapter, serve the main requirements of the elephant-catching industry in Assam, mela shikar is still a pastime with many people drawn from surprisingly varied sections of the community. Lawyers, doctors, tea-planters, schoolmasters, members of religious orders, village headmen and tribal peoples all take their chance in this most fascinating of gambles. Many families have been ruined, while others have become rich only to lose everything in a succession of bad seasons.

The case of the 'owner rider' is rare, most of the owners being staid or middle-aged individuals. But there are one or two notable exceptions. One of them, most surprisingly, was the son of a Raja. 'Lalji' as we all called him because of his fair complexion, took to mela shikar with his phandis for the sheer sport of it. He was a born elephant man, with a deep love for the animal and a most humane approach to the sometimes sordid business of elephant catching. He could always be relied upon to observe the rules scrupulously and had great control over his men, with whom he lived in the jungle.

I knew another *bhadralog* or 'gentleman' who became a successful phandi in his own right. He was Durganath Gogoi, the scion of a respectable Ahom family of Upper Assam and the son of a famous elephant man who did his last catching under me. Gogoi combined the natural dash of a young Assamese who had elephants in his blood with the discipline of an educated man. He lived with his men and shared their hardships and so earned their respect and affection. His father had lost his fortune in the elephant-catching business, but this did not deter young Durga Gogoi. He plunged into it after he left college but with this difference, that he started at the bottom rung of the ladder as a working phandi and finished up as a very successful mahaldar or lease-holder.

The expenses of fitting out a koonki are negligible when compared with the financing of a stockade and the small man is able to take part in elephant catching each cold weather season after the paddy has been planted. Most owners of good koonkis prefer the safe earnings to be had from hiring out their elephants to koonkidars, who finance the entire operation and who meet the costs of fitting out the elephant. The requirements are saddle pads, ropes, jute to make the noosing ropes or phands, and salaries and rations for the three men accompanying the elephant for six months, plus incidental expenses. The total outlay for a season in my day was about a hundred and fifty pounds and the rewards could be high in the event of good catches. Most of the famous koonkis are hired out for the whole season, sometimes at very high figures and the phandis or noosers are also engaged and paid according to their fame and skill.

There is the attraction of a good gamble for the catcher himself; for the koonkidar who looks forward to his trained animal capturing two or three elephant calves; for the mahaldar or lease owner of a good catching area; for the expert phandi who is eager to add to his score of captures; and for the humble stockade man who, as he ploughs his fields, is filled with exciting thoughts of

8 and 9. Young elephants enjoying a bath

10 and 11. Elephant caught in a pit in southern India

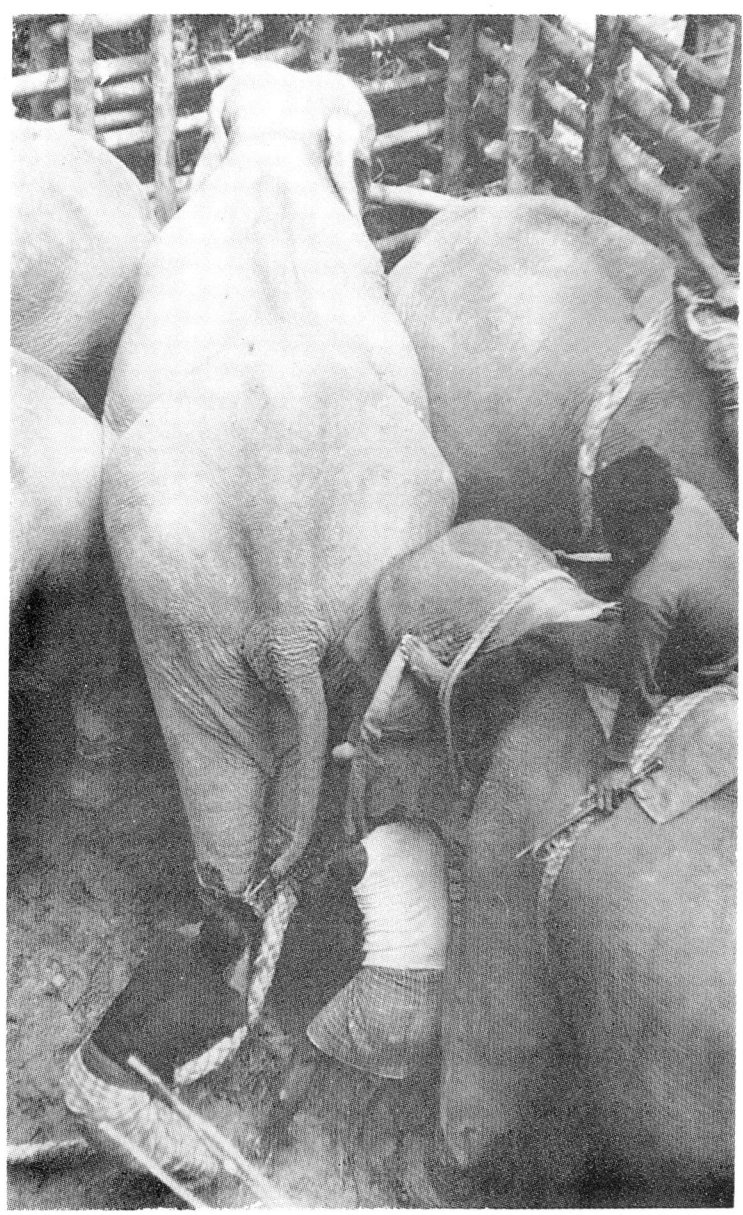

12. Roping in a Mysore stockade

13. Wild elephant tied to two tame ones for removal from a Mysore stockade

14. The catch in an Assam stockade

the coming cold weather operations. The work is intensely absorbing, spiced as it is with the prospect of a big catch and a high price, but it is hard and exhausting both for men and elephants. There are moments of despair when the elephants are elusive, or when the market is dull and traders have conspired to ring the auctions; but in spite of all this it is a sport which all concerned enjoy and look forward to every year.

Milroy tried to take some of the gamble out of elephant catching by organizing departmental kheddas in which all parties, including the government, took the risks of loss as well as a share in the profits. Instead of a flat royalty rate to be paid according to the sex and type of elephant captured, he introduced a share system whereby government, lease-holder, koonki owner and stockade man all had a stake in the sale price of the elephants caught. The operations were placed under a special officer and the whole-time services of a veterinary officer were provided; he was assisted by a jemadar or supervisor, himself a seasoned mahout, and in this way the confidence of everyone from catcher to purchaser was obtained. By using both the written rules and the traditions of the indigenous catchers, Milroy created an atmosphere in which the welfare of the elephant came first, last and every time. The lease-holder was generally responsible for any breach of the rules in his area; but the responsibility for a captured elephant until it was sold was fixed primarily on the phandi who caught it and brought it in.

A mela shikar team consists of three men: the phandi who does the actual noosing; the mahout who controls the koonki; and the grass-cutter who sees to its needs. The phandi first serves his apprenticeship for many years, having started from the bottom as a grass-cutter and then rising to be a mahout, before finally being elevated to the distinguished position of the expert who throws the phand over the elephant's head.

The mahout's place is at the rear end of the saddle pad and when in action he stands up holding on to a rope sling with one hand, while with the other he plies a goad to make the elephant go faster. In ancient times a spiked mallet was used. The spot pricked by the spear is always the same and in koonkis is marked during the catching season by a running sore and at other times by a white scar. The mahout is expected to play his full part in the handling of a koonki and its capture and in fact is only one place removed from that of a phandi; but he is not permitted by his master to handle the elephant except in simple operations until he has shown himself to be deft and useful.

The grass cutter or *kamla* as he is called in Assam, is the humblest of the hunting trio. His place is in the camp while the koonki is out hunting and when it returns, exhausted, his duty is to pour hot water on its back, a sort of fomentation of the spinal column and withers. If there is a catch in tow, he relieves the phandi and mahout while they eat. Perched on the neck of the koonki he lets it and the captive graze, keeping a wary eye open for trouble and ever ready to anticipate a turning movement by swinging his mount round the right way or by administering a blow with the koonki's head.

The essential details for mela shikar are the same everywhere – a skilful and courageous phandi, a fast, strong elephant and a thick rope. In the countries farther east the rope is made from fibrous tree bark and in Indo-China from raw hide, but in Assam and Bengal from the fibre of the cultivated jute plant. The most suitable elephants for mela shikar are females, though a good makhna or tuskless male is highly prized and by some is considered to be unbeatable. But on the whole male elephants are less effective than females as they are liable to be attacked by the herd bulls. Cow elephants are also less suspicious of their own sex and female koonkis can penetrate right into a herd. Tuskers are of very limited use except as a *tour de force* when it comes to dealing with wild males, as their tusks have the double disadvantage of impeding their progress through the jungle and frightening the wild elephants. The mela shikar koonki is like a racehorse in comparison with other horses and the head phandi is like a first-class jockey. The fame of a good koonki or the reputation of a skilled phandi are evergreen topics among elephant men, just as the skill and dash of a good jockey or the qualities of a good racehorse are among racing men.

Mela shikar koonkis hunt in small parties in order to be able to render assistance to each other. The daily search for the wild herd begins in the early hours of the morning and the camps are frequently shifted until contact has been made, the hunters remaining in the forest until they have made a catch or until their rations run out, whichever is earlier. In the meanwhile the koonkidar who has fitted out and financed the expedition is sitting in the depot anxiously waiting for news. Luck plays a great part in this operation and a koonki may strike a herd very soon after it goes out from the depot and be back in a few days with a capture. But skill is essential and a first-class phandi may capture anything up to half a dozen animals during the short catching season of six months provided his mount is equally good.

A few days after a phandi has taken his catch to the depot and handed it over for training he may be off again, but he is responsible for the animal he brings in until it has safely settled down under the severe régime of training. The little breather gives him and his fellow-hunters a chance to rest and replenish their gear and rations, which are of the simplest – rice, pulses, salt, mustard oil and a little sugar and tea, all carried in bamboo sections hung on the pad of the koonki. The little saddle pad is piled high with the simple belongings of the men, their bedding wrapped in old sacking and their few cooking utensils packed in net bags. A simple tarpaulin or gunny cloth tent completes the equipment.

While out hunting, phandis show their skill in picking out fresh tracks and here it is experience that counts. It is very important to find a hot trail, otherwise it would be impossible to catch up with a herd of feeding elephants, which are constantly on the move. Communication is by signs and whistles and very seldom are low words spoken. The approach to a herd is, of course, as silent and stealthy as possible, great care being taken to avoid the large bulls and solitaries which hang about on the outskirts. Generally only young elephants are the target for, apart from being easier to handle, they fetch the best prices. Little female elephants are in greatest demand and those under five feet three inches in height get a special concession on the railways when they are taken to the markets. Next in favour are young tuskers and sometimes rather larger tuskers, which in the old days could be sold to some ruling prince at a fancy price. Makhnas are unwelcome, but in the hurly burly of the chase it is often a case of taking what one can get. A cool and experienced phandi will select his quarry carefully but, although even a young tusker is generally easy to distinguish, to tell a female calf from a makhna is almost impossible, even in the depot. I remember a guffaw of laughter I once raised when I bent down to inspect a doubtful case from the rear!

A top class intelligent koonki will of its own accord and without any instruction from its rider use its trunk, head, legs and body to frustrate the attempts of the wild elephant to escape while the phandi is hauling in the slack preparatory to tying the check-rope. It is as if the tame elephant fully enters into the spirit of the capture. I have even heard of a koonki bringing the captive into camp by itself after its rider had been thrown and injured – and in one case killed – in the struggle that followed the noosing.

Mela shikar, in fact, depends upon perfect teamwork between the koonki, the mahout and the phandi; all three must constantly maintain a fine balance between good 'horsemanship', brute force and correct technique. Once the captive has been noosed, the phandi must prevent the rope from slipping off or from strangling the animal and he must shorten it at the first chance until at last the captive has been pulled in to the side of the koonki, when the check-rope is tied. This is applied to the noose to prevent strangulation; but it sometimes happens that even before the animal has been hauled in, its trachea may have been so badly crushed by the pressure of the noose that it may drop dead on the way to the depot. I remember a fairly large tusker caught near our depot which had struggled so violently that he collapsed and the phandis gave him up for dead. His breathing had apparently stopped, but they loosened the nooses round his neck and he suddenly came to and renewed the fight.

There are certain definite rules about the art of managing a koonki and of handling and tying the phand; if they are not strictly followed, it will lead to failure and sometimes to disaster. There is a right way and a wrong way for the noose end of the phand to take off from the koonki's side and only one way for it to be fixed to the girth rope if the animal is to give of its best.

Even the way of folding the phand on the koonki's back is pre-scribed, for it must be ready immediately when needed and must not become fouled up in the chase or when noosing in a stockade.

Once an elephant is tied to the side of a koonki, care must be taken to see that the rope does not become twisted and that the captive is always kept on the side on which the phand is attached to the girth rope. All the while the captive is plunging and dashing about, often getting on to the wrong side. When this happens, the phand will ride up and the phandi's waist and thighs will be severely rope-burnt, or he and the mahout may even be swept off the koonki. In the manoeuvring, the koonki has to be swung about like a polo pony and the phandi has to use his knees almost entirely for this as his hands are fully occupied with the phand. This is where the quality of a good koonki comes in, for some elephants are nippy and others are heavy and hard to turn.

The slickness and deftness which denotes an experienced phandi is the result of long apprenticeship, but it is intelligence and spirit which produce an outstanding elephant catcher. That almost instantaneous pulling upwards of the noose as it drops over the elephant's head, bringing it up tight where the questing trunk cannot grasp it; that swift pulling in of the phand at the precise moment when the 'fish' at the end of the line is slack; the knowledge of when to make the koonki go along with the heaving captive and when to anchor it; the final tying of the check-rope once the captive is fully under control – these are the hallmarks of an expert.

Gelai phandi and his koonki, a makhna named Shiva Prasad, were one of the best combinations I have ever known. Both were lean and sinewy from years of strenuous hunting and when I first met them neither was young. The koonki had the reputation of being very fleet-footed and the man was a renowned 'bor phandi' or great phandi. I never had the experience of going out on mela shikar with them, but I once had the pleasure of seeing them at work in a stockade.

The elephant looked lively and carried his head high, while the phandi was confident and alert. The preliminary business of butting and pushing the captives had just finished and the phandis and koonkis as well as the captured elephants were cooling off, the men wiping their foreheads with their cloths and the elephants vigorously flapping their ears, when Gelai, who had obviously been searching out the most likely elephant for noosing, quickly pushed his koonki in. With one swift, graceful movement he had his noose over the head of a little female and up safely under its chin, where he held it taut while 'going with' the tugging victim. Then in a moment of pause he shook the rope vigorously to make the noose settle and rapidly and dexterously took in the slack. Then the strenuously resisting animal was gently but firmly hauled out of the crush and the rope shortened in quick movements. It was the work of a master which contrasted strongly with the fumblings of some of the younger phandis and I was deeply impressed.

Capturing solitary elephants, particularly young and powerful males, has a peculiar attraction for the mela shikari and great is the kudos earned by a phandi who brings in a solitary male of any size. If he is powerful and puts up a fight, it is impossible for one koonki to handle the captive and several large elephants and more than one phand or rope has to be used. This is known as *dohar* or *tehar* (two or three phands) and all the koonkis share in the catch. There is an unwritten rule that a second phand cannot be thrown over an elephant's head unless the first phandi cannot control the captive and calls for help. As the second and subsequent koonkis all share in the reward, there is sometimes a dispute which the khedda officer has to settle; he must decide on the evidence available as to whether or not the second or third phand had been thrown without being called for.

One such case stands out in my memory. He was the biggest elephant that I ever saw captured in mela shikar and he was brought in by three big makhnas. He himself was fully grown, standing over nine feet at the shoulder and very powerful. It must have been a tremendous effort securing him and all four elephants were completely exhausted by their struggle, which took place near the Gabru depot, the scene of my first independent khedda in 1934. The elephant took three phands to hold him, but this was by no means a record as Milroy told me of an animal which had needed as many as seven phands.

Large male elephants are captured not infrequently, but usually they do not survive long and the elephant men say that they die of a broken heart. Big makhnas, as well as big cow elephants, sold at ridiculously low prices in our depots. In fact we had to persuade people to take them away at three hundred rupees (£23) each. This was the period of the great slump in elephant catching, an offshoot of the universal depression which was gripping India in common with the rest of the world during the nineteen-thirties.

Sometimes encounters with large solitary male elephants end in tragedy for the mela shikari. One such case occurred in the Garo Hills and resulted in the death of a famous koonki, Shivaji, which belonged to the Raja of Gauripur. Shivaji was leading a group of koonkis which were trying to get into a herd guarded by a big tusker. Again and again it turned up at whatever point the phandis attempted to penetrate the herd. Finally the other riders urged Shivaji's phandi to take on the tusker, promising to help him in the fight by attacking on the sides while Shivaji engaged him from the front. The men should have known better, for the wild tusker was defending his herd. In the battle Shivaji was knocked down and the phandi was trampled underfoot. Seeing this, the other phandis panicked and Shivaji was left alone to face a now thoroughly enraged animal. The battle was fought to the edge of a steep hill, where the tusker forced the tame elephant down to the bottom of the slope, tusking him mercilessly all the way. He stood over the dying koonki for two whole days, returning to the attack every time the gallant animal tried to rise until at last all was over. It was a pitiful ending to a fine koonki and so unnecessary.

The Nepal pitha-shikar (literally 'driving and catching') has something in common with the Assam mela shikar method of lassoing elephants and it also resembles a little the Mysore method. It is no longer practised to any extent, nor in fact does Nepal capture its own requirements in elephants these days, partly because herds are scarce there and partly because it is feared that any disturbance may drive away the elephants which that country shares with India. In 1850 Maharaja Jung Bahadur, the founder of the Rana dynasty in Nepal, had a thousand elephants; but the present number of domesticated elephants in Nepal is nowhere near the numbers which even twenty years ago could be assembled for the royal tiger shoots. For Queen Elizabeth's 1960 shoot, not more than three hundred elephants could be collected.

In the pitha-shikar of Nepal, solitary elephants are chased for great distance by men on fast, small koonkis until they become so exhausted that they seek a river or swamp, into which they plunge. The pursuit koonkis, which of course are changed frequently during the chase, surround the exhausted wild male and if he is small enough, two lassoes of thick rope are thrown over his head, one after the other, from the backs of the tame elephants. More often than not he is too big to be tackled in this way, in which case his hind-legs are tied with a cotton rope of great torque in a figure-of-eight manner. As can be well imagined, this is a most dangerous proceeding and the reward for the first man who succeeds in doing it is high. In those days it was two hundred rupees – a not inconsiderable sum. Competition is very keen and the men rush waist- or even neck-deep into the water and injuries are frequent. Once secured, a long length of rope is left dragging from the animal's hind-legs and he is released. For some days he is allowed to be free in the jungle, watched by men and koonkis of course, the idea apparently being to allow him to exhaust himself by his struggles. A neck-rope is then thrown over his head, the reward for this being half the previous reward; while the reward for tying the small check-rope necessary to prevent strangulation is half that again. The elephant is then tied to a tree by its legs and neck and broken in gradually, being taken out to graze during the day between two koonkis and kept tied only at night.

In Nepal the ropes are connected to the necks of the attendant koonkis – and not to their girths as in Assam; and accidents and deaths by strangulation sometimes occur during capture or while grazing in the forest, for the wild elephant often takes charge and bolts. We had some Tharu mahouts from Nepal with us in the 1935 and 1936 kheddas to which Nepal sent an agent to purchase elephants, and one day I arranged a demonstration of their methods of tying for the edification of our phandis. The latter were very amused when they saw the elephants being tied neck to neck and were unanimous in saying that such a method would never do, either in mela or khedda shikar, as the koonki would be unable to control the captive. These Tharus are the professional mahouts of Nepal and were a wild lot, but they were much inferior in daring to our elephant men and would hesitate to tackle an animal which would give no trouble to the average elephant attendant in any training depot in Assam. The two-week period allowed in our depots for breaking in a young elephant was too short for the Tharus; invariably we found their animals still in a very raw state when the time came to terminate the services of the koonkis and they would ask for extensions of time. Tharu men are not attractive but their women are said to be beautiful; the story goes that after the flower of Rajput chivalry had perished in the siege of Chitoor, their ancestors married the Rajput women who had been sent for protection from the Moghuls to the forests of the Himalayan *terai*.

The famous Balrampur kheddas of northern India, which had their heyday at the end of the last century, were a form of mela shikar in which large numbers of men armed with guns and a number of elephants were employed. The procedure was to cut off the herds in the narrow valleys and gullies which are a feature of the Siwaliks and outer Himalayas on either side of the Ganges river, armed men being used to guard the ridges and drive the elephants down to the lower, more open ground 'where they would be intercepted by the serried ranks of the khedda elephants previously drawn up in more or less crescentic form'. Fighting tuskers would engage the elephants and beat them into submission and then the nooses would be used from their backs, much as in the Assam mela shikar. These khedda operations used to be patronized by the Lieutenant-Governor of the province, who with his guests from Delhi and England, including ladies, would camp out and take an active part in the catching. Once the distinguished guest's elephant fell into a large hole while his private secretary fell off his mount and disappeared in the long grass. Some mahouts, mistaking his flounderings for the movements of a young elephant, surrounded the spot with the intention of using their nooses, only to discover their mistake, to their discomfiture and the amusement of everybody else.

The 1893 operations resulted in the death of Mrs Anson, the wife of the agent of the Balrampur estate. On this hunt two hundred men and ninety-six elephants were used and the line of elephants had not yet got into position when a large rogue tusker charged without warning as they were emerging from a narrow defile. It knocked down the elephant on which husband and wife were seated, gored it viciously and then fled. Mrs Anson, who was half crushed by the fallen elephant, was extricated by her husband and taken back to the camp on an elephant, but she died there. The rogue persistently followed them home and Major Anson had to take his wife off the elephant and up a steep bank for safety. The injured elephant was so badly gored that it had to be shot and the whole hunt was so disorganized that it had to be abandoned. The wild male was subsequently tracked and shot by the famous forest officer B. B. Osmaston, hero of another incident in which he saved the life of one of his students at the Dehra Dun Forest School from a man-eating tiger.

Early in my khedda days I was keen to sample the thrills of mela shikar. I got my first chance in the Dibru Reserve of Upper Assam, which was known as the *betoni*, the cane-mahal or lease-area, because of the dense cane growth which covered most of the forest and which was a perfect hiding place for wild elephants and buffaloes.

I had camped with the phandis in a lonely spot in the jungle and early in the morning we heard the noise of young elephants. From a distance this often resembles the roaring of a tiger, but it is more sustained. Generally it is made by the youngsters when they are frightened or hurt, or by calves unable to obtain milk, though I have also heard cow elephants make this noise when they do not welcome the attentions of amorous musth bulls and in resentment and fear at being pushed about.

The noises woke the phandis, who at once started up their fires and put their rice pots on to boil. It was not long before we were saddling up the elephants and loading on the big ropes or phands, tying the ends carefully round the girths of the koonkis, while the mahouts stood on the backs of their elephants and worked under the watchful eyes of their phandis. The koonkis, hurriedly dusted down, stood patiently during the process, sampling the morning air now and then with raised trunks as if aware of what was ahead of them. I was to act as mahout on one of the elephants and we set off.

It was not long before we picked up the tracks of the feeding herd, but they were moving away from us and it was some time before we caught up with them. The jungle was thick and the cane brakes were difficult to negotiate. In places we had to cut our way through. I was fascinated by the way in which the experienced phandis guided the more inexperienced ones by little signs, nods and shakes of the head. Not a word was spoken. Suddenly we came into a clearing and paused to get in touch with each other. We were just starting to move on, when a slight noise in the jungle on the other edge of the clearing attracted our attention. Then out stepped a young tusker with his ears cocked and his trunk questing for our scent.

Slowly and noiselessly he approached the group of immobile koonkis. Not one of them flapped their ears or made a movement, held tight as they were by the pressure of their riders' knees, only the tips of their trunks moving towards the intruder. I sat paralysed, wondering what would happen. Closer and closer the wild tusker came, obviously puzzled at the quiet group of elephants in front of him. When he was within a few yards of the leading elephant its phandi quietly tapped the sheath of his *dao*, the knife used for cutting jungle. The sudden noise in the tenseness of the moment was like a miniature explosion. The elephant whirled around immediately and in a few strides was gone. He had recognized the noise as that of man and was not prepared to face these dangerous, tame brothers of his. I heaved a sigh of relief and everybody relaxed, the elephants flapping their ears and the men stuffing betel into their stained mouths while they had a whispered consultation.

We went on. Suddenly, in rather an open bit of jungle, we came on the herd, which was grazing in groups and singly. We could detect the positions of individual animals by the movements of the foliage and an occasional back exposed above the level of the bushes. The koonkis fanned out so as to get at individual elephants, the phandis reaching backwards to unloose their phand. Gathering up the heavy rope and throwing the closed noose over one shoulder, they manoeuvred their mounts with their knees and an occasional prod from the goad.

Suddenly my koonki came upon a young elephant that was feeding with its head stuck half into a bush. It stood stock-still as we came up from the rear and for a couple of seconds the phandi held his noose poised, ready to throw. Then the little elephant suddenly withdrew its head from the jungle, giving the phandi a chance of throwing the phand in a half-casting half-throwing action. The noose fell square over the little elephant's head and at its touch he plunged forward into the jungle. The slack of the rope ran out with a jerk, a sure sign that the noose was well home. Immediately the phandi lent over to pick up the rope and to haul it in, at the same time putting his mount into motion to keep up with the tugging calf. It was a job for him to guide his koonki as well as to keep the rope taut, a task in which I should have been helping. But I was too busy holding on to the ropes of the pad with excitement.

Suddenly a cow elephant appeared from around a clump of cane bushes and came right up to our koonki, grabbing the phand in her trunk and checking us. The phandi threw his koonki hard against her but she held on, trying to bite the rope; she was the mother of the calf, which was still pulling at the end of the rope. Her gaping mouth with trunk curled back out of danger was close to my left knee and if she had wanted she could have grabbed me and pulled me off the elephant.

As a matter of fact it is very surprising that this does not often happen and one can only explain it by the great care which an elephant takes of its trunk, which is always kept out of danger. Even in a stockade, wild elephants never try to pull the riders off the koonkis. I have observed a phandi spitting at the waving tip of a trunk which was too near for comfort and it has immediately been withdrawn, the human effluvia being too strong for the elephant's sensitive nostrils.

I was holding on grimly, wondering what was going on behind the cow, whose body obscured her calf as she practically straddled the rope. Suddenly she stopped tugging and turned away. Simultaneously the rope fell slack. Obviously the calf had either slipped it off his head or had stepped through the noose. The mother with her baby in front of her, now running for dear life, shuffled away at an amazing speed, while we lost precious moments in pulling in the rope and re-noosing it. My phandi did his best, pounding his koonki's head with his goad, but we could not catch up with her. At last we stopped, breathless and crestfallen. My phandi was on the verge of tears with disappointment and I felt guilty. After a while we met the others. Not a single capture had been made and ours had been the only phandi to make a strike. From the talk as we wended our way home, I gathered that had our real mahout been on the koonki or had I known my job, it might have been different.

The elephant's sense of smell is its most powerful ally and the trunk its most wonderful asset. The elephant-catching phandi is often assisted by his mount's extraordinary powers of scent and the manner in which it uses its trunk. This is invariably the first indication of the presence of wild elephants and the rider is guided by the repeated and prolonged raising of the trunk and the deep breaths a koonki will take when a herd is near. When approaching a solitary elephant, the koonki will test the air in a less confident manner; it will start and shiver, all of which is communicated to the man on its neck. Every shikari who has come up with tiger on the one hand and less dangerous game such as deer and pig on the other, knows the different way in which an elephant will give the indication with its trunk. The nervous, yet threatening expelling of air from the trunk and the sharp rapping of its tip on the ground when tiger is encountered is characteristic.

The powerful homing instinct of elephants is almost entirely due to their wonderful sense of smell. Gogoi had a remarkable experience that illustrates this when he was out on mela shikar in the North Cachar Hills some years ago. With his chief phandi Purneswar, he had been chasing a herd for a whole day and late in the evening each managed to noose an elephant. Gogoi found himself separated from his fellow-catcher in the confusion of the chase and it was some time before he located him, only to find that he was in trouble. The phandi had had several of the nails of his right hand torn off in handling the roped calf and was in great pain, as well as in imminent danger of losing his capture, which was on the point of strangulation. The two men changed koonkis, Gogoi finishing the job of tying the check-rope after bringing the captured elephant under control. At the request of the injured phandi he remained on the latter's koonki, a famous makhna named Manik, and the party started for camp.

By this time it was pitch-dark and they had lost all their bearings and sense of direction. Exhausted and hungry as they were, it was vital that they reach their base. Purneswar asked his master to let Manik have his head saying that the elephant would take them home. Rather doubtfully, Gogoi removed his feet from the guiding neck-band of the elephant and hanging his legs freely, said to the elephant in an encouraging yet commanding tone, 'Go home! Go home!' The koonki hesitated for a while and then started moving, slowly at first and then more confidently, taking the scent several times with upraised trunk. Soon he settled down to one direction and Gogoi says that he was so tired that he fell face down on Manik's head and slept while the koonki proceeded, both controlling his capture and finding his way. He was awakened at dead of night by the excited shouts of the men in the camp, who had been alarmed on hearing the elephants approach silently, then reassured by the low rumbling noises given out by the koonkis as they reached their camp. According to Gogoi, it was a most impressive performance by the intelligent koonki. Whether the animal followed its own footsteps and those of the other tame elephant in the party, or whether it did a direct traverse led by its trunk, Gogoi was unable to say as he was sound asleep for most of the journey, but he thinks it was a combination of both. Still, to have been able to unravel their own tracks from among those of the many elephants which had moved about the forest and to have retained the necessary sense of direction was a feat which speaks volumes for the elephant's powers of scent as well as for its intelligent reasoning.

This is not the only incident of this nature which came to my notice. Just before I arrived in Assam, a party of Forest Officers was carrying out an inspection in the dreaded cane-bearing reserve of Upper Assam on elephant-back and were overtaken first by rain and then by darkness. They had completely lost their bearings and their plight can be imagined by anyone who knows how totally the sky can become overcast during a wet spell in this extreme corner of Assam, bounded on three sides by the mountains of China and Burma with their powerful influence on the local meteorological conditions. Yet their elephant brought them safely back to camp when given her head. There are also, of course, many instances of lost elephants returning home riderless, often after long periods and from long distances. This is also a manifestation of the homing instinct but with a difference – the remarkable readiness displayed in returning to captivity, when everything is in favour of the animal remaining free.

A classical instance of the homing instinct of a koonki was the case of a big makhna belonging to Bholobhadra Saikia. I had sold this animal to him in 1934 during my first khedda for a mere song. At the time he was less than six feet high, but within a few years he had become a first-class koonki and he used to hunt in company with a cow which I had also sold to Saikia. This animal had the hairiest head I have ever seen and a trunk with a cut in the wall through which water used to flow whenever it drank. The two elephants were engaged in mela shikar operations about eighty miles from home when one morning the phandi noosed a large male elephant. In the terrific struggle which ensued, the phandi and mahout were both swept off the back of the koonki when the noosed elephant had got on the wrong side. The other koonki was engaged with another capture and could not help and the big makhna was dragged farther and farther into the jungle. The men could do very little and after some time, giving up the koonki for lost, they returned to camp and eventually to Saikia's village where they reported the incident.

Nine months later, to the astonishment of everybody in the village, the koonki turned up at his home. The girth rope was still attached to its body and was cutting deep into the back, where there was a huge, running abscess. It was quite obvious what had happened. The koonki and his wild companion had remained attached to each other until wear and tear, caused by the continuous pulling, had finally severed the rope and the two elephants had been parted. The tame makhna could have remained· in freedom but he chose to come back across more than eighty miles of forest and open country, crossing two large rivers. Perhaps he came back to be freed of the agony of the rope, perhaps he was simply coming back to the place where he had spent fifteen years as a young elephant.

Another elephant which returned voluntarily to his home after the absence of a full year was the Kumar of Gauripur's tusker, Kishenlal. He had been captured in 1925 when he was about fifteen years old and grew up to be a beautiful 'sakhna' elephant (a male with short, upturning tusks). In 1942 he escaped during elephant-catching operations. Fully five years later he returned to Gauripur of his own accord, to the great surprise and delight of his owner Lalji, having traversed some fifty miles of mostly open, cultivated country. His tusks had grown long. He was put to work immediately on handling and training elephants and showed that he had forgotten nothing. We had in the forest department at least two cases of a runaway elephant returning like this. One of these animals was on the north bank, where it had been taken for the annual cold weather touring of the Conservator of Forests; it was carrying a deer which had been shot, along with the day's picnic lunch which included a box of soda-water bottles. The bursting of the bottles in a regular fusilade stampeded it and made it throw its mahout. The elephant was given up for lost and great was the surprise when it turned up at its home on the south bank in Kamrup several months later, complete with the remains of dead deer and picnic lunch tied on its back. I cannot here resist telling the story of another Conservator, a great believer in the pre-lunch

15. Fore- and hind-feet tied for training

16. Roped to two koonkis for training

17. An elephant being tied to a tree for training

18. An elephant being untied for exercise

bottle of beer who, at the end of a long and tiring march when the elephants had been unsaddled and camp was being made, discovered that the case of beer had been left behind at the last camp, up-saddled, turned around and marched all the way back to get it.

The other case concerned Sundarmala, who was a veteran escapee. She had got loose twice before I joined the department and she was always presenting us with calves on her recapture, born of the wild bulls who used to take her away and whose call she could not resist. On this occasion her mahout had failed to inform the range officer that her tethering chain was defective. He was in the habit of fastening the ends together with a piece of jute rope every night, instead of with the customary bolt and nut. So one day the tie broke and Sundarmala escaped.

I received the news with consternation, as it was a serious matter for a departmental elephant to escape. My assistant was as young as I was, and I took him severely to task; but as the head of the Division and so ultimately responsible I expected and duly received a severe rocket from Milroy, the last person to condone such a thing. I searched for Sundarmala for many days, but in vain. There were too many wild elephants and too many misleading tracks in the terrible cane of that reserve and we had to admit failure. This happened in 1933.

Fourteen years later, in the elephant-catching operations of 1947, she was recaptured. A party of mela shikar koonkis were hunting when they came on a cow elephant with two calves at heel, one of them a suckling calf. When she displayed no fear but stood looking at the tame elephants, one of the mahouts instinctively felt that she was an escapee. Taking a chance, he shouted loud and commandingly to her, 'Baito! Baito!' (Sit down! Sit down!) And to the astonishment of everyone the elephant sat down! Milroy had once written, many years earlier, that an escaped elephant never forgets the order to sit down and the elephant men know this. The phandi immediately jumped from his koonki and running up to the elephant, caught her by the ear and scrambled up on to her neck. The bigger of the two calves ran away, but the little one followed at her heels as she was ridden back to the depot in triumph, the centre of admiration and the

D

butt of the jokes of the elated men, who jeered at her stupidity in being recaptured so easily. The forest officers hurried to the spot on hearing the news and Sundarmala was recognized by her identification marks, which were recorded in her book which happily had been preserved. I was the head of the department by then and I received the news with astonishment. But there was no doubt that it was Sundarmala and she came back on to our books. Her calf, which we named Rupahi, went to Japan as a gift from Pandit Nehru in 1951. At the time of its dispatch in a railway wagon on the first leg of its journey to Calcutta there was, according to the young officer who supervised the business, a pathetic scene with both the calf and Sundarmala showing much grief. I was very angry when I learnt that the mother had been used to load her own calf into the elephant truck.

Sundarmala never escaped again. She was moved to another station and closely guarded and later I used her to train Shibo Singha, or rather to retrain him as he was still very raw when he arrived from the Singpho country where he had been captured. But she was always very wild and could not be worked much. I wish I could record that she was released or pensioned off, as was the custom in the old days; but times had changed and I was ordered to dispose of her and she was sold in 1954, after 'duly calling for tenders, being old and unserviceable'.

Sanderson has mentioned two other such cases of recaptured elephants. One was a cow which had escaped twelve years earlier and which when recaptured with a herd of forty-eight in his Chittagong khedda had three calves at heel. The rope marks on her legs gave her away and when she was pricked with a spear and told to kneel, she obeyed at once. Another runaway, which as a three-year captured koonki took fright in a drive and bolted, was recaptured after four and a half years, a hundred miles away from the scene of her escape, along with twenty other elephants and her calf. In three days she and another reclaimed runaway were being employed in the capture and training of her fellows.

These cases of recapture of elephants are unique in the proof they afford of the elephant's docility and retentivity of human discipline and the recovery of escaped elephants is a commonplace in Assam. In fact such cases often pose a problem for the Forest Officer and the administrator, because deciding the ownership of such animals is often difficult and disputes over their possession have sometimes led to protracted ~~legislation~~. Judgments on these cases of *res ferae*, which is the legal term for captured wild animals that have reverted to their native state, are recorded for the guidance of officers. It seems to be a question of prestige to establish ownership over such animals and it is surprising how tenaciously elephant owners will contest respective claims to a comparatively inferior animal which has escaped from custody years ago and which would be likely to escape again – for 'once an escapee always an escapee' is a pretty safe rule with elephants.

An interesting judgment by an appellate judge of Assam on an appeal against the decision of two lower courts, in an ownership suit concerning a lost and recaptured elephant, was in favour of the mahaldar who had recaptured the animal in the course of elephant-catching operations. This judgment was made over fifty years ago and has been supported by many others since. The judge quoted Blackstone's condensation from the Institute of the Roman Emperor Justinian, as follows: 'Wild beasts and birds and fishes, that is all animals which may be born on the earth, sea and sky, by the law of nations belong to their captor as soon as he catches them; for as they were nobody's property before, it stands to reason that they must belong to the person who seizes them. Such an animal is considered to be yours only so long as it remains in your keeping and once it returns to its natural liberty it ceases to be yours and becomes the property of the person who next captures it. It is understood to have recovered its natural liberty when it has either gone out of your sight for although you still see it, you cannot easily catch it.' The consequence is that even though the identity of an elephant can be proved, an original owner cannot have it automatically. In the case of Government elephants that have escaped, however, there is always a clause in the elephant-catching rules which makes their return obligatory, on payment of legitimate expenses of course.

I cannot resist recording the case of a search for a runaway elephant in the famous Nilambur Forests of the west coast of India, which had an unfortunate ending for the elephant. She was a cow named Bhagavati and on escaping had joined a wild herd. A ten-day search for her by the forest officers proved futile and as a last resort a Pamien named 'Billie' very pluckily offered to go in amongst the herd and endeavour to wound Bhagavati in the leg with his knife or mahout's staff, so as to prevent her from making off with the rest. He accordingly went in alone with his knife, staff and an old fashioned single-barrelled breech-loading ·500-bore rifle.

Suddenly without any warning there was a rush and about fifteen elephants, led by a tusker, charged towards him. On the spur of the moment he fired into the crowd and one elephant fell and the rest turned off. The elephant which fell was Bhagavati, a most extraordinary coincidence which is only equalled by the fact that a bullet fired from an old-fashioned gun by an inexperienced mahout killed an elephant at all. The bullet had entered the neck about nine inches from the ear-hole and had penetrated the lungs and the base of the heart, the full length of the penetration being about one yard. The hobble chain was still attached to the left leg but two links from the right leg-chain were broken off and the chain was old and worn.

The Pamien, on discovering that he had killed a Government elephant handed the rifle to the forester and requested that he should be shot, as a preferable alternative no doubt to being hanged, which he thought was the only possible sequel to the shooting of a Government elephant!

CHAPTER 7

ELEPHANT DRIVES

The most widely known method of capturing elephants is that of the khedda or stockade. The word is derived from the Hindi *khedna*, which in turn comes from the Sanskrit word *khet*, meaning to drive. Megasthenes was the first to leave a clear account of the khedda method of capturing elephants as practised in northern India in his day, probably in what is now south Bihar and neighbouring Orissa. In the original stockade method, as practised by the Aryans, a large space was enclosed by a circular trench, thirty feet wide and twenty-four feet deep, the soil being thrown up into a steep bank on the outside; the addition of wing walls to guide the elephants through regular gates was undoubtedly a later refinement. The only entrance to the enclosure was by a bridge covered with a deep layer of earth, turf and leaves. Female decoy elephants were driven into the enclosure and, from hiding places in the bank of earth, men kept watch for the wild herds; led by males attracted to the female decoys, the herds would sooner or later enter the trap. The appropriate moment would be chosen to demolish the bridge. The captives would be kept without food and water for some time to weaken them and then the bridge would be rebuilt and tame elephants introduced. A furious battle would rage between the tame and the wild animals and when the latter were thoroughly subdued, leg- and later neck-ropes would be put on, the necks being tied together. In order to bring about the speedier subjugation of the captives, their necks would be incised with knives in order to allow the rawhide ropes to bite into the flesh. Old and useless elephants and the very young were released. In these methods and practices we see the forerunner of much that survives in modern elephant catching including, as may be expected, the cruelty which has not been eliminated completely to this day.

The khedda of today is rather different, for a wall of wooden posts is the main stockade, the trench merely serving as a reinforcement, while there are wing walls and a gate. Decoy elephants have given place to drives, no doubt as man lost his fear of the elephant. Undoubtedly local conditions have influenced the design of the stockade and the methods employed in the various parts of the Indian sub-continent and in the neighbouring countries. For instance, where catching became a vocation of the common man, the stockades are small and the whole organization a sort of cottage industry, as in Assam, Bengal and Burma. Heavy expenditure on hiring and keeping tame elephants in readiness for a catch had of necessity to be avoided; this in turn led to the method of tying the legs of the captives to the walls of the stockade and to training devices, like the Karen stocks, the Upper Assam hal of the Morans and the south Indian kraal.

The evolution of the stockade in the different parts of the Indian sub-continent, influenced as it must have been by developments in adjoining countries like Burma, forms an interesting study. Since Assam is centrally situated between Burma and northern India, it was naturally the fusion point of ideas on capturing elephants. The trench round the inside of the stockade wall came from northern India, where it formed the original and at one time the only feature of the Aryan khedda. The generally softer nature of the soil in the eastern regions must have led the early elephant catchers to reinforce the trench with a palisade wall. Still farther east, in Burma, conditions were unsuitable for a trench of any kind and so the defence wall of the enclosure was carried out from a platform running all round the top of the stockade, as in the Shan khedda.

The Karen method of Burma comprises a simple stockade with a stout pair of funnel walls which taper gradually and end at a thick tree. Elephants are driven into this gully and cut off by drop

gates. They are then roped to the side walls and given a preliminary training *in situ*, as it were, until koonkis can be hired to take
them out. This economical method is reflected to some extent in
the Upper Assam hal, an enclosure resembling the ancient stocks
in which elephants are incarcerated for a period before being
trained, and also in the southern Indian kraal. But these more
leisurely devices for training elephants for some reason found no
favour with the Mysore authorities, although they are used in
neighbouring Madras and Travancore.

The Karen method of tying elephants' legs to the walls of the
stockade suggests connections with the systems of Orissa and
Chittagong. In both these areas, too, they employ vertically
dropping or 'flap' gates, a feature which was also introduced to
Mysore by Sanderson. The use of the drop gate farther east in the
Karen country raises the interesting question of whether the idea
went from India or came from Burma.

The small roping stockade is also a common feature of Orissa
and Mysore, but it is absent in Assam and Burma. A peculiar
feature of the Orissa, Chittagong and Mysore stockades is the
nature of the walls, which are openwork affairs of very heavy
timber in these areas whereas in Assam and Burma they are close-
knit structures of much lighter posts (see Plates 13 and 14).

So many resemblances in capturing and training methods, in
countries separated widely by seas and mountains, may be mere
coincidence; but more probably it is the result of contacts over
the centuries. The ancient Kalinga waves of colonization of the
eastern lands, which came from the shores of modern Orissa,
could have been responsible for the Chittagong and Tenasserim
coasts receiving the basic Aryan methods developed in northern
India. Bihar was apparently the centre of the early elephant trade
and certainly a key area for the exchange of information. Migration
routes from Burma must have taken both the Karen and the Shan
techniques into Assam.

Owing to the abundance of elephants in Bengal, Assam and
Burma, the practice of using koonkis for the noosing and removal
of elephants grew up in those countries. In Mysore, the first koonkis were imported from Burma and with them came the custom

of leading the captured elephant with long ropes or phands tied to two or more koonkis in front and behind. Strangely enough in Assam, which is so close to Burma, the captive is tied to the side of the koonki. This is again somewhat different to the Nepal method of tying the koonki and its captive together by the neck, which was the custom in the original Aryan khedda.

The elephant-catching industry of Assam, which has served the main markets of northern India throughout the ages, is based on the rapid breaking in of captives by picketing, the main training being done later. For this reason the Assam kheddas are not huge and spectacular showpieces like the leisurely yet elaborate Mysore kheddas of the south, which are staged only periodically. These used to be held mainly on the occasion of the visit of some distinguished person, such as the Viceroy or a member of royalty; but at the same time they served the purpose of thinning out stocks of elephants and of supplying them for the palace stables and the forest department. After Hyder Ali's failure to capture elephants by the stockade method and Colonel Pearse's unsuccessful efforts in 1867, Sanderson succeeded at his second attempt in 1874. On his return from Dacca he introduced his methods to Mysore, but the sites of the early stockades were different from that of the famous Kakankote khedda, which was used for the first time only in 1890. Sanderson developed his own ideas according to the local conditions. For instance, since elephants have to be brought in from long distances and sometimes across open country, large numbers of men and considerable force have to be employed. Elephant herds have to be moved in stages and held, if necessary, in position until the exact time when they would have to be rushed into the stockade; this final drive is witnessed by the distinguished guests and escape routes are blocked by deep trenches or stockade walls, while 'holding' and 'forcing' lines are arranged and cleared beforehand. Everything is timed to the last minute and the khedda involves months of preparations. As many as thirty or forty tame elephants and a thousand beaters may be engaged in the drive and in the final stages the length of the surround may be anything up to ten miles, every thirty or forty yards of the line being guarded at night by fires. At the fires the drive is halted and the beaters cook their food and sleep by turns. The forcing lines are ready laid in advance with heaps of firewood while blankets, liquor and food are supplied to the beaters, who are partly tribals used to living with elephants and partly ordinary cultivators recruited temporarily.

The final stages of the khedda, in which even the telephone system is used, are attended by numerous people for whom platforms are erected at vantage points overlooking the river. The elephants are driven for some distance and past these points before entering the stockade, where the main spectacle takes place. The roping of the captives takes several days and comfortable seats are provided for distinguished guests overlooking the small roping stockade attached to the main enclosure. This is a spectacle which is well worth seeing. The roping enclosure can take only a few animals at a time. The elephants are lured into the stockade by banana leaves and sugar-cane, or if necessary are hustled into it by the tame koonkis; they are then dealt with individually, being first tied by their legs to the stockade wall and later noosed by the neck. After the legs are tied, the neck-ropes are applied and the elephants are removed to a tying place outside. The men work partly from the ground under the protection of the tame elephants and partly from the back of the koonkis. The main duty of the koonkis is to press and confine the wild elephants between them. Several koonkis work on one elephant and squeeze it between them so that the men who are on the ground roping the legs can work in comparative safety. In Assam the phand or noose is first thrown and tied from the back of the koonki and it is only when the captive is brought out from the stockade that ropes are put round the legs. The Mysore method, though dangerous for the men who get down from the koonkis, is made comparatively safe by isolation of the elephants one by one within the roping stockade. Another main difference between the Mysore and Assam stockades is in the nature of the gate: in the original Mysore stockade a drop gate like a portcullis was employed; but this was later replaced by a 'flap' gate, horizontally hinged, so as to swing down over the mouth of the stockade when a rope is cut. To enter, the gate has to be lifted by the koonkis. The main stockade in Mysore is a very large enclosure, which may extend over five acres or more and is surrounded in places by deep V-shaped trenches which the biggest elephant cannot cross and reinforced by wooden walls where necessary. Where trenches cannot be dug, as in the river drive, wooden walls are built of stout squared timbers lashed to strong uprights with coir rope, the whole presenting an openwork enclosure of great strength.

The only elephant-catching operations which can compare with the Mysore khedda as a spectacle is that of Siam. The khedda here is of ancient origin and was formerly staged every few years near the city of Ayuthia, about one hundred and fifty miles from Bangkok. After a lapse of about thirty years it was revived in 1938 with great splendour under the supervision of the army but at a different site. The stockade was three times as large as the old stockade, the massive teak walls of which can still be seen at Ayuthia. The 1938 khedda was a gala affair and the profits went towards the construction of a military college for cadets. Charges were made for admission and it was estimated that twenty thousand people attended. The ropes used in Siam are of rattan cane and the nooses are held ready at the ends of long poles by the catchers who, mounted on tame elephants, chase the animals round the arena and seek an opportunity to slip the ropes over the hind legs; the other end of the leg-rope is then attached to the stockade wall and the necks are noosed.

In the Ceylon kraal operations, the last of which was held some years ago, the scale is comparable to that of Mysore and of Siam. Thousands of villagers take part in the drive, which lasts several days and covers from twenty-five to thirty square miles. At night the drive halts, fires are lit and cooking pots are set on them, while vendors of food make their rounds and there is much noise and gaiety. Hundreds of spectators hang on to the outskirts of the line during the day and the elephants are moved forward gradually until the kraal or stockade is reached, when with one final effort the herd is rushed into it.

The Assam kheddas are insignificant compared to these enormous affairs. The stockade does not exceed the size of a tennis court but is circular in shape and constructed of comparatively flimsy, junglewood poles. The wall, however, is well braced with cross-members and strutted from the outside with leaning poles, the base of the palisade being buried in and backed up by the earth excavated from the deep, V-shaped trench which runs all round the inside except in front of the gate opening. This trench effectively minimizes the force and power that the captured elephants can bring to bear on the stockade wall and without it no catch could be contained. Incidentally, the Khamtis and Itonias of Assam, who are Shans and the remnants of the Burmese invasion of that country, do not dig a trench but construct an elevated platform all round the stockade from which men armed with spears can keep off the elephants, but this results in severe body and head injuries to the animals. All the lashings are of cane and not a single nail is employed in the whole structure. The gate closes and opens most ingeniously. The enormous gate-post, fashioned from a single tree, pivots in a hollow cut in a log sunk in the ground and is held above by a lintel socketed to the top of another huge fixed post. The arrangement hinges the ponderous gate so lightly that one man can open or shut it.

There is a most simple closing arrangement, the motive power being provided by means of a young, straight tree which is bent like a spring-bow and fastened by a cane to the top of the gate in the open position. When the rope that is holding the gate open is severed, the bent tree springs upright, pulling the gate close and holding it there until it can be secured. As all driving is done at night, the responsibility of the gateman who is seated in a machan built against the stockade wall is heavy: in pitch darkness he has to judge accurately when the last elephant has entered before using his sharp dao or knife to make one swift cut on the stretched cane. The Karens suspend a bamboo in the gateway which knocks against a beam every time an elephant enters.

The Assam kheddas are built preferably near salt-licks or, where these are not available, astride elephant paths; in this case they have either one or two gates facing in opposite directions. A pair of funnel walls for each gate is obligatory and sometimes a double stockade – which is merely one leading into another – is built to facilitate the handling of large catches. It sometimes happens that while a catch is in a stockade and before it can be removed, a second herd appears in the neighbourhood; if there is a double stockade, the elephants already inside can be moved to the adjoining enclosure to make room for the second herd.

Catches in Assam are generally quite small, up to twelve or fifteen elephants or a family group. Occasionally larger catches are made, particularly when stockades are situated near salt-licks, or in areas with large elephant populations, or in places where catching has not been done for some years. Sanderson speaks of as many as 118 elephants secured in one drive in Chittagong in the 1880s and my own record, which I shall describe later, was fifty-four animals in the Bhagti stockade in 1936. There was one stockade named Soraimari near Jamuguri, situated in the plains some distance from the Naga Hills, which had a phenomenal run of successes in the years 1935-7. The total bag for the first season was 130 elephants in six successive catches – the biggest single catch was some thirty-five animals – and the total for the second and third season was over a hundred. The lease-holder, Durganath Gogoi, I have already mentioned as being one of the few 'gentleman' catchers who used to work as a phandi with his men on mela shikar. He used to bring in elephants on a level with the best of professionals. But in those days of slump I am afraid Gogoi did not make as much as others thought he did out of his stockade, which twenty years earlier would have made him a rich man.

In the days when I was a khedda officer, the preliminary outlay on a stockade was about four thousand rupees, or nearly three hundred pounds. This sum covered the food and keep of a group of twenty-five stockade men for six months. The mahaldar or lease-holder who finances the venture should easily recover his outlay from profits made on the catch; but a poor season may result in a dead loss to the mahaldar and no earnings for the koonkidars, while the government of course will not receive the anticipated royalties. It is here that the great advantage of the departmental khedda is apparent, where several parties – government, mahaldars, koonkidars and stockade men – share the risk.

An Assam khedda calls for only a small complement of men, not more than about twenty-five and armed with four guns firing blank ammunition; to achieve success, therefore, it needs great skill, courage and hard work. And yet it is exceptional for a stockade to fail to capture elephants. In Assam, koonkis are not used to help in the drive, as they are in Mysore, for men are found to be better for this work. Elephants brought from long distances are driven by parties of picked men armed with one or two guns. This is known as *kukur singia*, literally 'dog tracking'. With slight noises, such as the tapping on a tree with a dao or a distant gunshot, the men alarm the herd and start it moving in the required direction. The art of the drive lies in keeping the herd on the move the whole time without stampeding it. When the elephants are near the stockade, they have to be moved cautiously within the surround area, which is demarcated by a cleared trace. They are kept there until after dark, when the final drive starts. The small force of men could never succeed during the daytime, so the final drive into the stockade is always done at night.

In the case of stockades built close to salt-licks, there is none of this preliminary bringing up of the herd from a distance; instead, it is a game of patience, waiting for elephants to visit the salt-lick, which they generally do on moonless nights. A heavy responsibility rests on the watchers, who listen all night from machans built in convenient trees. When they are sure that the elephants are at the lick, they get down from their perches and proceed quickly to the main camp to warn the others. In the inky darkness of the forest, where even the starlight fails to penetrate, this requires nerve and courage. There is always the risk of running into the herd bull, who may be encountered standing absolutely still beside the path where he suspects there may be danger.

Hurriedly the men assemble, carrying bundles of dry sticks or bamboos to be lit as torches. Once the first shot is fired to signal the start of the beat, the men gathered in the surround let themselves go – shouting, banging on tins, shaking wooden clappers and firing blank shots. As the drive moves forward, the positions of the men on the holding lines are revealed by the flames and noise. At last, with a final rush, the elephants are in the stockade. It is a scene, as Sanderson has said, 'which cannot fade from the memory of anyone who has witnessed it'.

Equally memorable is the business of removing elephants from a stockade. It attracts the whole countryside and people come from long distances to make a picnic of it. The removal may go on for one or more days, depending on the size of the catch and the number of koonkis available. In removing an elephant from a stockade, it is essential to use a koonki powerful enough to control it. A strong, and above all an intelligent koonki, makes the task of the phandi easier, both in the stockade and while the captive is being removed to the depot or to the first temporary tying place near the stockade. It is a real pleasure to see a first-class koonki at work. Ratnamala was one such elephant – a beautiful *koomeriah bandh* or 'royal' animal, middle-aged when I first saw her, but powerful enough to handle the biggest female elephant. With ears flapping – the only sign of strain she allowed herself – she would haul the big elephants out of the stockade unceremoniously and then march them away, head erect but ever ready to deal her captive a good blow to restrain it and bring it into the line of march. She would use her powerful, wrinkled trunk to hold down her opposite number and her raised knee to throw back those sideways rushes which the phandi constantly has to look out for. On occasions she would even take the top edge of the captive's ear in her mouth – all without being told by her rider. When there were a number of little elephants to deal with, we would make her take one on either side of her and it was fascinating yet somehow laughable to see how easily she would handle the recalcitrant youngsters.

Old and unsaleable elephants, pregnant mothers and cows with calves are not roped. Although the occasion is a sort of Roman holiday for the people, it is at the expense of the poor elephants. The dispirited and exhausted animals have long ago given up the fight after the severe pommelling they have received from the koonkis, the customary prelude to the roping. Mothers try to keep their offspring close to them while treating other calves with roughness. The young tuskers use their tusks to push aside their companions or to throw the calves out of their way. There is a continual boring inwards on the part of the younger animals, only the old *dhuis* or cow elephants standing statuesque and forlorn. The planted vegetation put there for camouflage has long ago been trampled down. Elephant dung is everywhere and the stench of their urine rises from the arena. The captured animals are too restless to eat and fodder thrown to them is kicked and trampled down, while the hollowed-out log holding water which is pushed through a hole in the stockade wall meets with the same fate. The elephants are caked with the moist mud which they throw on themselves to cool their overheated bodies.

When the roping starts it is the smaller elephants which are removed first, though if there is a very troublesome cow elephant which is at the same time saleable she is removed before them. As the phandis share in the rewards for removal of the catch in accordance with the price each elephant fetches, there is much competition to throw the first phand, the target being the best looking young female elephant.

These sometimes put up unexpected resistance although the rule 'the bigger the elephant the less the resistance' holds good for both males and females. Sanderson narrates how a seven-foot-high *sarin* (a female which has not yet calved) dragged a koonki 8 ft. 3 inches high all over the place from eleven am to four pm and the situation was saved only by the arrival of a second koonki. The mahout of the koonki lost his nerve. 'The *sarin* fought more like a fighting ram than an elephant and made repeated attempts to pull him off his mount. She would have succeeded eventually had we not got at her with spears and distracted her attention when things we're getting really bad.'

Mothers do everything possible to block and obstruct the attempts to remove their offspring, pulling at the taut rope with their trunks and trying to bite through it. They interpose their heads between the koonkis and their calves, roughly pulling the babies close to them with their trunks. The large cows take on the koonkis in their desperation, standing up to the severe battering they receive from tusks and foreheads. The milling

elephants go round in circles to the accompaniment of the bellowing and trumpeting of the youngsters, the admonishments of the
sweating phandis and the excited shouts of the spectators, who
have no time to feel pity for the captured elephants.

I shall never forget the magnificent resistance which a grand old
dhui put up for her little male calf. She gathered him under her
belly with her forelegs, practically kneeling over him while she
chewed at the rope. Again and again she was hurled aside by the
koonkis, urged to their maximum efforts by the phandis on their
necks. Once she nearly killed the little fellow by straddling him
protectively in the ditch, where he hung half strangled by the
merciless phand that stretched tight to the side of the koonki.
I could stand it no longer and ordered him to be freed. Nobody
objected, for the gallant mother had made a deep impression on
us all. It was a moving sight to see her as she left the stockade at
the end of the day, pushing before her the little chap with the cut
noose still round his neck.

Released mothers sometimes come to the tying place to search
out their calves. In my first kheddas of 1931 in the North Cachar
Hills, we were tying up the catch some distance from the stockade
when a mother came rushing to the spot and finding her calf,
attempted to free it. We had to drive her off with koonkis but she
hung about all night, only kept away by the fires we lit. In an
account of elephant-catching operations in Perak some fifty
years ago we are told how a mother elephant located her calf in
this manner and actually commenced to suckle it, making no
attempts to free the baby. When daylight came she would not be
driven away. The Raja Muda of Perak was so moved that he
ordered the calf to be released.

In the Linlithgow khedda of Mysore in 1939, a cow that had
been separated from her calf literally fought her way through the
line of men, crossing the deep trench under a shower of stones,
blows and shots. She rushed to the place where part of the catch
was tethered and went from calf to calf, but not finding hers
among them she disappeared into the jungle. The next day she
appeared at another camp a full day's march away, where she
found her calf. Her performance astounded and so moved the

authorities that they set the calf free. It is not all elephant mothers which are so determined, however. In fact it is the exception rather than the rule.

Large male elephants are by no means welcomed by elephant catchers because of the impossibility of handling them with the available koonkis and because of the damage they inflict on the smaller elephants in the stockade. A group of captured elephants is a group of frightened wild creatures; huddled together head to tail, the picture is a pathetic one. In the pushing, seething mass the adolescents bear in towards the centre, trying to hide their heads like ostriches under the adults. The larger elephants are more dignified, but the strain and tension tells on them too and occasionally they burst into furious assault on each other. Particu-larly unfortunate are the calves which have got separated from their mothers. Tusks are used freely to push aside those elephants which get in the way, while tails are bitten and makhnas and females open their mouths wide and use their tushes to bear downwards on head and shoulder. Kicking and butting add to the damage, which is only revealed later in the depot and sometimes seriously affects the prices fetched.

Sanderson relates an incident which took place in the Chitta-gong kheddas: a large male continuously attacked a younger one, chasing him all over the stockade; the younger one in his fright took it out on the rest of the catch, with the result that out of forty-eight elephants captured, four young ones and a large makhna were killed. What a scene of animal ferocity and human futility it must have been, a sad commentary on man's dominion over animals.

Although we were occasionally forced to shoot elephants which could not be controlled, we never had to do so on the scale of Sanderson's kheddas. In his book *Thirteen Years among the Wild Beasts of India*, we read of his execution of elephants which were considered too old or too dangerous to release. In 1889, twenty-four elephants were shot; in 1890, during the first Kakankote khedda, eighteen were shot; and in 1891 the total was sixteen. In 1896, fifty-eight were killed out of 170 captured by Sanderson's successor 'Khedda' Shamiengar. Speaking from my experience of

elephant catching and quite objectively and dispassionately, one
is at a loss to account for this slaughter. The fact that it was given
up soon afterwards proves that it was unnecessary.

Whenever possible I used to turn big elephants out of stockades
rather than shoot them and often used large tuskers to help,
borrowing from neighbouring stockades when necessary. On one
occasion we captured three large elephants, a tusker and two
makhnas, which had visited the salt-lick together one night. When
the news was brought to me in the depot, I collected one or two
of the leading traders and told them that if they fancied any of the
elephants I would try to take them out with big koonkis as a
special case. Sabul Hussain, a young trader who was always on
the look out for good tuskers for his clients (among whom were
a couple of Maharajas) accompanied me eagerly. But when we
reached the stockade one glance told me that it was hopeless. The
tusker was a beautiful specimen – which was why the stockade
men had sent me word instead of releasing the elephants at once –
but he was long past his prime. It had been a difficult task to keep
the animals from breaking out of the stockade and the men were
glad to see me. Much as Hussain admired the tusker he shook his
head. Had it been the beginning of the cold weather season, he
and I might have risked it; but the season was nearly over and
the chances of such a large elephant surviving the breaking-in
period were small. The makhnas attracted no attention and so the
order was given to open the gates.

The first principle in stockade operations is, of course, to keep
the captives as intact and as free from injuries as possible; that is
why the rules of the Assam Forest Department insist on the speedy
removal of a catch, which must be completed within four days of
capture at the outside. This period is generally long enough for
the news of a catch to reach the men with the koonkis, who are
posted some ten to fifteen miles away from the stockade – at such
a distance that their presence will not be detected by the wild
herds. This is not too far for them to make the journey to the site
and remove the catch within the specified period, provided of
course that the catch is not abnormally large.

Koonkis stationed within this distance of a stockade in readiness for a catch are not allowed to take part in mela shikar under any circumstances, as this would seriously disturb and disperse the wild herds. Unscrupulous phandis, however, will sometimes poach near a stockade and this can cause a lot of trouble. I have heard of cases of a capture being literally snatched from the mouth of a stockade, but they are rare. It was partly to obviate such happenings that Milroy adopted the snare system for departmental kheddas. Since mela shikar is so much sought after, to give everyone a chance koonkis have to do stockade duty by turns. The biggest tuskers, which are generally ineffective in mela shikar but are essential for the stockades, get a slightly increased share.

CHAPTER 8

HANDLING AND TRAINING

While the art of handling elephants has been known to certain Asian peoples for nearly two thousand years, it has to be admitted that some of the beliefs on which the methods are based have their foundations on superstition and myth rather than on scientific truths. Even in modern times, it is not an easy matter to rid such a profession of its load of tradition. Also, the art of elephant handling is so specialized that there is an inclination to be over-reverent towards those who are considered to be experts. Laymen fear to tread where professional elephant men walk boldly, secure in the inherited and acquired knowledge of centuries.

The general level of education and enlightenment of the average elephant trainer is so low that he can be forgiven for persisting in some of his superstitious beliefs which may cause him to indulge in cruel practices. What is more surprising and less excusable is to find how little the authorities have interfered with native elephant catching and training methods. 'The elephant is essentially a native's animal,' wrote Sanderson over seventy-five years ago. 'Natives alone have fully studied his peculiarities and classified him into castes; his capture, training and keeping are in native hands as well as the trade and the native standard of merit regulates the market.' So for many years the native elephant man was left alone, secure in his methods and beliefs. It was only men like Sanderson, the father of the stockade method in Mysore, and Milroy in Assam, who ventured to break into the realm of the elephant men to any extent.

Anyone who is not acquainted with the elephant trade may still be shocked at what appears to be unnecessary cruelty; it is not realized that the handling of such a large and strong animal is not an easy task and must involve at least some force and firmness. From the earliest times, severe belabouring of captives, both by trained elephants and men, and the use of iron-tipped spears, knives and fire have been the rule. Starvation in the initial stages of capture was once considered essential. All this was designed to break the spirit of the animals and reduce them to speedy submission. But the essentially noble character of the elephant has the effect of so endearing it to its captors that in a very short time the application of kindness based on real affection usually prevails. There are sadists among elephant men, however, and all rules of procedure and training are aimed at them.

In the old days in Bengal and Assam, the business was entirely in the hands of the local people – some of whom would be financed by British adventurers – and the authorities did very little, apart from realizing royalties on the captured elephants. Casualties were extremely heavy, elephants being kept in the stockade for long periods until purchasers had been found for them. Immediate commencement of training was not insisted on and the exclusive services of one koonki per captive was unknown. It is to the credit of Assam and its Forest Department – and largely due to the initiative of Milroy – that nearly forty years ago rules were introduced to remove some of the cruel and harmful aspects of the trade.

Milroy realized that the debilitating effects of prolonged incarceration within a stockade are so great that the animals are severely handicapped during the breaking-in period that follows. He therefore insisted that the elephants should be removed within a short time and that training should begin and be completed within a fixed period. The present rules in Assam specify removal from the stockade within four days of capture, the operations to begin within two days and to be completed within another two days. This is made possible by holding at all times a certain number of koonkis in readiness within a reasonable distance of the stockade. After the elephant's arrival at the depot, training or breaking in must begin within one day. Milroy also used to insist on the sale of a capture as soon as possible for 'an ownerless elephant is an elephant without a future'.

The use of metal-tipped spears was banned and Milroy demonstrated that an elephant can be controlled effectively with a long, sharp stick. Well do I remember the old Doctor Babu walking about with a couple of metal-tipped spears he had confiscated from traders and the wrath that descended on the men's heads. The tradition-ridden phandis had a custom of cutting the nape of the neck of a troublesome elephant, or of putting damp sand under the phand so that the rope cut into the flesh, so that the captive could be brought under control more speedily; this cruel practice, which resulted in horrible neck-wounds, was also stamped out. There was another custom of cutting a small vein at the back of the elephant's ear after the phand was tied, a form of blood-letting very effective in controlling a fractious captive – it was as if the elephant feared the smell of its own blood. I shut a blind eye to this after I saw how innocuous it was, for the small cut soon closes.

It was also made obligatory for a lease-holder to provide a large and capable koonki, preferably a tusker, for each stockade in order to cope with big elephants. I have already described how I used to employ these 'sirdari' or chief koonkis to turn big males out of stockades instead of shooting them. The rules insist on at least four koonkis per stockade being kept in readiness, but we would frown on a lease-holder attempting to interpret this rule too literally. In actual practice enough koonkis were on hand at all times to deal with a catch within the stipulated periods and if all koonkis were occupied in training captives at the depot, the stockade was kept closed. Koonkis were to be of a minimum height of seven feet and experienced in handling captives, though sometimes we would register small and inexperienced koonkis for such work as fetching in fodder. It is amazing to see how soon a newly-captured elephant can be turned into a koonki and used to catch and train its fellows. One such elephant comes to my mind. He was a young tusker rising seven and a half feet in height with the most beautiful turned-up tusks I have ever seen – they used to remind me of Kitchener's whiskers! In the very year after his own capture he was training elephants and in the second year he was removing elephants from a stockade. He was the pride of the whole depot and when suddenly and for no explicable reason he died, his owner wept as for a lost child. I think it was due to the premature strain he had been put to and the Phookans, whose young half-brother owned him, should have known better.

Milroy insisted on the journey to the depot being done in easy stages and woe betide any phandi who lost his elephant on the march. Strangulation and heart failure are generally the result of harsh handling, though occasionally a strong and high-spirited captive would literally kill itself. Apart from the fact that royalty has to be paid on an elephant that dies in a stockade or while being handled, the only salutary deterrent to rough handling was and still is, black-listing. This is, moreover, the main restraint on greed, which can play a large part in cruelty in the elephant-catching business.

Every effort was made to minimize the rate of casualties, which was reduced dramatically from nearly thirty per cent to under five per cent as the result of the new methods Milroy introduced. If an elephant exhibited dangerous symptoms during the breaking-in period, it was promptly released and the money was refunded to the purchaser. The authority of the khedda officer was final in these matters. The heavy mortality rate with pregnant elephants was always a headache, since the signs of advanced pregnancy in elephants is difficult to detect. In the case of tame elephants, they are generally laid off work well ahead; but when one is dealing with a wild elephant, subjected to severe strains, it is another matter. We used to take no risks and rigidly enforced the rules regarding elephants suspected to be pregnant or with suckling calves, which were on no account to be captured or retained.

As a young khedda officer, Milroy had been trying out his humane methods since 1918 in the conviction that elephants trained by gentler methods had a better chance of survival in the long run. He never told me, but I think he was as sure as I am today that the majority of elephants captured and exported out of Assam to the markets of northern India could not survive for more than a few years. Otherwise how is one to explain the continuous demand for elephants in what amounts to an 'elephant slave traffic'? He realized that this demand could not be stilled, but he tried to make it easier for the elephant. I shall never forget how he described his early attempts at persuading the elephant catchers of Assam to fall in with his ideas and to join in the first departmental kheddas in the nineteen-twenties; these aimed at retaining the essential elements of the 'cottage industry' type of elephant catching peculiar to Assam, with certain humane refinements.

This was the atmosphere in which I was lucky enough to take over the mantle of khedda officer. Unfortunately the system of departmental kheddas more or less died with Milroy and catching today takes place in small operations by individual lease-holders. Thus the risk has reverted entirely to the private catcher, but fortunately the enlightened rules governing catching and training are still there and to a large extent the same standards of procedure and discipline are being maintained today. In these respects Assam is enjoying the fruits of those early departmental kheddas and sound and humane catching is the rule.

There is something about the atmosphere and smell of a *pilkhana* or training depot which is subtly exciting – that typical but not unpleasant smell of burning elephant dung and refuse combined with the sweet resinous odour of crushed elephant grass; the sight of the straight rows of standings or *thans* and the smooth tethering posts to which are tied the restless captives, shaking their ears and swinging their tails while they eat. When the fires push back the darkness and the plaintive singing which accompanies the night training flows into grass hut or canvas tent, there is no need for excuses in congratulating oneself on a khedda officer's life.

Every night we would go round with a lantern to see if there was enough fodder in front of each animal. An elephant is almost a twenty-four-hour feeder, lying down for very short periods; when it sleeps, it does so rather heavily and sometimes it snores stertorously. In addition to a large amount of vegetation, elephants

under training need titbits and delicacies which they do not normally require when in sound health. It was our business – and
later the business of the purchaser – to provide an adequate
quantity and variety of fodder and, equally important, to see that
the animal eats at all times.

A feature of the training of elephants used for timber dragging
– which is their main occupation in southern India – is the large
amount of cooked food they receive. Forest department elephants
are fed with concentrated and easily digested foods such as rice,
or pulses cooked and made up into large, square cakes; these are
given according to a prescribed ration and make up for the feed
the animals miss while working. I have even heard of sick elephants in Malabar being fed on mutton and chicken flesh! This is
a distinctive feature of the south, unlike in Assam where the
elephant is treated very much as a child of nature and gets only a
nominal ration of rice or paddy with a little salt. In northern
India, elephants are fed on large, thick chapattis containing quite
a substantial quantity of wheat flour. They are also given sugar-
cane where this is available. All this, of course, is in addition to
the basic feed of greenstuffs, mainly grasses in eastern India and
figleaves and branches elsewhere.

The traders, mainly Muslims from Bihar, would invariably
take pains over their purchases and there would generally be an
attendant constantly on duty at the tying places, stroking and
talking to the elephant or feeding it with juicy mouthfuls of
grass, made into little balls with a sprinkling of raw rice and salt
water to make them more palatable. The only weapon of these
attendants was a short stick to restrain the animal when needed.
In the evening, the piles of fodder or banana stems would imply
forethought for the night's fodder requirements. Elephants who
received such treatment would always be in good condition and
quite docile when dispatched to the melas or elephant fairs.

Training in the depot follows a strict routine and the average
time required for a small- to medium-sized elephant to be broken
in is two weeks. For a larger animal, the period may be extended
to four weeks; but invariably within six weeks of being brought
in, an elephant comes and goes unaccompanied and carries its own

fodder. It was the Doctor Babu's responsibility to see to the welfare of the elephants and if these periods were not adhered to, he would be very severe on the owners.

In the earlier stages of training, a koonki is needed on either side of the captive; as training progresses, one elephant would be removed and later the second one – usually the koonki that brought in the captive. At first this koonki is retained on a long phand, then unattached but in close attendance. These stages are known as the 'one-koonki' stage and the 'two-koonki' stage respectively.

The tying of an elephant is subjected to strict and time-honoured rules, the result of generations of experience. The native catchers have nothing to learn in these particulars but best of all were the traders. Stripped to their vests and with a loincloth tight around their buttocks, thus eliminating any loose ends which the elephant could seize, the men would get to work. Those working at the rear would keep complete silence. They would slip in between the legs of the attendant koonkis and seek for an opportunity of slipping the noose end of a slim but strong rope around the captive's ankle, while someone dangled a titbit in front of the elephant to keep its trunk occupied. It was always a job to get the first leg-rope on and the process of tying up all four legs might take a couple of hours in the case of a big elephant. It was the rule for everyone handy to assist and the first tying of an elephant was something of a ceremony in the depot. Once the legs were securely tied, the phand would be run out by the koonki and the end brought back and a couple of turns taken with it around the tying post. Then everyone would give a hand in hauling on it until the neck of the captive was pulled tight against the post. This is the position in which the animal is held for the first few days, except at nights when the phand is loosened to allow it to lie down. Every time the animal is taken to water and for exercise, which is twice a day morning and evening, the phand is fastened to the side of the attendant koonki, a second rope being applied by another elephant in the earlier stages of training. Throughout the training the key rope is the phand, which is never far away and is used to control the elephant at all stages until it is thoroughly broken in. And should the elephant die, its phand is buried with it, symbol of its capture and slavery!

When an elephant is tied for the first time after capture in mela shikar or in removal from a stockade, a particular method is followed. The hind-legs are bound securely together with a rope in a figure-of-eight tie which is called a *degi* and the legs are then fastened to the base of a convenient tree. The phand, which emerges outwards from the top of the head instead of from beneath the chin, is run out to its full length to a tree in front and is tied at such a height that the captive cannot get its mouth up to the rope. On the second and subsequent occasions, while the animal is on the way from the stockade to the depot and before it is picketed out for the training to begin, the elephant is merely fastened by its neck to a straight, smooth tree-trunk with its phand in such a way that the rope has two loops, turned at right angles to each other. This most ingenious tie, which is called the *galla ghuronia* or 'neck round', enables the elephant to move freely round the tree with its neck held close to the bole. Once the elephant reaches the depot, both its fore- and hind-feet are tied with figure-of-eight ropes called *banda* and *degi* respectively; others are tied to strong stakes fore and aft, while the phand is drawn close to the main tying post. This is a stout length of tree whose bark has been removed before it is buried firmly in the ground; it must be of a soft texture, for in its struggles the elephant uses its mouth and tusks or tushes to split the wood, often injuring or even breaking off the tips of these modified teeth.

In Assam, tethering is done with a chain fetter in the shape of a figure-of-eight, the two open ends being fastened with a bolt and nut around the ankles of the forelegs. When the animal is released in the forest at night to graze, a length of chain is added. Even with this impediment, an elephant can wander away more than a mile, but tracking next morning is simplified by signs of the chain, which often gets entangled in bushes and tree-stumps. Often one will be able to tell a koonki suddenly encountered in the jungle from a wild elephant only by the clinking of this chain and by the elephant's shuffling. One of our departmental elephants Manik, a fine tusker, on one occasion while he was in musth unscrewed the nut of the bolt which secured the chain fetter and escaped, alas to his eventual death.

The Upper Assam people and particularly the Miris and Morans – both large elephant-owning classes – use as a substitute for the iron fetter a circle of several strands of thick, twisted cane. After being put over the feet of the elephant it is pulled in at the middle by a short length of rope to form an oval. Although the cane fetter is more than strong enough to resist the attempts of even the largest elephant to burst it, the rope is the weak link and many escapes can be attributed to it.

In Madras, leather gaiters are first tied round the elephant's legs when it is inside the kraal as a preliminary to the fitting of hobbles and training chains. The use of these protective devices, added to the fact that the employment of the kraal postpones the application of ropes until the animal is docile, results in very few leg injuries. It is interesting to note that fifty years ago the head of the Madras Forest Department tried to persuade the Maharaja of Mysore to adopt this training device for his kheddas, but without success.

Attention is paid not only to the ropes and the tying post, but also to the actual ground on which the elephant is tied. The locality is always a soft river-bank, carefully prepared by removing all roots and buried stumps and liberally sprinkled with sand. These are important precautions because the animal in its rage – and also in order to obtain earth to throw over itself – kicks the ground repeatedly. It can injure its toenails badly in the process and they become loose; the leg may then become highly inflamed and septic, when the nails will fall off. Such animals suffer a slight depreciation in value when they go to the markets, though not as much as when they lose the end of the tail; but the traders are very clever at fixing on temporary tails to deceive purchasers.

Every morning and evening the otherwise deserted sands by the river come to life and, to the accompaniment of the traditional training commands, the elephants are marched up and down. They are made to perform simple evolutions such as stopping, going backwards, and turning round. The words of command are sung to the elephant and are accompanied at first by severe

thwacks with sticks and pokes from sharpened poles, the attendant elephants assisting and performing the same gyrations. The
elephant has a set of body ropes, to which the rider on its neck
can cling when the animal shakes its body violently and flings
itself about. This is customary in the early stages particularly and
great care has to be taken that the animal does not bolt or hurt
itself. One attendant walks in front with a long, sharp wooden
spear while another trails at the back, holding on to the tail if
possible. The monotonous but musical chanting eventually lulls
the animal as much as the continuous patter of the human
attendants, who take every opportunity to rub and stroke the
elephant. The training is terminated by a bath and drink at
the river. The whole procedure presents an animated picture to
the visitor, which is heightened when he witnesses the evening training.

This is performed after dark and is something to which everybody in the depot looks forward. The phand is pulled tight so
that the elephant cannot injure anybody. Then, in the smoke of
burning torches the men gather round the captive and sing to it,
rubbing its body down with straw and branches of leaves, while
a rider perched on its back clings on for all his worth while the
struggling captive throws itself about. When it reaches out with
its trunk, it is beaten and intimidated by a torch thrust at its face.
Trunk curled up to avoid the smoking flames, moisture trickling
down from its eyes – whether real tears as the elephant men swear
they are or natural exudation of moisture caused by the smoke –
the elephant presents a pathetic sight. If it falls down in its struggles it is poked and made to rise. Eventually its spirit is broken
and it stands drooping, apparently enjoying, if such can really be
the case, the singing and stroking.

All the training is done to the accompaniment of talking and
singing, the meaning of the words being praise of the animal and
encouragement to it to become docile and obedient. The psychological approach is one of force and kindness, command and
cajolery, admonishment and praise. The songs tell of the capture
of the beautiful elephant by the big strong koonki, of the happy
life ahead as a fine cow or a noble tusker which will do valiant

deeds. The men urge the captive to be gentle and brave, powerful and swift, intelligent and obedient. The words are simple and the theme beautiful. In the sombre light of the fire and the flickering torches the words seem very moving – the epitome of the pain and cruelty of elephant catching as well as its achievements and rewards.

This, then, is the art of elephant handling and training. It can only be learnt by a long apprenticeship on a humble salary and two meals of rice a day, clothes dirty and in rags from the jungle and its thorns, hair uncut for many weeks, body fined down through hard work during the long six months of the cold weather catching. As the spring approaches, restlessness begins to overtake everybody including, it seems, the elephants. The close of the operation is approaching and all feel the urge to go home. Some have had a good season, others have not been so lucky. Once the four main markets are over, those elephants left unsold must be held over until next year. The traders leave one by one and finally the last koonkis depart. The khedda officer's duty is to inspect the stockades to see if the gates have been cut down, so as to leave the traditional elephant paths free for the herds to use again. The melancholy smell of burning dung drifts across the empty depot while the crows turn over the last of the refuse. The jungle prepares to close in again and the spirits of the elephants which have been trained here, and of those that lie buried not so far away, seem to hover for the last time before departing too.

So far I have described the breaking-in period of a wild elephant's domestication; the completion of its training is accomplished afterwards by its first or subsequent owner. Early schooling is important and the cliché 'the elephant never forgets' is most apt. An elephant's memory, or its power of retaining or reproducing mental or sensory impressions as the dictionary puts it, really is remarkable. It learns quickly but there are, of course, clever elephants and others not so clever. Sanderson has recorded the case of a young female which had been worked from the age of eight years learning its task in the short space of ten days and pulling logs eighteen feet long and fifty inches in girth, although she was only 5 feet 8 inches in height herself. Durganath Gogoi described to me how he trained a young makhna, which he bought for a few hundred rupees in our kheddas, to drag timber without a rider on its neck. All that was required were men on the ground to tie and untie the chain round the log and the elephant would do the rest, marching up and down between two points half a mile apart with the log in tow. It is said that in the timber-yards of Burma elephants stack the logs while their mahouts smoke cheroots and gossip under a tree.

In India working elephants are, early on, trained to put aside branches and creepers when going through jungle with persons on their backs and to pick up articles dropped by their riders and will go on doing these things automatically thereafter. A friend described to me how he once unknowingly dropped his cigarette case from his elephant's back and it was only when the elephant stopped with a jerk and would not go on that, realizing something was wrong, the mahout looked down and saw the case on the ground. Some elephants will pick up things dropped on the march automatically or with very little urging; but on the other hand I have come across cases where the animal was either too dull or too timid to pick up the article and the mahout has had to climb down for it.

There are also varying degrees of retentivity of what an elephant has been taught and individuals can become very rusty or indifferent to what constitutes the code of good elephantine behaviour, such as not reaching into its throat for a little of that mysterious store of saliva which it is in the habit of squirting over itself (and its riders) on a hot march, or not reaching out for a titbit of jungle at some critical moment when being taken up to an animal in a shoot and thus alerting or startling the quarry. The case of Lalji's koonki being successfully put to work at training captured elephants soon after his voluntary return after an absence of five years in the wilds, and the instance of Sundarmala obeying the order to sit down after nearly fourteen years of freedom, which I have already described, are of course outstanding examples of an elephant's powers of memory.

Although the sagacity of the elephant has been questioned, some instances which have come to my notice deserve to be recorded as evidence of their natural intelligence. On my first kheddas our Doctor Babu used to tell me of the alertness of a certain big tusker named Manik which we used to use as our 'dressing elephant' when treating sick elephants. According to the old vet, Manik had once saved him from being trampled by a captive tusker when he was underneath its body, dressing some leg wounds. Of course there was a mahout on Manik's neck as he, along with another big elephant, was being used to 'crush' the tethered sick elephant during the treatment; but according to the Doctor Babu, the man could not have intervened in time to save him. Suddenly the tusker grabbed his arm and it was only Manik's instantaneous response, and the savage jab which he administered to the aggressor with his heavy tusks, that saved the situation.

There was a much-publicized case of an elephant's sagacity resulting in a cat being saved from death. On the west coast of India, when important religious festivals are celebrated by Hindu temples, a huge shed is erected. The central post is made from a tall, straight tree, generally of jack-fruit, which is coated with saffron paste and erected at an auspicious hour, fixed by the priests, with the aid of an elephant. On one occasion a large tusker, which had dragged the tree into the centre of a large gathering assembled to witness the ceremony, refused to lower the post into the hole. After all the commands and persuasions of the mahout had failed, it was found that a black cat was cowering at the bottom of the pit. What is more – according to a witness who described the scene – the elephant actually lifted the cat out of the hole, though this was probably done at the command of its rider. Was it nervousness that made the elephant refuse to lower the post, or might it have been its regard for another animal? Whatever the basic emotion, it does seem to reveal a certain intelligence.

Another remarkable story concerns an African elephant, nicknamed 'The Lord Mayor of Paraa', in the Murchison Falls National Park of Uganda, which learnt to turn on the water hydrant to obtain a drink. This acquired ability must have resulted from an unexpected success after several fumblings with the

19. The daily bath

20. Enjoying a titbit

21. Lal Bahadur (*see page 173*)

faucet of the pipe; if the animal had learnt to turn it off again after quenching its thirst, it would have been far more remarkable!

But there have been several cases of elephants in Assam escaping by unscrewing the nut of the bolt on the leg fetter (one such escape occurred during my time). Obviously the elephants had grasped that the bolts, and in particular the screwing and unscrewing of them, had some direct bearing on their loss of freedom and it is surely significant that they used this knowledge when the urge to be free came upon them.

Manik, one of our finest elephants whom I mentioned above, once unscrewed the nut of the bolt which secured his chain fetter and escaped. At the time I was looking for suitable elephants to reinforce the ageing Akbar and Sher Khan at Kazaringa and decided to withdraw two from the Sadiya Division, which involved crossing the Brahmaputra and a march of some two hundred miles. The two elephants, Manik and Mohan, were companions of several years and a support to each other in their annual periods of musth. As soon as one of them came into that condition, he would be tied securely and the other would administer to his needs in the way of fodder collection and general security. As luck would have it, Manik came into musth just before the journey was about to begin and the foolish divisional officer, instead of postponing it, sent Mohan to Kazaringa alone. Manik was stationed near a Miri village a few miles outside Sadiya, where plenty of fodder and water were available. All the precautions that the little Abor mahout took was to move Manik a little distance away into the forest and tether him to a tree – and a rotten tree at that! In the night, the elephant overturned the tree and cleverly unscrewed the bolt of his fetter.

When the escape was discovered next morning, the first thing the worried attendants did was to release a female elephant to keep Manik from straying too far away. They then informed the Divisional Forest Officer. It was a serious business to lose a departmental elephant and the officer immediately sent me a telegram. Unfortunately I had already left Shillong on the start of a long tour, which was to end in that very division; yet it did not strike the DFO to send me a message to one of my camps, nor even to mention the incident when I met him by chance in the Tinsukia bazaar. The same evening I crossed the Brahmaputra and next morning went up to the foothills headquarters of the local Political Officer at Pasighat. I was horrified when he handed me a telegram from his colleague in Sadiya to the effect that he intended to have Manik destroyed as he was proving a menace to the district.

There was nothing I could do, as I was not in possession of the facts, and in any case I was due to reach Sadiya the next day. I spent a disturbed night at my camp at Murkongesellek, which was destroyed by the Brahmaputra's floods after the 1950 earthquake, along with the town of Sadiya and much else in the area. Early next morning I set off, but it was a whole day's journey, involving crossing and recrossing the great river with my vehicle on a ferry boat, and it was late in the evening when we reached the little town of Sadiya on the north bank. As we made fast I caught sight of a group of my officers among the crowd on the landing stage and one glance at their downcast faces told me the worst. Manik had been shot dead the previous evening by an Assam rifleman.

I listened to the full details, holding back my recriminations as best I could. Apparently every effort to recapture Manik had proved unsuccessful, but the staff had done a very good job by keeping in touch with him. The elephant had not attempted to go very far and once he had satisfied his sexual urge on the cow elephant which had been released to restrain him, he had hung about the village. At night he used to visit it looking for a chance of a drink of Miri liquor, of which he was very fond. This liquor is brewed in quantities and stored in large jorums made of earth, kept by the Miris on the platforms of their stilt-houses. These riverine tribesmen used to allow their elephants a drink of liquor now and then, a custom which had been part of Manik's upbringing. He visited a different house every night, pushing in the fragile walls and platforms in his deranged state of musth. The terrified villagers had gone to the Political Officer, a plainsman who was nervous in his first posting as a district official. In their quaint way of pronouncing Assamese, they threatened to send a telegram to Shillong and have the officer removed if he did not do something immediately. And so Manik's fate was sealed.

Some Assam riflemen were posted at the village, but with no very clear orders as far as I could make out in the inquiry I held after my arrival. For some evenings Manik stayed away and the men, who were constantly on his track, reported that his musth condition was subsiding. Then early one evening, while it was still daylight, he was seen on the outskirts of the village. The alarm was raised and the only rifleman available ran to the spot. While Manik was hanging about the little Gurkha, thinking it was his function to guard the village, took up his position in front of the hut nearest to the forest. When the elephant saw the man he came forward and, while he was kicking up the dust and demonstrating, the rifleman fired a shot. Naturally the wounded elephant charged and the man, as he admitted to me later, lost his head (the actual idiom is 'the head got hot'). He fired bullet after bullet into the unfortunate elephant and it took over thirty ·303 bullets to fell him. I found him lying half on the river-bank and the vultures were already whitening his great bulk with their dung as they waited for the skin to soften and give them a chance to pierce the swollen body with their rapacious beaks. His musth condition had cleared up and his temples were free from the flow of the oily fluid, though the cheeks were deeply discoloured. The men said that when he began to come out of musth, he remembered the evening ration of a bucketful of salted paddy which all the Forest Department elephants get; it is like sweets to a child and I could well believe that he was on his way to his old standing on the edge of the village when the trigger-happy rifleman found him. I stood by Manik's side mourning his so unnecessary death with tears in my eyes.

Apart from their intelligence and aptitude for carrying out routine tasks, elephants can display the most astonishing aptitude for performing tricks. There was an elephant near Golaghat in Central Assam which used to play with a football, kicking, bouncing and throwing the ball about with its feet and trunk with the greatest gusto and every sign of enjoyment. He was bought by the agent of a Burma teak firm solely because of this ability. Most elephants when trained young can acquire amazing virtuosity. In south India this is a feature of young elephants captured in pits, every effort being made to attract circus proprietors by a repertoire of ready-learnt tricks. Kind treatment and regular rewards for cleverness and aptitude are the secrets of quickly and successfully training an elephant, though firmness is very essential. In the forest department depots of south India timber-dragging elephants are taught over forty basic commands for different operations, which illustrates what has come to be expected of an elephant.

For aptitude, docility and faithfully carrying out orders once it has learnt the tasks and the meanings of the commands there is surely no wild animal to equal the elephant. Plutarch in his essay on Fortune says: 'what is more huge or formidable than the elephant in appearance? Yet it becomes man's diversion and a turn at public games, for which it learns to dance and to kneel. And all such sights are not idly introduced but to the end that they may teach us to what height reason raises man and over what it sets him and how it makes him master over everything.'

CHAPTER 9

DOCTORING ELEPHANTS

For an elephant to survive its training in good condition depends not only on the care and attention it receives at the depot, but on the amount of strain to which it was subjected during its capture and immediately after. Sometimes animals arrived at the depot very badly damaged during removal from stockades; but we prided ourselves on our low casualty rate, which was very largely due to careful handling both in catching and removal.

Many wounds which might appear alarming to an inexperienced observer are merely surface injuries which heal quite quickly, but those caused by ropes are often more serious. What the khedda officer dreads most of all is a rope cutting through nerves and tendons and pressure must be removed immediately. Big elephants gave most trouble in training: their very strength was their worst enemy, for they would injure themselves in their fierce struggles and greater force would be needed to subdue them. Severe rope galls on ankles and necks were the commonest injuries and the first lesson we impressed on our men was to prevent ropes rubbing unnecessarily on open wounds, by adjusting and supporting them above the sore place and tying them to the body ropes. We always worked on the principle of trying to prevent rather than cure. The chafing of limbs could be prevented by providing bedding of dry grass and rejected fodder on either side of the elephant and this was well worth the trouble. Falls had to be prevented as much as possible, for wounds on elbows and knees could result in severe swelling, while pitching forward violently on face and trunk could mean nasty wounds caused by broken tusks and tushes.

The khedda officer's and the Doctor Babu's attention was continuously absorbed by such things as the problem of maintaining the strength of a large elephant suffering from septicaemia, or the struggle to keep alive a suckling calf which had been separated from its mother. Then there is the continual battle against flies, which lay their eggs in wounds and the eggs in due course hatch out into maggots; this is a feature of camp life which is, of course, intimately connected with the cleanliness of the surroundings and it is a campaign in itself. There are also the crucial decisions which must be taken with regard to the release of an elephant on the verge of collapse from injuries or the rigours of training, or from some obscure internal ailment – decisions which have to be taken in the face of objections from the purchaser, who sees his money lost, and from the catchers who see their earnings disappearing.

As a young khedda officer in my first elephant-catching season I had a very good example of the difficult business of nursing a big sick elephant. The Doctor Babu had taken particular pains to introduce me to the treatment of wounds on what I could see was his pet patient. This was a large tusker which through rough handling had developed severe injuries on its legs and neck. We suspected that the nape of the neck had been cut to bring the animal under control. When I saw the elephant it had an enormous swollen fore-leg and its neck wound was several inches across – the wound was so deep that I could put my hand under the fold of skin on the neck. The smell from the rotting flesh around the toenails and on the ankles was almost intolerable. The animal had not lain down for more than ten days.

The daily treatment consisted of syringing the affected parts with a solution of permanganate of potash, followed by a tepid solution of iodine and water. Large wads of medicated wool soaked with oil-salve were packed into the wound on his neck and wherever flies had laid their eggs and maggots had formed – the most certain indication being the smell of putrefied flesh – we applied raw phenyle, taking care to avoid the healthy skin.

Suppurating toenails and peeling sole were treated with Stockholm tar. All open wound surfaces were continuously smeared with a fly dressing made from such simple ingredients as pulverized clay boiled with rosin, phenyle, and camphor applied cold with jute swabs. The animal was in an advanced stage of septicaemia but we did not know the use of sulpha drugs nor of penicillin in those days and all our efforts were directed to keeping up the animal's strength. But his drooping, sleepy eyes caused the Doctor Babu much anxiety. True enough, after more than a month on his feet his heart failed him just as we had got his wounds under control and, much to everybody's chagrin and sorrow, he collapsed and died.

One of the most serious wounds I ever had to dress was in the case of a koonki which had been attacked by a wild tusker. A line of koonkis had been going through the forest in single file when a tusker, which had been lying in wait by the side of the path, suddenly rushed out and gored the last koonki deeply in the side. I hurried with whatever medicines and dressings I could collect to the spot where the unfortunate animal was standing, crippled and unable to move. I could put my arm up to the elbow in his side and all I could do was to plug the hole with yards of lint soaked in a medicated oil dressing, after syringing out the wound with a mild potassium permanganate solution followed by iodine. Luckily the tusks had not pierced the stomach, but they had entered the groin. The wound was a clean one, but it took several months of treatment before the koonki recovered. He was never the same elephant again and the Phookans who owned him could only use him for depot work after that. It was a sobering warning to me that the presence of big male elephants with a herd is always a deterrent in elephant catching, particularly in mela shikar.

Seriously sick elephants were the object of interest and sympathy for everyone in the depot. In their spare time, the Bihar elephant purchasers would wander over to the sick animals and give suggestions and advice. We had great faith in these men, who could be relied upon to pull a sick elephant or a suckling calf through if it were at all possible. They had their own secret native medicines and drugs which we knew very little about, but which we suspected they used in addition to those administered by our veterinary doctor. But they were nevertheless very amenable to our discipline and as a class they were worthy of admiration.

Elephants which showed no chance of recovery would be released when possible in the neighbouring forests. It was a delicate business deciding when this should be done. The Doctor Babu and I used to work in close support of each other and the moment he gave me the word, I would act. In our departmental kheddas we had considerable freedom in such matters. The main thing was not to leave the release too late in the interest of the elephant, though there was always the inevitable tussle with the catchers and the purchaser, both of whom had a financial stake in the elephant.

Although elephants which develop serious illnesses never lie down and will sleep standing for long periods, they will eat to the last in an instinctive effort to maintain their failing strength. Strangely enough, in such condition they would make no attempt to escape although all ropes except the bare minimum were removed.

The use of a sling to raise a sick animal off the ground and support it on its feet has never found a place in the treatment of elephants so far as I am aware, but I believe it would save many an animal doomed to continue lying prone through its natural fear of trusting to its legs when it is weakening. I did once experiment with such a contrivance, which was invented by a lease-holder named Goramuriya Goswami, head of one of the Vaishnavite Hindu monasteries in Assam located in the Majuli, which is said to be the biggest riverine island in the world. Like many people in Assam he had been drawn to the highly speculative business of elephant catching not for personal gain but to support his monastery, which had fallen into decay. He lost a lot of money in the years before I came to Assam and then got caught up in politics and served his term in prison. He was now staging a comeback in the hope of retrieving some of his losses. He was a man of very dignified presence and idealistic outlook and, by the very nature of his religious position and his high caste as a Brahmin, of austere and frugal living.

The Goswami was always trying experiments, not invariably successful in practice but generally based on sound ideas. He was dissatisfied with the method of removing big elephants from a stockade and felt that the custom of tying the phand round the girth of a koonki imposed a great strain on it and also did not allow it to exert its maximum power. He was in favour of some arrangement whereby the strain was taken on the chest as used in timber dragging in Burma. He had a six-inch-wide breastband prepared out of plaited jute ropes with a view to trying it out on the first possible occasion; but somehow the occasion never came, for various reasons connected with the busy comings and goings of the Goswami.

I once took the contrivance out to where a young tusker had collapsed because of a leg injury and tried to raise the animal and support it with the broad band under the chest, with the hauling end slung over the limb of a convenient tree. But not even a dozen men could raise the elephant to its feet; it gave no help whatever, lying limp in the sling and bawling with fright throughout the operation. Reluctantly I had to give up the attempt, but if only I had had a pulley to overcome the friction it might have been different. In the end I had to shoot the elephant and this was a great ordeal for me, as always.

The Goswami also tried the experiment of bringing a party of Morans from upper Assam to build a hal for us and demonstrate its use. The hal, which as I have said resembles nothing so much as the ancient stocks, should prevent the injuries which are sometimes severe in big elephants when they are trained by the ordinary methods. The structure consists of uprights and side and cross bars of stout timber, all ingeniously put together to form an open crib. The most important element is the pair of uprights, between which the animal's neck is held so as to prevent its head from moving freely. Its movements are thus greatly restricted and attendants can handle it in the hal with safety from the very first day, provided that they keep away from the trunk. Also, there is no furious tugging on leg- and neck-ropes as in the usual method.

We used the Goswami's hal to train two big elephants – his own tusker eight feet ten inches in height and a makhna over nine feet tall. The traders marvelled at the results, but said it would never do for them because they had to train their elephants quickly in order to catch the markets in North Bihar. For an average elephant they took from two to three weeks, whereas by the hal method it would take double that time.

Suckling calves were always a very difficult problem. Every little calf will play about with grass, putting it into its mouth and chewing at it and this is often claimed as a sign of it having reached the stage of eating solids. But it must be remembered that elephant calves go on suckling their mothers long after they have had a baby brother or sister. I have personally seen an old *dhui* or cow elephant in a stockade with as many as three calves at heel, all of them taking a turn at suckling her although the little one got the preference. Punishing a phandi who brought in a suckling calf was all very well, but we dared not release the baby in the forest lest it fell a victim to a tiger. So often we were compelled to try and rear the animal but invariably with very poor results. Cow's or buffalo's milk is a poor substitute for elephant's milk and infant calves brought up on it rapidly lost condition and developed stomach disorders. We did not know in those days that elephant's milk is very rich in albumen or we might have added the whites of sufficient eggs to the milk we were using; nor did we know much about vitamins and calcium substitutes.

Feeding was generally done with a length of bamboo, cut at one end so as to form a spout, though if one had a rubber tube and a douche-can this was the best. The men would resort to soft boiled rice mixed with *gur* (crude brown sugar) or even lentils. The Bihari traders were the best people to be entrusted with these little calves, but I am convinced that the unfortunate animals never survived for more than a few months after being sold in the markets. When Gee, the naturalist tea-planter of Assam, sent Dumbo to the London Zoo in 1949 she was a suckling calf and had been separated from her mother. She had staggered into a depot starving and looking for help from the very men who had probably taken her mother. The animal was then three feet two inches in height and was estimated to be about five months old. Gee kept her alive for a month and a half on fresh cow's milk mixed with one-fourth water and also a little boiled rice and lentils. She took to nibbling green food and was fond of *gur*. He flew her to London, provisions for the journey consisting of tinned milk and cornflakes. On arrival in London she was put on a special feed based on a calf-milk meal, balanced and enriched to simulate elephant's milk. Six months later she was taking an increasing amount of solids, but was expected to depend on liquid food for some time after that. Lucky Dumbo! I wish we could have had the use of such enlightened diets for elephant calves in those days. The golden rule was not to bring in a doubtful elephant if one could help it and later, when I became Conservator, I enforced a minimum height of four feet for elephant calves.

Several times in the course of my service, elephant calves which had been separated from their mothers were found. I always encouraged my staff to make immediate arrangements with any reliable and knowledgeable person to take over and care for the animal, instead of putting it to auction as 'government property' in the rather heartless way ordained by red tape. Giving away the animal unconditionally would have been best under the circumstances, but there is a lot of truth in the saying that 'nothing is valued if it is not paid for'. We used to ask the custodian to pay the royalty on the animal in the event of its survival, but I am sorry to say that the Government very seldom got the money. Surprisingly enough, I never came across the case of foster-mothering by other elephants, though it may have existed with the Assamese elephant owners. The fact of the matter is that in our commercial khedda operations there was no room for a cow koonki with a suckling calf which we might have tried to use as a foster mother. Incidentally I seldom heard of the system of 'elephant aunts', which appears to be common among the teak elephants of Burma.

Frank Nicholls, a veteran planter and wild life enthusiast, has described the poignant situation when a mother elephant came to him for help when her calf was hamstrung as a result of the attacks

of a tiger; on hearing Frank's elephant passing, she came out of
the jungle where she had been keeping the tiger at bay and,
fearlessly placing her trunk on the head of the tame elephant as if
asking for help, led them to the spot where her little calf was
standing with one leg almost severed at the lowest joint. I have
had the experience of a wild elephant calf, which had also been
attacked by tigers and had been separated from its mother and the
herd, coming boldly up to a lonely railway gangman's hut in the
middle of the forest at the foot of the Naga Hills, obviously in
search of help and food. It staggered up to a pool at which a
woman was washing her clothes with its little trunk outstretched
and fell at the edge of the water. What was the instinct which made
these elephants act as they did, or was it simply intelligence?

Elephants are notoriously gentle with their young. The love of
a mother elephant for her calf is well known, of course, but the
behaviour of large males towards little ones is also characterized by
gentleness, except in a stockade when calves which get in the way
are pushed aside impatiently by the big males and are often injured
or even killed outright. But in the desperate press of a stockade
even cows will turn on each other and on each other's calves.

The trusting nature of a little elephant where big ones are
concerned was brought home to me on one occasion when my
mahouts and I unexpectedly came upon a herd that was feeding in
open *sal* forest. It was a wonderful sight and we skirted the herd
cautiously in order not to disturb them and then turned away to
go about our business. Suddenly I found a little tusker, not more
than four feet in height, behind my elephant Mohan Prasad. He
had followed us for at least a hundred yards from the rest of the
herd and if I had not detected him I do not know how much
farther he would have come. His curiosity had been aroused by
Mohan Prasad and his little trunk now and then took the scent of
the big elephant as he walked behind. Only when I stopped him
did Mohan Prasad realize that he was being followed and as usual
he spun round with a start, but there was no anger when he saw
the little fellow. He stretched out his trunk and the little elephant
did likewise and so they greeted each other. When we spoke out
loud to send the little chap back to his mother he got a start and

went off with his ears stretched wide, his tail up and out in that characteristic elephant manner. All the while the herd had been quite unconscious of our presence, although we must have been clearly visible to them in the open forest. But the wind was right, which would account for their not detecting us.

The wonderful attachment between elephant mothers and their calves was always the cause of much unhappiness, both to them and to us, when the time came to separate them. The depot would ring with the pathetic bawlings of the little ones tied apart in a corner and the roarings and rumblings of their mothers, unable to see their offspring yet acutely aware of their presence. Even when we sold a calf along with its mother, her milk would generally dry up under the stresses and strains of the training and once this happened, the mother often developed an antipathy towards her calf. So if the calf was a steady fodder eater it was always better to separate it from the mother straight away.

One sometimes felt that the whole of the elephant-catching industry deserved the appellation of a brutal and cruel business; but we were part of a system which had persisted for thousands of years and mere cogs in a machinery which had to be kept in motion. Our function was to take all unnecessary cruelty and suffering out of the trade and this is what we tried to do.

A frequent cause of death soon after capture is attributable to colic followed by pneumonia, brought about by allowing a heated elephant to drink or bathe in cold water. The phandis were most particular about this and used to rush the new captives through a stream if one had to be crossed on the way from a stockade or on mela shikar. It is firmly believed that drinking or dallying in water when the animal's system is overheated after its struggles brings on an acute attack of colic, particularly if the elephant lies on the spot for any length of time; but it has always struck me as strange that in southern India a newly-captured elephant is given water freely to cool its system.

As the result of non-observance of this rule, one of our departmental elephants, Mohan Prasad, which had particular associations for me, met with his death prematurely. He had been ill and not in use for some months before the last and fatal occasion he was taken out. It was during a whole day's inspection in September, one of the most sultry months of the year, and he was made to cross several swollen streams. On his return to base he collapsed and never recovered. The post-mortem revealed pneumonia. Mohan Prasad was not a very old animal and had still many years of service in him. His going left a void in the elephant establishment of the famous Goalpara Division and meant a great loss to me personally, for he had been my faithful mount and companion on all my big shoots. Another rather similar case was the loss of a beautiful young female, rising six feet and probably going to have her first calf; I had purchased her for the department fresh from an elephant depot soon after the war and named her after my wife. She was being moved to Assam from the Surma valley after her training period was over and her inexperienced mahout, guided by the phandi of the escorting koonki who was in a hurry for some reason or another, marched her some fourteen miles on a hot day in May across open country. Just as they were nearing the end of the march they had to cross a river. Instead of camping on the near side of the river, she was taken through it in her heated condition, with the result that she collapsed after going some way on the farther bank. In her run-down condition she contracted pneumonia and died where she fell in spite of every effort to save her, to my great rage and bitter disappointment.

The Asian elephant is a powerful swimmer. Sanderson has stated with reference to the old Bengal khedda department, that 'large numbers of elephants are annually swum across the tideway of the combined Ganges and Brahmaputra between Dacca and Barackpore and they are sometimes six consecutive hours without touching bottom'. He had seen an elephant swim a river three hundred yards wide with its hind legs tied together. It is all the more extraordinary therefore, to read Commander Blunt's assertion that elephants in Africa cannot swim and prefer to walk on the beds of the rivers with the tips of their trunks projecting above the surface, in which state they are easy prey to native hunters, who spear the trunks from boats. Elephants have a natural buoyancy and after a certain depth it is difficult to make them walk, for they would much rather swim.

I well remember, on my first khedda, crossing the upper reaches of the Bhorelli river on elephant back when it was in spate. I had gone to inspect a stockade and in the morning the river was knee-deep; but on our return in the evening we found it a roaring torrent, flooded half-way to its banks by some unexpected cloud-burst in the hills. We were a party of three elephants and I was on the biggest, a fine tusker. There was trepidation on the faces of the riders but there was nothing to be done except to venture the crossing, for the river was between us and the camp. Keeping the smallest elephant upstream we entered the river, setting a course at an angle downstream. The lease-holder who was accompanying me muttered prayers and threw some coins in the river. We were soon in a rushing nightmare of white-capped waves, with the roaring of loose boulders turning over in the river-bed and on which our elephants slipped and floundered, nearly losing their footing more than once. I observed my mahout beating the elephant over the head repeatedly and when I remonstrated with him he said the elephant wanted to swim. Had it done so and given up its laborious and careful picking of its way across the river, its trunk alternatively feeling the bottom and pointing out over the troubled waters to the opposite bank, I would not be here to tell the tale, for I am no swimmer. How we got across was a wonder and I was frankly terrified. Once the little elephant was swept off its feet and came crashing into my mount and against my leg, which was severely jarred, but the big tusker steadied him. Our pad was almost awash at the deepest point and it was with tremendous relief that at last I observed the level of the water receding and I could lower my eyes to the rushing river.

In Assam crossing the Brahmaputra is nothing to elephants, yet the animals that come from the hills are sometimes nervous at being asked to cross the mighty river. I remember the case of the beautiful tusker caught in one of Goramuriya Goswami's stockades in my kheddas of 1935–6 and the trouble he gave when he was first taken across the river to his new home in the Majuli. He was being escorted by the Goswami's great koonki, Jung

Bahadur, who had brought the young elephant out of the stockade and had trained him. When the two elephants, roped together, were ridden into the river swollen by early floods, the young elephant panicked. Shaking off his mahout he climbed on to the shoulders of his escort, whose rider in turn was dislodged. Getting both his front legs across Jung Bahadur's back he hung on, compelling the koonki to swim for his life. The two elephants without riders on their backs were carried downstream seven miles, Jung Bahadur swimming desperately to support himself and his unwelcome load. The men followed in boats, frightened for the fate of the elephants. But somehow they survived the swim. When at last they stepped ashore on the other bank and the younger elephant had got off the back of the koonki, Jung Bahadur waited a minute or so to recover from his titanic effort and then turned on his companion and gave him a tremendous hammering, as much as to say 'don't you ever try that again'.

These two elephants were in another drama which ended less happily some six months later. They had returned to the same lease area mahal for the next cold weather operations, the young elephant this time having given no trouble in crossing the Brahmaputra, and were marching together with some other koonkis through the forest, when a lone bull buffalo suddenly dashed across the path and stampeded them. Both the elephants threw their mahouts and ran into the jungle. The young elephant was never recaptured; in fact he resisted all efforts to catch him and suddenly became very fierce, as if he had realized that he had regained his freedom in the very jungles where he had been captured. Goramuriya Goswami, who was ill when the incident occurred and so could not do much personally to assist in the attempts, was broken-hearted but I blamed him for having brought the animal back as a koonki to his home jungles so soon after capture.

There is an annual swimming race for elephants across the Brahmaputra near Gauhati and it is fascinating to see the great animals bobbing about in the water, like black rocks, sometimes almost completely awash with only the tops of their skulls and their backs showing, at other times rising high out of the water,

22. Wild tusker in musth

23. A two-year-old elephant up for sale

24. Udaigiri, ceremonial elephant of the President of India

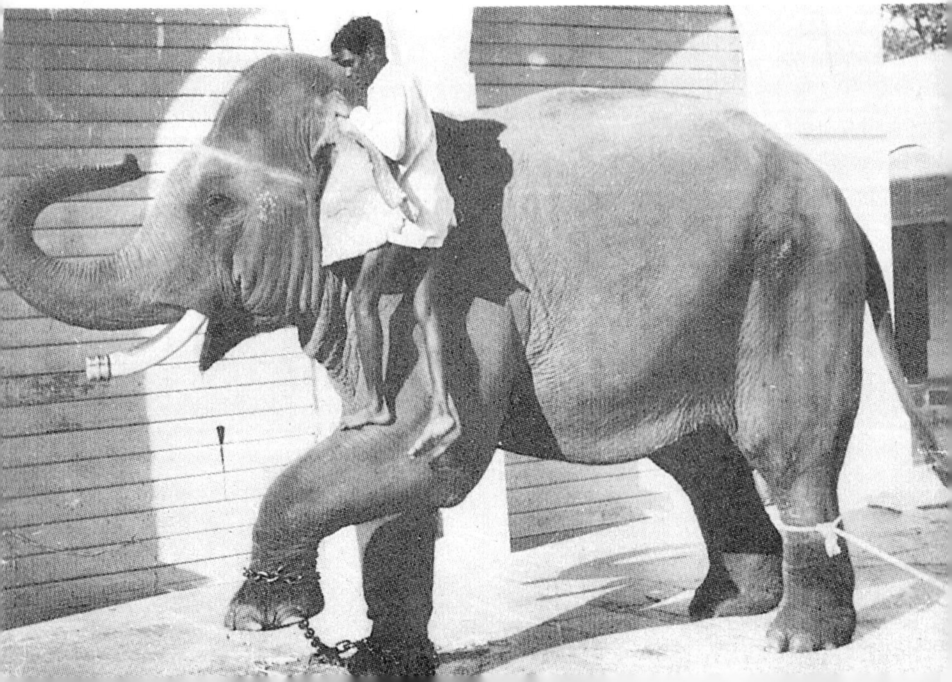

25 and 26. Work in the teak forests of Burma

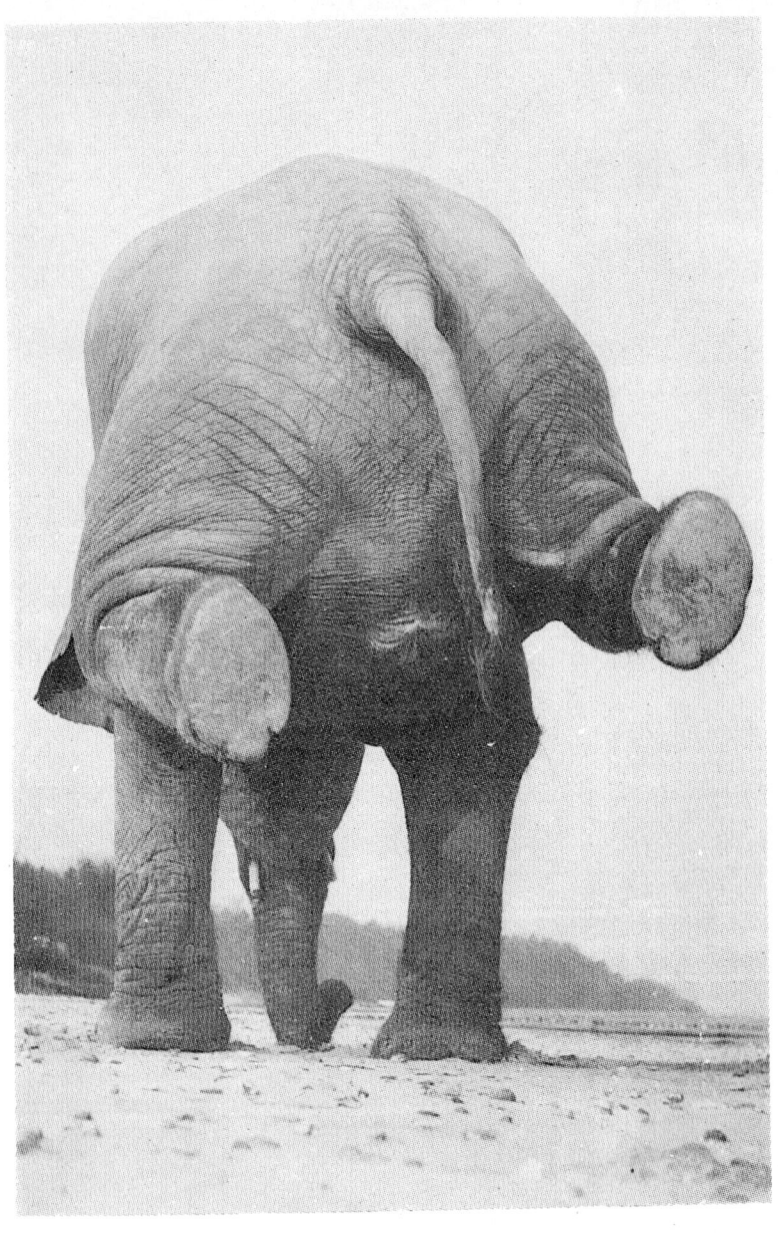

27. 'Thy impudence hath a monstrous beauty, like the hind-quarters of an elephant' (Flecker: *Hassan*)

the tips of their trunks breaking the surface periodically for air. Elephants roll about a lot when swimming and obviously use their trunks as well as their feet. It is very difficult for elephants to drown but they must not be faced upstream or forced to swim against the current, as they are liable to become exhausted.

Quicksands are, however, a great danger to elephants – in fact all elephants are naturally nervous of entering boggy ground and of crossing rivers with treacherous bottoms. Some years ago a large wild tusker became bogged in the Chakardeo swamp near Gauhati when it came down from the hills to feed on the lush *dal* grass and his end was observed by many. In his titanic desperate struggles, the elephant broke off one of its tusks and its piteous calls were heard all night. I have read an account of an elephant being bogged on the edge of the Brahmaputra, where his struggles were observed by the passengers in a passing river steamer. One of our elephants was saved when the pad of his companion was thrown to him; this proved to be of great assistance. During my first kheddas in Darrang in 1934 I got news of a captured elephant which had become bogged in a deep and treacherous stream on its way to the depot. The koonki in attendance had managed to get out of the morass but the wild animal, apparently weak after its capture and long march from the stockade at the other end of the district, was unable to summon the strength to save itself. There would have been no doubt of the eventual result if the spot had not been close to the depot. Collecting two or three of the biggest koonkis available, I rushed to the spot. The unfortunate makhna was almost up to his eyes in the mud and had apparently given up the struggle. I at once put Kan Sira ('Torn Ear') in with his rider, a young and dashing phandi who had the reputation of being one of the few men who could manage this koonki, who was a rather stubborn and temperamental animal though a wonderful worker. They managed to get hold of the victim's phand, which was still around its neck though deep in the mud, and this was attached to Kan Sira's girth-rope. Then, using his short goad on his koonki's head and a spear with which he prodded the wild elephant's ear mercilessly, the young phandi got both animals moving. Inch by inch they moved, the one pulling the other and both using their last reserves of strength under the goading, until at last they were on firm land, encouraged by the shouting of the spectators on the bridge above the mud hole. It was a wonderful example of determination and I rewarded the phandi well from the phandi's fund; the same reserve also provided a jar of Miri liquor for Kan Sira, who was reputed to be inordinately fond of the stuff.

CHAPTER 10

STOCKADE DAYS

My first experience of driving elephants was in the cane-bearing lease area of Durganath Gogoi, the very successful 'gentleman' catcher whom I mentioned earlier. He had invited me to inspect his completed stockade and on arrival I was pleasantly surprised to be told that there was a herd of elephants near by and that the men had been sent out to try and persuade them into the surround. My camp was being made and I had just settled down with my back against a tree to eat some sandwiches, when two men came running breathlessly to say that the herd had crossed the surround path. Immediately all was bustle in the camp. The stockade men ran to take up their respective positions for the drive. Gogoi and I went along the cleared path linking the ends of the funnel walls, he to inspect the arrangements and I to make myself familiar with the surroundings. We proceeded in complete silence, almost on tiptoe so as not to alert the herd which was feeding inside the quadrant of enclosed forest.

At intervals we met groups of tense, waiting men with unlighted torches in their hands and we were approaching the end of the path when suddenly we heard a slight noise in the jungle. As we froze behind a tree, a large tusker stepped out of cover on to the path. He stood there uncertainly for some time, his ears cocked and his trunk obviously investigating the meaning of the smells which came up to him from the well-trampled path. His tusks met at the tips and actually crossed each other – a bad omen, Gogoi whispered to me. The elephant was highly suspicious and he took in all the signs as he looked up and down the path. Then, convinced of danger, he quietly stepped back into the surround area, vanishing silently into the forest. My companion clicked his tongue with disappointment and whispered that it would now be very awkward, as we had the herd bull within the surround and if he were driven into the stockade there would be great difficulty in handling him.

Word was immediately passed round that we had a 'goonda' within the area; this is the term for a large makhna among elephant men, but it may be used loosely to include any large and probably dangerous male elephant. The Hindustani meaning of the word is a bad character or rowdy. In this particular case the old tusker was too cunning to linger where there was danger and he went right across the front of the stockade to the other wing wall, where he repeated his examination of the cleared path in full view of the machan, on which the man who had to cut the control rope of the stockade gate was already in position. Presently word came round that the 'goonda' had vanished again and we breathed a sigh of relief.

The afternoon wore on and the men went in relays from their posts to snatch a cup of tea, which was drunk in brass mugs without milk but with plenty of sugar. I took my full share and this was the first time I had shared the elephant catchers' food. The experience of drinking milk out of a bamboo 'bottle', or of eating rice which has been steamed in a bamboo and served on leaves, was then strange; but today these are among my most happy recollections of the exhilarating business of elephant catching.

At last evening was approaching and still all was quiet. We were in our places and I was near one of the wing walls. Suddenly in the distance the first shot was fired, followed by a terrific din of shouts, beating of tins and clapping with bamboo clappers. The drive was on! My heart missed a beat and my chest was bursting almost to the point of suffocation. We waited, tense and quiet, as it grew dark rapidly.

I found myself shivering. This shivering experienced by persons in the vicinity of elephants is something unique which has to be experienced to be appreciated. The men call it *hathi jokar* or literally 'elephant shivers'. Well do I remember, in a subsequent khedda, having to shake by the shoulders a strongly-built young Assamese stockade man who was afflicted with an uncontrollable bout of shivering. He could not move along the path on which he and I were standing in the dark with our torches ready but unlit, because there was a big, solitary elephant approaching the line within unguessable distance from us. I literally had to shake him out of the shivers before we could tiptoe away along the path, which I had to feel with my feet in the dark, guided only by the white ribbon below.

The din and noise continued, with occasional gunshots, sometimes coming from near at hand and then appearing to recede to a confusing distance. Durga Gogoi, who was by my side, was obviously puzzled as to what was happening. When at last we heard the moving elephants it was apparent even to me that they were split up in more than one group and that they were not coming forward as rapidly as we expected. Obviously something had gone wrong and Gogoi started to fidget. It was now well past seven o'clock and the night was inky black. According to his calculations, if all had gone according to plan, the herd should have been driven into the stockade by this time. Whispering to me that I should stay where I was and leaving a man to look after me, he disappeared along the path. After waiting for what seemed an eternity, straining my ears and trying to pick up the meaning of the sounds I could hear, I became impatient. Grabbing the arm of my silent companion I slipped around the back of the stockade to the other wing wall, passing under the machan with its patient gate man, and made my way cautiously along the circular path in the opposite direction.

As I got closer to the din, my Assamese companion put me wise as to what was happening. The herd had refused to be driven in and was trying to break back. We pushed on and suddenly a group of hurrying men with smoky flares in their hands came through the forest, all bunched together and obviously demoralized. We questioned them and by their crestfallen demeanour it was obvious that they had let part of the herd slip through. Calling to them to follow me, I dashed along the path to try and cut off the rest of the elephants. From what I could pick up in the darkness, it was obvious that there were still a few elephants within the surround and we put ourselves between them and freedom.

The elephants were making short sharp rushes, pausing to listen and take stock now and then, but steadily coming forward to join those which had escaped. I had an electric torch and the others had burning flares. Unluckily we had no gun with us. This might have made all the difference and I sent two of the men. running to fetch a gun if they could get one. Meanwhile we did our best to hold the elephants. By this time the noise had died down elsewhere but we were shouting and yelling at the top of our voices. I now had only two men with me and their torches were giving out. These torches are prepared ahead of the drive and are stacked at convenient strategic points, but apparently they were all exhausted by now. At any rate the men made no effort to get fresh brands and presently we were left with only my torch.

Nearer and nearer the elephants came in short, sidelong rushes while I danced up and down the path, turning an elephant back here and another there by flashing the torch into their eyes. I had quite lost control over myself by this time, though my companions who stuck close to me did their best. But the elephants were determined to rejoin their companions and finally we had to give way. I jumped aside when a big cow dashed across the path within a few yards of me with a calf at her heels. We had lost the fight.

Dispiritedly we made our way back to camp and held a post-mortem in the light of the fires and of the kerosene lanterns hanging from the trees. It became clear to me after some time that our stockade men were comparatively inexperienced raw hands; Gogoi cursed them long and loud in Assamese, which I could then barely understand. We had our meal of rice and vegetables in silence, broken now and then by the recriminations of Gogoi and his stockade sirdar or leader against the unfortunate stockade men. Then the whole camp fell asleep at last, exhausted.

Four years later I was to take part in another drive, this time at Gogoi's famous Soraimari stockade. On this occasion his sirdar had mistaken the presence of a couple of solitary elephants at the salt-lick for a small herd and had started the drive. Soon we suspected that they were only *mal jooria* elephants (an association of two or three bulls) but by then it was impossible to call off the drive. The men were thoroughly worked up and were determined to get the elephants in. I ran and shouted and waved torches with the best of them and once caught my toe and fell headlong in the dark, winding myself badly. Since there were just two or three elephants, the men could concentrate on them and I was amazed at the determination they displayed in ringing the animals and constantly blocking their attempts to escape. This was a very different crowd to the one which Gogoi had had before and indeed they were crack stockade men, as their catch record showed.

Finally we managed to force one elephant into the stockade, only to discover to our dismay that he was a great makhna in full musth! The men clambered up the stockade wall shouting the bad news to each other, while the elephant walked around the enclosure with his ears widespread as if taking in the situation. Then he stepped down to the V-shaped trench and pushed with his head at the stout wall – once, twice until the whole section rocked violently. He then moved on and repeated it, searching for the weakest spot in a ponderous but extremely menacing manner, as if to tell us that the worst was yet to come.

I had in my camp the young British DFO from a neighbouring division with his mother and sister, who had come out from England for the cold weather, and they were perched up on the gate machan while all this was going on. The elephant's attacks on the stockade wall were becoming more determined and I was frightened for their safety. We had long ago decided that we could do nothing with the makhna and the men were busy splicing the cane rope which had been cut to pull the gate shut. Actually it must have been a couple of minutes before the gate creaked open but it seemed like hours. At last the makhna was free to go, but it took him a few seconds to realize that the opening was there. Then he left, slowly and majestically, his ears spread wide and his head moving from side to side, while the men speeded him with shouts and whistles. I learnt later that the stockade men had imagined that they were to get the elephants in at any cost in honour of our guests, hence their determination.

My record catch was made in the Bhagti stockade of the Naga Hills in 1936. The Inner Line country was closed at the time and it was only by special permission that we could build stockades there. The people were curious but not unfriendly and I shall never forget the beautiful Naga girls bare to the waist harvesting the crops or walking past us on the narrow paths with bundles of large sections of bamboo for holding water; nor shall I forget our welcome with the inevitable mugs of *zu* or rice beer drunk with the red-blanketed village headmen on the rear porches of their long huts, perched high over dizzy slopes. It was magnificent country with a magnificent people.

We captured fifty-four elephants in the Bhagti stockade in one drive, a figure which surpassed one of Kingsley's catches in a Goalpara stockade twenty-five years before by a narrow margin. Kingsley had been unable to hold his large catch, which burst the stockade and escaped, while my catch was reduced by more than half through deaths and releases necessitated by the inadequacy of koonkis. But that catch was abnormal from several points of view and the circumstances were so favourable as to defy repetition. The Bhagti stockade was strategically situated in a valley and commanded the main elephant path leading over the ridge separating the Doyang from a tributary stream. The local people had taken me to the saddle on the five-thousand-foot ridge over which they said the elephants always crossed and I could see that it was a 'natural'. And events proved it so. The Nagas who enrolled as drivers did their part almost too well and surrounding all the elephants in the next valley drove them over the ridge and into the stockade for us.

There were several large elephants in the catch and three of them – one tusker and two makhnas – had to be shot before the catch could be removed. I did not reach the spot until it was all over and I was glad, for I could not have stomached the killing. The scene was bad enough when I arrived, some forty-eight hours after receiving news of the catch at my distant depot in Dimapur.

From there I set off immediately on a forced march which must
have broken some of the records. The catch had almost all been
removed by then and the stockade presented a ghastly sight, with
three dead elephants lying swollen and distorted, while a pathetic
looking group of cows and calves were being hurried and hustled
by the koonkis as the roping went on. The elephants had been
killed by the *dak wala* or mail runner, Naga Sonowal, a dashing
young Assamese whom I subsequently employed as a mahout for
one of our departmental elephants which had escaped and needed
a good man. He had arrived soon after the catch had been made
and the rifle he was taking to the stockade for use in just such an
emergency had proved most useful. He had never fired a shot in
his life from such a heavy weapon, let alone to kill an elephant;
but when he was called upon to do so by the stockade sirdar or
leader, who was becoming frantic at the damage which the large
elephants were inflicting on the rest of the catch in the crowded
stockade, he did his part well. At an expenditure of four or five
rounds he killed all three elephants as cleanly as an expert would
have done. The mahaldar or lease-holder – father of Durganath
Gogoi and a famous catcher in his day – had been able to command
not more than a dozen koonkis with which he had started the
removal of the catch and I had arrived in the nick of time with
ten or twelve more, commandeered from among those available
at the depot. The catch was really too big to be economic, particularly in such an inaccessible spot and there was nothing we
could do except to select the very best animals and release the
rest. We started our march out of the hills with less than half the
elephants we had captured and the number was still further reduced by casualties on the way.

That was a nightmare Hannibal-like journey and I was glad to
be there to lend a hand. The narrow bridle path was never meant
for marching elephants two – and sometimes three – abreast and
for the greater part of the journey we had to proceed with leng-
thened phand ropes, with the koonki leading and gently dragging
the captive. The pace was funereal, but fortunately the captives
were too frightened to give much trouble. One wretched beast
slipped over the edge of a near precipice and only the quick action

of the phandi on the attendant koonki in cutting the rope saved his own mount from being pulled over. For some seconds the roaring of the frightened elephant and the crashing of the under-growth and trees could be heard and then all was silence. Some of the men said that they could see some movement at the bottom of the hill and I sent Naga Sonowal and another man down to the spot with the rifle by an easier route with instructions to put the wretched animal out of its misery if necessary. They rejoined us at the camp ahead to say that they had found the captive on its feet apparently only suffering from shock and that on their approach it had slowly moved off. I was glad. We had to release some more elephants before that march was over for I always reckoned that a free elephant was better than a dead elephant. I was glad to be there to take the decisions myself, because every elephant released meant so much less profit for the Government and, what was really more important, for the mahaldar who in ordinary circum-stances would have been most reluctant to release elephants while there was the slightest chance of taking them to the traders. It took us six days to cover what was normally a three-day march from Sanis to railhead at Jamuguri. There I held an immediate and special auction, to which I summoned all the traders from the Dimapur depot in order to save the elephants any further mar-ching and in the hopes of finding them owners as soon as possible. But we were to have further casualties in training and all told that record catch was very disappointing financially. Today there is a jeep road over the knife-like Bhandari ridge between Merapani at the foot of the hills and Sanis and one can do the journey, which cost us so much effort, in three hours – but now there are no elephants in the Bhagti valley, only fields and villages. The disturbed conditions following the war, combined with the predi-liction of the Nagas for meat of any kind and the abundance of weapons which fell into their hands, has been responsible for the disappearance of elephants in the area. The same process is going on on the borders of the Lushai Hills in the other valley and only strong action can stop it.

Garampani, ten miles from Golaghat, was and still is one of the most famous stockades in Assam. The word Garampani means 'hot water' and on the bank of the Nambar there is a natural salt-earth, with hot water bubbling up from the ground, where people have always bathed. The water is said to be good for skin complaints. There are several salt-licks dotted around, including the main one at which the stockade is built. The area is now a one-square-mile sanctuary for the animals and birds which visit the area for the salt-impregnated water and mud, which they suck up greedily. Such salt-earths are wonderful pigeon-shooting areas, being favourites with the great Imperial pigeon.

For generations, the stockade has been built on the main path leading down to the salt-lick and as a matter of fact this site is as well known as the famous Kakankote stockade of Mysore, where there is a permanent trench dating from Sanderson's time. When kheddas are held at Garampani, almost the identical spot is used each time and in the many photographs which have been taken of the place, I keep on recognizing the same old tree, which stands to one side of the enclosure.

The Garampani site was very well constituted to receive the elephants of both the Mikir and the Naga Hills, being situated on the main path. The Nambar Reserve was at one time the largest single forest in India, before it was broken up by the opening of a corridor on both sides of the railway line to Upper Assam in the nineteen-thirties; before this, it was one of the main elephant areas of Assam. Herds moved freely up and down the wide elephant path stretching between the Naga and Mikir Hills, along which were sited the Garampani, Gellipung and Pabojan stockades. Today, Pabojan has disappeared in a sea of paddy cultivation and Gellipung is but a shadow of its former self, though when I was catching elephants the forest link was still there. Garampani was always considered a prize mahal and is stockaded every few years, but the elephants are not there in their old numbers any longer and catches are generally small these days.

One night I was camping in the forest bungalow near Garampani with David Flaherty of *Elephant Boy* fame and his young and attractive niece Barbara. His brother Robert Flaherty, then at the height of his career as a maker of documentary films, was in India to make *Elephant Boy* for Alexander Korda. The film was based on Kipling's *Toomai of the Elephants*, and the location selected was Mysore and the famous Kakankote stockade. I had been on leave in Bangalore before taking on my big kheddas of 1935 and had heard of the project. I at once contacted the Flahertys. 'Why not consider Assam for the shooting of the elephant scenes?' I asked. 'Never heard of Assam' was the answer! Soon after I got back to Assam I received a mile-long telegram from David. The company was considering my suggestion and would like to inspect Assam: could I make the necessary arrangements? For the next fortnight, the telegraph authorities must have earned a packet – it was my first experience of American hustle. Then one morning David and Barbara, complete with cameraman, camera and mounds of equipment, landed up at the little railway station of Jamuguri. There was no plane service in those days and the journey from Bangalore had taken them four days.

'You are in luck,' I told them, as I motored them to the forest bungalow where I was staying. 'There was a catch last night in Gellipung stockade and after breakfast we will move camp to Garampani bungalow which is near by.' David raised his expressive eyebrows while Barbara said something about washing her hair. Presently they were to taste something of *my* brand of hustle.

Equipping the little forest bungalow with a few extra things for the Flahertys had not been really difficult, except for the sanitary arrangements. The bungalow had bathrooms but only a 'long drop', to which people had to go across the compound. I was literally living in my boxes in those days, moving about in my old Chevrolet car with my gun, my dog and a single man, with the camp stuff tied on to the back of the car. I had no furniture and lived in forest bungalows or grass huts which could be made extremely cosy, complete with fireplaces and bamboo beds. So the first thing I had to think of was a commode for Barbara – a 'thunder box' as the planters used to call it – and luckily I found one in a Golaghat shop, where I also bought a mirror.

After a bath and breakfast, I called up my two elephants Loftus and Shiv Dutt and we started loading the kit preparatory to sending them through the forest to Garampani. We were to motor round by the circuitous PWD road. While loading up the heavy batteries which David had brought along a little acid fell on the rump of Loftus. The mahouts did not know what it was – they were only used to the dangers of letting kerosene oil touch an elephant's skin – but I washed the place down quickly and applied some oil. It left a dark angry-looking mark, though luckily the skin did not blister. It is amazing how tender an elephant's skin really is; even large horseflies will draw blood and it is a sickening sight to see these monster flies clinging to an elephant's head during a forest march in the summer or rains.

The Flahertys had their first experience of photographing captured elephants that very afternoon at Gellipung and I thought David and the cameraman would never stop filming. Exhilarated but relaxed after warm baths and a good dinner, we eventually went to bed. It was past midnight when I was aroused by my men. '*Hathi porise!*' (literally, 'the elephants have fallen!') were the magic words which immediately banished all vestiges of sleep from my eyes. There had been a catch in the Garampani stockade, which was a little more than a mile from the bungalow and one of the elephants was a large tusker. I immediately pulled on my clothes and taking my torch, left David still sleeping soundly and accompanied the man to the stockade along the dew-drenched path in the silence of the night. As we were nearing the stockade we could hear the shouts of the men and an occasional gunshot, testifying to their efforts to keep the freshly-captured animals from breaking out.

It was a wild scene which presented itself to me when we reached the place. Fires had been lit all around the stockade and men were running about with wooden-tipped spears, jabbing at the elephants through the openings between the junglewood poles which constituted the stockade wall, while now and then a blank shot was heard. Live cartridges were not allowed in khedda operations, but it was almost impossible to prevent the stockade sirdars from concealing one or two and even buckshot for an emergency. In fact I know of at least one case where a large troublesome elephant was shot dead with a single charge of buckshot in its temple at point-blank range, fired by a desperate stockade sirdar who was frantic at the damage being inflicted on valuable young calves, while waiting for the rifle that never arrived. Goramuriya Goswami, the stockade lease-holder whom I mentioned earlier, was waiting for me.

The Goswami loved elephants and was the owner of a particularly large and powerful tusker named Jung Bahadur, which he treated as his child and which he had taught to perform simple tricks at his command. The koonki was a particularly menacing-looking animal with his rather ugly head and short, powerful up-turning tusks but his appearance belied his temperament. He became troublesome only when in musth and on one occasion when he had broken away in one of these spells, the Goswami had got up from a sickbed and recovered him when all others had failed. Tonight I found him agitated. 'The big tusker will give us trouble and I do not want to have to shoot him,' he said, after greeting me and apologizing for having got me out of bed. We proceeded to climb up the stockade wall to inspect the catch and the big elephant in particular. The latter was indeed a magnificent animal and at one glance it was apparent that he could not be controlled by any of our koonkis single-handed. I was in entire agreement that he should not be shot if we could help it, but what could we do?

The Goswami and I had urgent consultations. I felt that there was an outside chance of being able to control the big elephant with two or three large koonkis. There was Jung Bahadur and another big tusker available on the spot. But the biggest of all and the most experienced elephant in my whole khedda establishment was Errol Grey's old tusker Joy Bahadur, which was now owned by his former stockade sirdar Chowngion Gohain who had one of the adjoining lease areas. He was at the moment in the training depot some fifteen miles away, in a direct line through the forest. I knew we had to have him.

I hurried back to the bungalow and drove the twenty-odd miles to the depot. It was still moonlight and the depot presented an eerie picture with the sleeping men by the dying fires and the ghostly elephants, some still eating, some sleeping on their feet and others sound asleep on their sides. I picked my way through the depot, flashing my torch here and there until I found the big elephant. Near him his three attendants were sleeping. The phandi, a Shan tribesman called Imet Khamti, was a confirmed opium addict and it was difficult to arouse him. When I did succeed in shaking him awake, I told him the plan. He was to take his big elephant through the jungle by a direct path and reach Garampani by ten o'clock in the morning. It was already two am so I insisted on his waking the men and putting the cooking pot on to the fire; I assured myself that they were all thoroughly awake before I left them. I got back to Garampani bungalow completely exhausted and fell asleep on my camp bed immediately.

It seemed as if I had just put my head on my pillow when it was dawn and my bearer came in with the tea-tray. David, who had slept through it all, was told the news. He was as excited as a schoolboy at the prospect of more pictures, particularly of the anticipated struggle to remove the big elephant from the catch. 'You are lousy with elephants here,' he said. 'I'm going to bring the whole outfit up to Assam, Pat.' I nodded my head but my mind was far away as we ate breakfast and there were the usual stomach flutters as I tensed myself for what was ahead. We were going to attempt something that was normally not done. In another stockade and at another time the big elephant would have been shot dead by this time, but the Goswami and I both hated this wretched business of executing big elephants in stockades. I count myself fortunate that I have never had to do it, nor have any such elephants been shot in my presence, I am glad to say. It is one thing pitting oneself against a rogue or bad elephant in the forest but quite another executing a herd bull in the presence of his cows and calves. I just could not do it, nor could the Goswami. When discussing it with him on one occasion I had even considered using powerful electric batteries mounted on a koonki's back with which to keep off a big elephant, while we removed the catch or shoved him out of the stockade. A friend of mine from Calcutta whose firm manufactured storage batteries for tea-gardens assured me that it would be simple. But such innovations needed time and money, both of which were denied to us in our commercial kheddas.

By the time we had breakfasted news came from the stockade. The Goswami was anxious as the wild tusker was showing signs of becoming restive and dangerous. We hurried to the stockade. The big koonki had not yet arrived and I insisted on the elimination of all unnecessary noise, for although the stockade men were on their toes with anxiety for the safety of the catch, they were inclined to shout and fire shots in the air. At last about eleven o'clock Joy Bahadur arrived, much to the relief of everybody. There were willing hands to unload the big elephant of its bundles of catchers' belongings and ropes and while the phandi and his assistants were given some refreshment and, I suspected, a smoke of opium, the koonki was led to a heap of freshly-cut fodder at which he set to greedily. This business of opium addiction was beginning to die out when I joined kheddas, but in the old days the khedda officer had to carry stocks of the drug (which he drew from the Government treasury) for issue to the licensed opium smokers among his men. Otherwise it would have been impossible to get any work out of them when they were cut off from the opium shops. We used to arrange with the nearest opium shop for the registered addicts among the elephant men to draw their weekly ration in bulk for a month or so.

After an hour's rest the koonki was saddled up again with the stout noosing phand and Imet tied the thin check-rope round his waist and adjusted his little jockey cap on his head. Jung Bahadur, the Goswami's own koonki, was ready; so was the other elephant we were going to put in, a lean old animal long past his best but possessing what is a great advantage in an elephant, a long pair of tusks. It is like a boxer having a long reach. There was tense silence as the three large koonkis, with Joy Bahadur leading, lined up outside the enclosure. The men sent up the usual prayer to Hori to bless their efforts and then with shouts of encouragement from the crowd the gate was pulled open, the leading koonki assisting with its head. I had assured the men that I was standing by with my rifle in case they were unable to control the tusker and they went in with a good show of confidence. The koonkis seemed their usual unconcerned selves, merely stretching their trunks out and taking the scent of the catch and no doubt of the big tusker.

For a few seconds the phandis sat tensely but quiet on their mounts. There was complete silence while the elephants quested each other with outstretched trunks. Then there was a shout as the large tusker came forward with ears cocked and his trunk out at full length. The phandis hesitated for a moment. Then Imet Khamti advanced, a lean rakish-looking figure perched upon his elephant, and in a minute there was a clashing of tusks amidst the wild shouts of the spectators. I shouted to the other two phandis and they urged their elephants forward to attack the wild tusker simultaneously.

It was a grand sight to see the three koonkis working together as a team. The situation hung on their efforts and on the courage of their phandis. Jab for jab and push for push went the two main contestants in the centre, while the two side koonkis took every opportunity to hammer the wild tusker on his sides and flanks. The struggle lasted for about ten minutes, the koonkis at no time allowing the wild tusker to get in between them and presenting a formidable wall of strength and tusks. Then suddenly it was all over. The wild tusker backed into the midst of his herd, which all this while had been standing crowded together. Simultaneously the koonkis stood back for a breather, all three elephants flapping their ears and blowing dust noisily over themselves. We knew we had 'broken the wild elephant's courage', as the Goswami expressed it, and we all heaved a sigh of relief. It might have been much more difficult and we had been lucky that is was over so quickly. We would have to be on the alert, however, for any signs of further trouble.

I stilled the shouts and well-meant directions which were coming from the men clinging to the stockade walls and, warning the gun-men to stand by in case of trouble and the three phandis inside to keep their eyes open, I climbed down and held a hurried council of war with the Goswami and the stockade leader, in which the three phandis joined from inside the stockade. We decided to cut out the big elephant and push him out of the stockade and for this we would need more help. We opened the gate again and introduced some more koonkis, the best that we had with us. They were to control the cows and young bulls

F

while the big tuskers concentrated on cutting out the herd bull and pushing him out of the stockade.

It was easier said than done. It is very difficult to separate an elephant from the rest of a catch and it required much skilful work on the part of the phandis. Luckily all the fight had been taken out of the big male by now, otherwise it would have been an impossible task. Though the gate was wide open he resisted, with heels dug in and stiff fore-legs, just like a human being under similar circumstances, while the three big elephants pushed and prodded him from the rear.

Suddenly he caught sight of David and his camera man, standing on the machan above the stockade wall and filming away for all they were worth. Immediately his rage flared up. Taking three rapid strides forward, he jabbed at the edge of the open gate with his tusks, lifting it and the huge gate post several inches from the ground at each jab and shaking the whole stockade wall. David and the camera man were taken completely unawares and just had time to grab the stand and camera before they were thrown to the floor of the machan. The lens box was toppled over, spilling its contents through the floor of the machan. As for Barbara, she had been standing on the broad top of the gate post itself concentrating on taking pictures with her still camera and she managed to step back and steady herself in the nick of time. Had she toppled into the stockade there would have been a tragedy.

The koonkis seized the opportunity and renewed their attack from the rear. Inch by inch the wild tusker was moved nearer the open gate, which yawned wide in front of him. Then suddenly he realized that ahead lay the jungle and freedom and he stepped forward of his own accord, at first rather cautiously and suspiciously and then with increasing boldness, finally stepping outside into freedom. Triumphantly the men raised a shout and a shot was fired into the air to speed him on his way. Even then he went in a dignified manner, looking to the right and left with ears outstretched and questing trunk. We had succeeded. The big tusker had been given his freedom. He had been saved from being shot dead and trodden upon by his family in the mud and filth of the stockade. We were glad.

Thereafter the removal of the rest of the catch passed off without incident, though the roping gave us the usual thrills. The Flahertys had their fill of filming and in the afternoon David returned to the bungalow to write to his brother that 'Assam was lousy with elephants' and that the whole outfit should come away from Mysore and make the film here. Why that did not materialize is a different story. Suffice to say that the authorities in the most progressive native State in India in those days were not slow to appreciate the publicity they would get from the making of *Elephant Boy* in Mysore and they laid on a real khedda in place of the fake drive which they had originally offered. And so the Assam khedda lost its chance of world publicity.

CHAPTER 11

ROGUES AND KILLERS

What makes the solitary elephant and what the rogue and killer? I have differentiated between them, for all solitaries are not rogues. Correctly, the term 'rogue' should be applied only to a really bad elephant, one which raids crops, attacks houses and kills human beings. It is unafraid of man and his attempts to drive it away and in the worst cases it will ambush travellers on foot or in carts and will even attack cars and buses on the forest highways. Cases have been recorded of elephants waylaying inoffensive pilgrims on their way to temples in the jungles of southern India and Ceylon. A real rogue will so demoralize a whole locality that it can cause almost a complete suspension of human activities.

Many theories have been advanced to account for the solitary male elephant and many reasons have been adduced to explain a rogue. A solitary elephant is often said to be one that is turned out of the herd when it is no longer fit for breeding; but at least two reliable observers and old elephant catchers have told me that it is the minor bulls which have to leave the herd in fear of the master bull. This I am inclined to believe, for several circumstances point to it as being the real explanation of semi-solitaries. Many apparently solitary elephants are comparatively young or at any rate are not the old and useless animals which the first theory would require them to be. Sanderson's view that most solitaries are 'lords of some herd not far away' would thus be partially correct. Even the master-bull may occasionally leave his herd, but not for long.

Some of the really solitary elephants, of course, must have left the herd because of their inherent desire to lead a solitary life. In Assam the high proportion of tuskless makhnas complicates things, for there is no doubt about it that these elephants are at both a psychological and physical disadvantage when it comes to standing up to the tuskers of the herd in competition. I have often found a large makhna hanging about the outskirts of a herd obviously waiting for the opportunity to sneak in and snatch a cow, which he promptly takes to some distance.

Another factor which tends to obscure the issue, particularly for the casual observer, is that male elephants have a natural tendency to stray in search of food or crops. In fact they are seldom actually found with the herd, which is led by an old and experienced cow elephant, except when they want to satisfy their sexual urge. The master-bulls invariably keep to the outskirts and the secondary bulls generally remain aloof from the herds, keeping in touch with the cows and commuting between them and selected feeding grounds or crops. These semi-solitary bulls often move in pairs and sometimes in threes and the Assamese have a name for this association of bull elephants which they call *mal jooria*. Invariably the association is that of a makhna and a tusker or two makhnas and a tusker or the other way round. Sometimes a young bull will keep the company of an old animal, to whom he serves as a sentinel and some sort of natural protection from shikaris and hunters, who become confused between the tracks. There is no basis for the belief that makhnas are more bad tempered than tuskers and in south India, where the proportion of makhnas to tuskers is much less than in Assam, they are generally considered to be rather docile and harmless.

Every solitary elephant that one meets in the forests is not necessarily one which has severed its connection with the herd. There are of course the real solitaries, generally very big and old elephants, but it may not necessarily be incapacity that makes the bull lead a solitary life. As in the human race, individuals may be irritable or placid, surly or good tempered, courageous or cowardly, though naturally sexual incapacity would be expected to encourage mildness of disposition and a desire for seclusion.

I have known many solitary large males to be completely inoffensive creatures.

Some males on the other hand are naturally bolder and more truculent than others, showing no fear of human passers-by. Such animals are totally unafraid of noises and even of gunshots in paddy fields. Others are more timid and will invariably put a great distance between themselves and human beings, particularly those whom they suspect to have evil intentions, pausing now and then in the early stages of flight to investigate the cause of suspicion before finally deciding on a rapid get-away. It is this characteristic which has gained for the average solitary elephant a reputation for cowardice which is really undeserved. For flight from man, particularly man behaving in a suspicious or threatening manner is one thing and refusal to fight or attack when cornered is another.

Any large male elephant will sometimes demonstrate in a menacing way if he is caught near a road, particularly if he is in the process of crossing it. There was a famous case in my early years in Assam when a big tusker had a pushing match with a car on the road leading to Shillong. The terrified driver could only hold on to the wheel while the tusker jabbed and prodded the old machine, steadily pushing it backwards, while the occupants, a family of Assamese, screamed and clung to each other. The incident might have ended tragically for the occupants of the car had not the radiator cap suddenly come off, sending a spurt of steam and hot water into the face of the elephant, which promptly turned and bolted! The car miraculously came to a stop on the brink of a steep drop.

I once had an interesting experience of this kind. I was driving a distinguished person, complete with his liveried *chaprassi* and a brother officer from our district headquarters along a lonely forest road, when we suddenly ran into a herd of elephants feeding. The first intimation I had of anything unusual was the agitated cry of 'Hathi! Hathi!' from the driver, who was sitting in the rear seat. At the same moment I saw a young tusker careering down the road with its tail up, twisted in that funny manner of elephants. I automatically braked hard and the engine stalled. Suddenly a cow elephant appeared in front of us and with trunk curled tight, bent her head to push in the front of the car. She looked really menacing. All I could do was to press the button of the horn, by instinct more than anything else, and this so startled her that she desisted from her intention and made off. The whole thing was over in a flash and only then did I become aware of the crashings in the jungle and the trumpetings of elephants all round. By this time panic was reigning in the car and the distinguished person was literally almost in my lap while the people in the back seat were stiff with fright. I pressed the self-starter but it was dead. 'Wind the starting handle!' I shouted to the driver but all he did was to wind up the glass on his side, stuttering 'I cannot wind the handle!' I was nervous at the prospect of meeting the herd bull, which I had seen at the same spot only a day or two before so I jumped out and seizing the handle, somehow started the car.

When we were safely away and had got our breath we compared notes. It seemed that I had missed by inches a baby elephant which had run across the front of the car while my attention had been concentrated on the young tusker farther down the road. This is what had caused the cow elephant to attack us. My 'presence of mind', as the distinguished person called it later, in blowing the horn was, I feel, on a par with the driver's presence of mind in rolling up his window glass against an elephant.

But frankly, what does one do under such circumstances? Randolph Morris, a famous coffee-planter of the south who had much experience of elephants, once ran right into a tusker around a bend in a hill road and it damaged his jeep severely before it made off. Ingty, an Assam official, was chased in his jeep for some distance on the Manipur Road of war-time fame by an elephant which he tried to pass and he swears the animal followed him for a considerable distance.

Some visitors to the famous Top Slip Forests of south India in October 1957 had a very nasty experience with an elephant which damaged a car severely, injuring the occupants. They met the animal near the road in broad daylight and it held up the first car that passed. The driver had the presence of mind to take off his dhoti and throw it to the elephant, which promptly attacked the white cloth and while it was doing so, he dashed past. The second car which was following close behind was not so lucky and ran right into the tusker on the road. After smashing up the front of the car, the animal left the scene. Now there had been no previous incidents of this kind in that locality and one can only conclude that it was merely an unfortunate coincidence meeting the elephant and, I suspect, bad judgement of the driver in trying to pass the animal. On the same road two years later, a party of forestry students in a lorry met a large 'gonesh' (single tusker) which promptly attacked. It drove its tusk viciously into the front of the lorry and according to one of the occupants of the driver's cab, had it had two tusks the other would have impaled him. The driver of the lorry kept his head and drove his vehicle hard, literally pushing the elephant backwards and off the road. In the confusion one of the students in the back of the lorry lost his hat and jumped off to pick it up – this was not discovered for some time and it was lucky he was not attacked. These forests and this road in particular were well known for such incidents and the lorry drivers who drove under such conditions generally displayed coolness above the ordinary. One night a lorry with two Forest Officers was going up the ghat section when it encountered an elephant obviously feeding on the road. Instead of giving the animal plenty of time to get away they followed it up the road, driving and stopping alternately. Suddenly, round one of the sharp bends where there was no room to pass and where the elephant must have felt trapped, it turned to demonstrate. One lucky shot from the rifle of one of the officers prevented what might have been a nasty incident.

Once we met an elephant on this road in our jeep. We came round a sharp bend and there was the animal, a fairly large makhna, ahead of us and about thirty or forty yards away. He had heard us coming and was trying to get away and was actually in the act of slithering down the steep edge of the road with his hind legs folded, his trunk questing the soft earth ahead of him. We stopped to let him get on with the job, while I got out of the jeep and went forward cautiously to see him more clearly. I have always had an insatiable curiosity about wild elephants and cannot resist the urge to go and observe them whenever the opportunity arises. In this case there was no danger, as the elephant was getting down to a lower level. This he did, quickly but in a dignified manner, moving slowly away and observing us the whole time until he was lost to sight in the bamboos.

I was once held up by an elephant on a forest road in one of my divisions in Assam and the incident is worth repeating from the point of view of the animal's psychology in the circumstances. I had a friend and two ladies with me and was making for camp late in the evening when an elephant crossed the road in front of us. I stopped the jeep to observe the makhna, which took up his stand about twenty yards from the road and refused to budge. I had stopped about a hundred yards away and when I noticed the unusual behaviour of the animal I hesitated to go on. He must have held us up for nearly half an hour like this. He merely stood quietly under a tree, occasionally shifting his position slightly and hardly visible in the fading light. We discussed him in whispers and once or twice I switched on my lights to see if he had gone. At first I kept my engine running, uncertain whether to try to dash past or not and then I switched it off. I was ready to start backing should he come for us, for in our position there was no possibility of turning the car round because of the narrow road and deep drains on either side. The situation was becoming a little boring but the more the elephant stayed there the more suspicious I grew of his intentions. After some time he began to move away but very slowly, as if deciding we were harmless, and when he was far enough from the edge of the road for safety I made a dash for it, blowing my horn.

In this case I feel it was a case of curiosity rather than of evil intentions and in support I quote another most interesting story. A German dentist who lives in Shillong and who has his practice in Upper Assam, had an enormous truck which he had acquired from 'disposals' at the end of the war and which he had fitted up as a travelling surgery. In this he was in the habit of driving long distances from town to town, mostly at night after his work was over and because he wished to have a clear road. Late one night he was driving along the trunk road which runs past the famous

G

Kaziranga Sanctuary when he spotted a large tusker in the head-lights of his truck. It was bang in the middle of the road and when it showed no signs of moving away, the dentist ordered his driver to stop and switch off the truck lights and the engine. After about half a minute he switched on the lights, to find to his conster-nation that the elephant was moving up the road towards them, slowly but with a certain determination which made him shiver. Hurriedly switching off the lights again, the two men waited tensely in the closed cab of the truck and presently the ghostly shape of the elephant, with its tusks gleaming, loomed into sight. Slowly it circled the vehicle, while the two men sat petrified. The driver was by this trembling violently and the dentist is always at his best as he narrates how he sat stroking the driver's arm and whispering 'silence, *sala*' (the Hindi name for brother-in-law which, perhaps understandably, is used as a term of abuse among common people) while in his other hand a lighted cigarette had burnt down to the end without his having felt it.

Whether the elephant could see them in the darkened cab was doubtful, but he was either very suspicious or very curious, for he gave the truck a thorough inspection. The only damage was to the bent-back arm of the driving mirror which, projecting outwards, had naturally suffered slightly. It was an absolutely silent circumambulation of the truck, which lasted a few seconds but to the two men in the cab it seemed like hours. Then, appar-ently still deeply suspicious and dissatisfied with this huge, silent monster almost bigger than himself and smelling of heat and oil and petrol fumes, the tusker quietly left the scene, vanishing into the forest by the side of the road. Immediately afterwards the huddling men heard the breaking of trees and the loud rumblings of his obvious displeasure and anger at their presence, a favourite trick of large elephants when they want to drive anyone away.

A planter friend of mine told me how he met elephants on two occasions·in his jeep in the Bengal Duars. On the first occasion he was driving in the middle of the day along a winding road and came round a bend almost to run into a makhna which was going in the opposite direction. He stopped immediately and the animal turned and looked at the jeep, then after thtewing some earth over his head, he slowly moved off the road. On another occasion, this time at night on his way to the club, his headlights picked up a large makhna standing broadside on in the middle of the road. As the animal showed no signs of moving, he stopped and switched off his lights. On switching them on again he found the elephant still there, standing in the same position. By this time other cars had come up behind but my friend made no effort to pass the elephant, which continued to stand in the same position in spite of the lights and the occasional hooting from impatient planters eager to get to their first chota-pegs. After about twenty minutes the elephant moved away and the procession of cars passed.

Early in 1963, a grim tragedy took place in the NEFA (North East Frontier Agency) when a rogue tusker overturned a truck and kicked it down a three hundred-foot-deep gorge, resulting in the deaths of nine people. The victims were personnel of the Border Road Construction Department, who were engaged in road-making in the mountains recently overrun by the Chinese. Ironically, this organization was known as 'Tusker' and had an elephant as its emblem. The rogue in question was called the 'Monarch' of Khooni Pahar and in his attempt to defend the frontiers of his domain against people who in fact were defending it for him, he sealed his own fate. The incident took place at night and perhaps if the driver of the truck had stopped and switched off the lights, the tusker might have left it alone. It is stated that the driver made 'frantic efforts' to elude the rogue and the noise and confusion may well have provided an additional incentive to attack.

All these experiences go to show that the wisest procedure when one meets an elephant on a road is to stop and do nothing to attract or annoy the animal, though it is another matter, of course, when your car runs right into it round a bend. It is largely a matter of luck and the particular temperament or mood of the elephant one meets, but it is clear that big males are inclined to dispute the right of way on roads in their own domain.

Such maliciously dangerous animals as justify the appellation of 'rogues' seem to be more common in certain tracts of southern

India and Mysore than in Bengal and Assam, perhaps because of the comparatively more opened-up conditions in the south. In the prolonged clash between elephants and man resulting from the expansion of cultivation – particularly of coffee and tea – in certain parts of India from the middle of the nineteenth century onwards, Assam was less affected as it was the last area to be annexed by the British. It is only within the last fifty years that the opening up of the country has proceeded rapidly.

The old tea-planters and Forest Officers had their share of troublesome elephants no doubt, but there was room and to spare for everybody in those days, including the elephant, and there were plenty of forests to which it could retreat. It is significant that Milroy, a few years after I went to Assam in 1930, introduced the Elephant Control Scheme which was aimed at keeping down the bad ones. In the years when I was first catching and then shooting elephants, there were plenty of cases of assaults by wild elephants, but few that I can remember of deliberate and murderous attacks over continuous periods and involving a number of lives. Elephants have killed villagers in paddy fields and hunters and catchers in the jungles; but for sheer murderous terrorism of inoffensive human beings, some of the south Indian rogues which have been reported must be the worst.

Sportsmen who have shot 'rogue' elephants have often reported abnormalities in these animals and have attributed their bad temper to these defects. There are elephant-shooters who claim that all rogues have injuries at the base of a tusk, or have bad teeth; while others base their views on the fact that some of the elephants they have shot had bitten-off tails, or abscesses at the root of the tail. I shot one elephant with an enormous cancerous growth beneath its tail, which was bitten off. Baldwin also killed an elephant with such an affliction, but neither of these were 'rogues' in the usual sense. It is the unpleasant practice of elephants in fighting to grab each other's tails in their mouth and to chew on them, while jabbing with their tusks at their opponents' rears. Held in this position, an elephant is particularly vulnerable to serious injury, while the vertebrae of the tail can be dislocated in the jaws of its adversary or even crushed, despite the fact that the vertebrae are stout enough to bear the weight of a man when the tail is held in a loop for use as a ladder in mounting.

Once an elephant suffers such painful injuries it is quite likely to react violently against other elephants and men. These two causes – tusk and tail injuries – might well be the explanation of rogue tendencies. But the really bad-tempered elephant has often been attributed, and correctly so, to gunshot wounds received from hunters who have bungled their business and such animals can be very dangerous indeed.

A recent case of such a rogue, which fell to the muzzle-loader of an enraged villager after terrorizing the locality, revealed that it was riddled with bullets from crop-protection weapons. This happened in the Lansdowne forests west of the Ganges in UP. The animal was also in the habit of pulling down the machans of sportsmen sitting up for tiger and on one occasion had killed an inoffensive buffalo calf which had been tied out as bait. The elephant, which had one of its tusks broken, charged but failed to gore the calf. It killed the buffalo with a kick of its hind leg and then, after trampling on it in fury, picked up the mangled body and hurled it twenty-five yards away – all in full view of the petrified occupant of the machan, who was in any case under the impression that he could not legally shoot the elephant!

There can be very real danger in taking one's elephant up to a strange wild male, as the following incident shows. It was on the occasion of the visit of the Shah of Persia to India in 1956 and his brother had expressed his desire to shoot an elephant while in East Pakistan. He was duly invited to the Chittagong Hill Tracts, where elaborate preparations were made. A camp was pitched in the heart of the jungle and Lal Bahadur, the biggest tusker of the forest department and an animal which had been in many khedda operations, was provided for his use. There was reputed to be a rogue elephant in the neighbourhood and when it was located by trackers, the distinguished guest went out on the big tusker accompanied by the Commissioner, Colonel Niblett.

The Prince, who had no experience of big-game shooting, fired at the rogue from a distance of about twenty-five to thirty yards, letting off both barrels of his heavy rifle. The elephant was not killed immediately, but staggered and made off; later it was found dead, in a decomposed condition, some miles away.

Lal Bahadur had shied after the shots, throwing his mahout to the ground; he then bolted, with the Prince and Colonel Niblett hanging on grimly. He went along a path on the edge of a hill, through bamboo jungle, and with a swamp on one side. The two men had great difficulty in staying on the pad and eventually the Prince, who was in front, was swept off the elephant and fell to the ground. He saw Colonel Niblett trying to crawl to the neck of the runaway elephant, hoping to get it under control; but he in turn was swept off and fell towards the hillside. When the Prince got up to him, he found that the Colonel's left arm was fractured and was hanging by the skin, while his left thigh was also badly crushed. He had obviously been 'run over' by Lal Bahadur, who went on for some distance and was eventually recovered.

Colonel Niblett inquired after the Prince's safety, then expressed his conviction that he was going to die and became unconscious. His daughter, who had been hostess to the Prince in the absence of her mother, forced a way through the swamp in a jeep and reached her dying father's side.

Naturally there was a lot of publicity over the tragic affair and garbled versions of how Colonel Niblett had been killed by his own elephant appeared in the press. Lal Bahadur narrowly escaped being executed by the authorities, but there is no doubt that it was a pure accident. Lal Bahadur was of somewhat uncertain temperament and Niblett's predecessor in the Chittagong Hill Tracts, Colonel Hyde, had once been tossed by him. Colonel Niblett himself once had to reprimand the unruly tusker and as a punishment made him swim across the Karnaphuli river! The Colonel was over sixty when he died and was perhaps a little too old for such dangerous ventures.

I have collected every case I have been able to lay my hands on of elephants indulging in unexpected and apparently unprovoked killings in an effort to throw light on this gruesomely fascinating problem; but I have confined my observations and conclusions only to those incidents of which I have had either first-hand knowledge or have had authentic details given to me by reliable observers.

Early in my khedda days I ran up against an unexpected killing by one of my own elephants, Shiv Dutt. He was a tusker who along with Loftus, an enormous makhna worthy of his name, was allotted to me during my kheddas. I was breakfasting in a little forest bungalow by the side of the Dhansiri river, when Shiv Dutt's mahout came running to tell me that the elephant had killed his grass cutter. It seemed that the incident happened almost before the very eyes of the mahout, who was getting ready for the day's march.

The grass cutter had taken Shiv Dutt down to the river to bathe him preparatory to saddling him up. The elephant was standing in the shallow waters and the man who had been washing him bent down to pick up some sand with which to clean the elephant's tusks, when in a flash the animal threw him down and crushed him between his feet. It then stood perfectly still and the mahout, who was cooking the morning meal nearby and who somehow overcame his natural shock and fear, was able to lead him up from the water and to shackle his legs.

I ran to the scene of the accident but there was nothing that I could do. I questioned the mahout closely and the only conclusion I could draw was that the animal had resented the cleaning of his tusks. Then I remembered that I had told the attendants some days before to polish the tusks of the elephant as they were very dirty. This, perhaps, was the result. I had a most uneasy feeling for a long time after the death of the unfortunate man.

I sent a telegram to Milroy and informed the police. I had left Loftus behind for some reason which I cannot remember now and I had to wait until he and another large koonki arrived. Then we marched the murderer Shiv Dutt, who all the while remained placid and calm, back to the depot. Milroy instructed me to send the killer to join his own elephants in the North Cachar Hills, where he was on tour, which I did under an escort of a koonki. Two weeks later we got the news that Shiv Dutt had disembowelled his new grass cutter, for no apparent reason, right in Milroy's own camp.

From then on Shiv Dutt killed men in monotonous succession, both while he was in our possession and after he had been sold, not long after, to the large British timber company which was operating in Upper Assam. Altogether Shiv Dutt killed some eighteen men. He was a very good worker and that is what saved him from being executed. His end came nearly fifteen years later at the hands of a wild tusker, which attacked him when he was tethered to graze in the forest one night as usual.

It may have been more than a coincidence that Shiv Dutt was a particularly cowardly elephant and was useless on shikar, even hesitating to cross a stream which was strange to him. I remember taking him one day to test a river crossing before selecting the site as our depot. All the training of captured elephants is done on stretches of sand along the banks of rivers; both captive and tame elephants may have to cross and recross the river for fetching fodder and it is essential to establish that the bottom is hard. I had ordered Shiv Dutt to be taken down the steep bank, which was covered with suspicious looking mud after the rains, and Shiv Dutt would have none of it. Again and again the mahout tried to force him to cross and there was no real danger, for the moment he began to show signs of bogging he would have been pulled back; yet he shook his head and snorted and flapped his ears and would go no farther than the edge of the bank, where, in typical elephant fashion, he knelt down on his hind-legs. In exasperation I picked up a length of sapling which was lying nearby and belaboured him on the hind-quarters, shouting at him to go forward. In a flash and with a swoosh he turned on me and it was all I could do to step back hurriedly out of his reach while the mahout dug the goad into his ear and pulled his head back sharply. We did not know then that Shiv Dutt was a potential killer and I realized only later how narrow my escape had been.

Another cowardly elephant was John Bahadur, who was trained under Mohan Prasad in the Goalpara West Division. He was also 'bad' in the sense that although he had not killed anyone, he used to misbehave and attack people on occasions and was generally disobedient and mischievous, unlike Mohan Prasad who was the essence of docility. The mahouts used to say that his unreliability was due to the fact that he was a home-born elephant. Such animals are reputed to be troublesome and elephant men say that they imbibe through their early association with human beings all the bad qualities of man, for whom they gradually lose all fear and respect. This was a widespread belief in Assam and I think a very well-founded one. It was certainly extraordinary to find comparatively large wild elephants, captured in some cases after they had attained maturity, becoming completely obedient and reliable; while elephants born in captivity, and which had grown up from babyhood with other tame elephants and elephant men, were often vicious and in some cases even became man-killers.

These man-killing elephants were notorious and also famous in their own way. The Raja of Bijni had such an animal whose record was nearly a dozen men killed, yet he was an asset while on a shoot and continued to be used in spite of his long record of killings. This makhna, Ram Prasad, was one of the most miserable-looking animals I have ever seen but he was a very steady shikar elephant and was always in great demand for the Governor's shoots. Once I borrowed him for my Christmas shoot, to which I had invited some friends. One of them was Frugtneit, inevitably known as 'Fruity' and the butt of everyone's wit. He was allotted Ram Prasad for the morning chukker in the forest and as I was putting the guests up on their respective elephants, I casually mentioned to Fruity that his mount had killed only eleven men. His reaction was immediate: 'Do you expect *me* to get up on *that* elephant?' he asked dramatically, emphasizing the words with his finger and repeating them once again before flatly refusing to mount the already kneeling animal. There was nothing for me to do but to give him another elephant and I asked my wife to change over, which she promptly did. Fruity, nothing abashed at a lady giving way to him on a little matter of riding a man-killing elephant, could not understand why we found it difficult to stop laughing.

When men were killed in those days, compensation was generally paid to the relatives of the unfortunate victims but certainly nobody thought very much of it until the next incident.

Sometimes an animal would be tied up for a few days after the attack, but when there was obviously nothing wrong with it the owners would resume working it.

One large tusker which was not only a man-killer and a bolter but which had a reputation for attacking other tame elephants that came near it, arrived at Gauripur from the Maharaja of Cooch Behar while I was in Goalpara, some time in the early years of the war. This elephant was treated by the other mahouts with the utmost respect and they would angrily warn his mahout if he was brought too close to their own mounts. When grazing, he carried an ankle fetter with a long length of chain. Generally it was kept hoisted up on the pad, but it could be thrown down at a moment's notice to serve as a sort of anchor for the bolting animal. This formidable looking elephant with his clanking fetters looked so much like the conventional figure of an old time convict with a ball and chain round his ankle that I could not help being amused whenever I saw him.

Akbar, the big departmental tusker who was once Milroy's elephant and later the showpiece of Kaziranga Sanctuary, was normally the most placid of elephants; but he had two killings to his credit – or discredit. The first, in 1942, was easy to understand for it is said that his grass cutter had been prodding him with a spear to prevent him from eating some banana or plaintain trees after a long day's march. It was possibly more than a coincidence that the tragedy occurred a short time after his musth period was over.

The second time, ten years later, he was coming back to the camp with a load of fodder on his back, on the top of which was sitting the grass cutter in the usual careless manner; he had reached the grass huts of the mahouts, when suddenly he attacked another attendant who was standing in front of the hut. The story is that this man was holding up a pumpkin to show Akbar's grass cutter, when in a flash the elephant charged him. The man turned to flee but came up against the wall of the hut. Akbar, who had overtaken him in two strides, thrust his tusk through his back. His own rider having fallen off his back with the load of fodder, Akbar then calmly walked away into an adjoining field, where his mahout found him quietly grazing. It was suspected that the victim had been in the habit of stealing Akbar's grain ration and the feeling was that it was a case of revenge killing. Or was he provoked by the man holding up the pumpkin, which he probably thought was being withheld from him?

A few years later an incident occurred on the north bank of the Brahmaputra which caused a sensation. An elephant was standing idly in a village street, with its attendant sitting carelessly on its neck and chatting to a woman who was seated on the ground in front of a hut cleaning some rice. The woman had a baby tied with a cloth on her hips. Suddenly the tusker without any warning and before the man who was on his neck could do anything to control him, lunged forward and attacked the woman, one tusk transfixing the child who was killed instantaneously, the other narrowly missing the woman's other hip. Apart from the blow from the elephant's trunk as he lunged, she suffered no harm from the attack, which was all over in a few seconds.

Nobody could explain why the elephant had attacked her. Food again, perhaps, but it is impossible to be certain about this. Could it have been some sudden movement on her part which irritated the elephant and which it associated with the withdrawal of a proffered titbit of grain?

In 1944 a mahout in Assam who had changed over from a tusker to another elephant, was killed by his old mount in very peculiar circumstances. The two elephants with their riders were returning to camp and the men stopped for a chat and a smoke, neither dismounting from the neck of his elephant. While the mahout of the tusker was passing a cigarette across to his friend, the animal suddenly grabbed its old master from the neck of the other elephant and despite the efforts of its rider to control it, gored the unfortunate man and then repeatedly trod on him. The reason given, whether true or not, was that the man had beaten the tusker on one occasion when he had been in charge of it and the incident was put down as an example of an elephant's revenge.

In 1956 on the west coast of India, a tusker killed its mahout in the courtyard of the house to which it had been taken to give the children a joy-ride, when the man was in the act of offering it a coconut after the children's outing was over. It was said the elephant had been ill for some time before.

The extraordinary case of Dolly, a circus elephant who picked up and crushed to death a five-year-old boy in Florida because, it was said, he had been stealing pea-nuts from under her trunk, is worthy of mention as being one of the few cases of a female elephant taking such revenge. Poor Dolly was executed with cyanide. Perhaps in other circumstances and times she would have received more understanding treatment.

Quite different are killings which occur when elephants run amuck, either during attacks of musth or when they become 'mad'. An elephant on the rampage is a terror indeed and when attempts are made to stop and recapture them, the consequences for the persons concerned are likely to be fatal. Sometimes male elephants escape and roam about. They naturally inspire fear in their beholders, who run and scream and do foolish things. Sudden noises, such as are made by passing trucks or trains only frighten the animals the more and they start dashing madly about. Thus a sort of chain reaction is set up which leads inevitably to the death of the elephant. And for days the reasons will be hotly debated – was the elephant mad or was it merely frightened?

One such unfortunate case occurred in Delhi in 1955. A circus elephant had been left starving and unattended in a Delhi suburb. It broke its chain and went to the nearest *peepul* tree to feed. People began to panic. Soon a call went out from the municipality to the police to destroy the elephant, but no less than ten shots from .303 service rifles had no effect. Then started the real chase which ended in the elephant being killed in a field miles away, after it had injured three people. 'All were in agreement that the killing was badly handled', said the newspaper report. Some people later stated that the elephant had been off his food and had exhibited signs of musth.

Recapturing a large runaway elephant is a job for experts. A favourite means of bringing the animal to bay is to shoot him in the legs. Then there is the iron contrivance consisting of a claw-like grip with sharp teeth, which when clipped on to the hind-leg of an elephant brings it to a halt. This was the method used in northern India in the princely states to put an end to elephant fights. Both methods were used to bring Jung Bahadur in when he broke loose in one of his attacks of musth, shortly before his death at Gauripur in 1945. He had remained at large for more than a week but Lalji had recovered him, by patient and sustained efforts during a chase which covered many villages whose banana groves he had raided. When his death occurred soon afterwards, Lalji put it down to the strain he had undergone during the exhausting period of his freedom and chase. And so ended the career of one of the tallest recorded elephants in India, an animal famous in the old Raja's time for tiger shooting and the hero of many a shikar story in the Gauripur family.

One cannot help feeling a pang of regret for the fate of elephants such as the circus elephants of Delhi, or of Udaigiri, the President's elephant, of whom I have written earlier, or even of the tusker which, in April 1962, met its death when being taken to the famous Kumbh Mela at Hardwar. Near Muzaffangar, when nearing a bus stand, it got out of control. Was it startled by some inconsiderate motor driver or the heedless revving of an engine in a crowded city street, so alien to its natural haunts? Whatever the reason, the animal killed its mahout, trampled on another man and smashed up two buses. Orderlies from nearby police lines fired at it, hitting it at least twenty times before it was killed. But one has less sympathy, somehow, for the type of elephant exemplified in the famous case of a musth elephant in Borpeta, on the north bank of the Brahmaputra, many years ago.

This animal, a normally inoffensive and well-behaved makhna living in typical rural surroundings, suddenly escaped after knocking down its mahout and commenced a reign of terror in the locality which lasted for almost a week. It killed and disembowelled a man whom it pulled from a shed on the bank of the river, then roamed about attacking boats at the ghat, knocking down houses and giving chase to all and sundry. Human voices put it into a violent temper and one man escaped only by spearing it, the spear-head remaining stuck in the forehead. Some phandis tried to noose it from a tree but failed: the elephant remained under the tree for a day and a night hoping to get them. It attacked the tree furiously at intervals, breaking off both its tusks, one at the root. The Deputy Commissioner decided to shoot it and embarked in a boat, which the elephant promptly charged, to be turned away by a volley of bullets. Finally it was captured on the bank of the Manas river. It was fed with food in which opium was concealed and nooses were then spread on the river bank. After several fruitless attempts and when it was somewhat calmed down, its legs were finally noosed and it was recaptured. The rather unctuous ending of the tale to the effect that 'it was indeed a mercy that a great public danger was averted without inflicting ruinous loss on a loyal mauzadar (tax-collector) by having to destroy his valuable elephant', is an eloquent commentary on those times, at the close of the last century, when apparently human life was cheaper than that of an elephant.

I had the experience of meeting a determined killer, this time a wild elephant, some years ago, though it was never established as to whether or not he was in musth. It was in the Darrang forests not very far from the route traversed by the Dalai Lama when he entered India on the final stages of his escape from Tibet in 1958. I was living in a tent on a river-bank and used to go out with my assistants to mark trees for felling every morning, returning late in the evening. Often very tired, I used to get to bed early and sometimes soon after dinner, a fact so unusual for me that it induced occasional nightmares. This particular night I dreamt that an elephant was outside my tent and in fact the crunch of his feet on the gravel on which my tent was pitched was so clear that I leapt up, shouting, and tore through my mosquito net and out of the tent. There I stood until I came to and realized that it was just another bad dream. I went into the tent again rather shamefacedly and as I climbed into my camp bed my two dogs started growling. Silencing them, I fell asleep.

Next morning imagine my amazement when I found clear, fresh footprints on the gravel, right up against the wall of the tent, of a smallish elephant. I called for my men and inquired if my own elephant had been brought to the camp the previous day but they said no. Still doubting my eyes and the recollections of those crunching footsteps in the night, I tracked the footsteps past my camp bathroom and down to the river, which it was obvious the elephant had crossed. I thought nothing more of the incident until on my way out to the forest after breakfast I found the footprints leading right from the spot where we had stopped work and come out on the road the previous evening. It was obvious that the elephant had followed us home and had had evil designs on my tent, which only my nightmarish shouting had frustrated. It was eerie but there was more to come.

The next day news came to us from a sawyer's camp farther downstream that an elephant had pulled a man out of his shelter and killed him. Two days later an elephant pulled an old woman out of her hut and crushed her to death. It was said that the animal was looking for salt or rice. Then there were no more reports and a few days later I broke up my camp and moved down to the grass country nearer the Brahmaputra for a tiger shoot with some American airmen. We had had a pleasant week, which however yielded only one tiger, and the party had broken up and I was about to return to my headquarters when news came of a wild elephant which was terrorizing the locality I had just left, killing people and behaving in a mad manner. It was reported to be a small makhna which was coming right out in the open ignoring people, then disappearing only to turn up at night at a lonely hut and attacking silently. I at once decided to go after it as I had my rifle and elephants for tracking it in the thick stuff in which it used to lie up. I made all preparations for an early start next morning, when that very night the big tusker which I had intended to take with me ran amuck and almost hammered the life out of one of the smaller animals in the camp. They were both borrowed animals and I had to see to the tying of the large elephant in case he was getting into musth and to attend to the treatment of the smaller animal, for which I had to await the arrival of the veterinarian from headquarters. It was two more days before I could get away on my own cow elephant and when I reached the place there was no sign of the elephant I had come to kill nor did several days of search bring success. He had disappeared, as silently as he had approached my tent that night, leaving the most extraordinary record of silent and unprovoked killings I have yet come across. Nor was he ever heard of again.

Elephants are very vindictive in combat and fight to the death, the victor leaving the scene only when his opponent has been killed. Many years ago a case was reported from the Ghatsila copper mine in Orissa of a fatal combat between two large wild males. It took place right inside the settlement, from which the terrified occupants had to flee. After the fight one elephant was found dead with his tusks broken off. His conqueror had retreated to the neighbouring jungle, from where he emitted roars and grumbling noises; shortly afterwards, he too was found dead, with one of the tusks of the victim deeply embedded in his palate and the other in his trunk. During the kheddas of 1935-6 the local Jamuguri Forest villagers told us of a fight which had taken place in the bed of the Doyang river in full view of the awed human spectators; the battle lasted for two whole days until the victim was killed.

In view of the characteristic gentleness of male elephants for their offspring and for those of others, the wanton killing of a small calf by a wild tusker, reported by my friend Frank Nicholls, seems extraordinary. At the foot of a sloping bank, he found the body of a young elephant with a large gaping hole in its back and above it there were footprints of a big elephant. There could be only one possible reconstruction of the signs: the tusker must have chased the little elephant down the bank and gored him in the back, killing him instantaneously. The reason for such a murderous attack could only be confirmed bad temper in a solitary that hated its own kind, or perhaps a sudden fit of irritation on the part of a herd bull in musth.

Battles for herd leadership or when in musth are easier to understand than the unexpected killing propensities displayed sometimes by tame elephants. Such animals are generally placid by disposition, but some are highly temperamental. Most elephants are easily startled and upset by sudden noises, or by animals running towards them unexpectedly, and are liable to bolt, particularly when they cannot see the object that has startled them.

There is a Sanskrit saying to the effect that if elephants were not so nervous, snakes so sluggish and Brahmins not so given to quarrelling, other men would have no chance! I am inclined to conclude from all the evidence that the tendency to be easily startled is the root cause of elephants killing human beings in a sudden frenzy, only to behave perfectly normally afterwards. Milroy used to say that one should never go near strange male elephants without some sort of weapon in the hand, even a small stick. Yet one sees elephant keepers, mahouts and others taking the utmost liberties with their charges and the mysterious and wholly unexpected tragedies one hears about are very rare.

Sudden killings, in which the whole business is over in a minute or even a few seconds, sometimes appear to be quite unprovoked. Some of these cases may perhaps be associated with revenge and the expression 'the elephant never forgets' is often used to explain the killing of someone who is presumed to have outraged the elephant's feelings on some occasion. For instance the death of someone who has been responsible for feeding it has often led observers to conclude that the elephant killed because it had been deprived of food by a rascally keeper.

It is perfectly true that elephants have a long memory for places, persons and associations; but to credit them with the ability to store up recollections of continued injustices or remembrances of deprivations of food, and to assume that the animal has been waiting for a long time for an opportunity to attack the oppressor, seems distinctly far-fetched. Why not have killed at the first instance of injustice? If the ability to store up feelings of revenge is indeed granted to the elephant, it would mean crediting it with just those very powers of reasoning which critics of its brain capacity deny.

Scientists have fallen back on the size and structure of the brain to explain the sudden mental black-outs during which elephants commit murder. It has been said that the rationalizing areas of the brain are not large and that the elephant's reputation for sagacity is largely undeserved. Is then the ability of a trained Burma elephant to pick out the key log in a river blockage and free it so that the obstruction is removed the result of nothing more than training and obedience rather than reasoning?

Many facts may be responsible for an elephant's bad temper and readiness to vent his rage on human beings or even on other animals. Just before I went to Assam there had been a sensational case of a pair of large elephants attacking a convoy of buffalo carts carrying logs in the forest, tusking and killing a buffalo apiece. It was an isolated forest which was being worked for the first time and the incident was never repeated. Could it have been sheer resentment at the invasion of their sanctuary by man? Perhaps this was also the explanation in the case of the elephant attacking a car in the Top Slip Forests, an incident which I have described earlier in this chapter.

The whole subject is a fascinating one, like that of the man-eating tiger, and one for which all the answers will never be forthcoming. One thing is certain, however, and that is that the one-hundred-year-old and eleven-foot-high Asian elephant – if he exists at all – will be found only among the solitaries or rogues; and this, to my mind, gives them a special niche of their own.

CHAPTER 12

SHOOTING ELEPHANTS

Elephants can be very destructive creatures and in parts of Assam they are really troublesome. But this is only to be expected in a country where the forests are so closely interlocked with inhabited areas, forming a hinterland around the fertile valleys which have been cleared for cultivation and tea – a natural buffer, as it were, between the mountains and the plains. Here the elephants can live unmolested except for the periodic catching operations, though the rapid clearance of the jungles outside the reserves has exposed them increasingly to contact with man. It is this encroachment on their habitat which is mainly responsible for the existence of crop raiders and rogue elephants.

Just about the time I had finished with elephant catching, Milroy introduced the Elephant Control Scheme and he urged me to take to elephant destruction under it. I was reluctant to do so until I could obtain a good rifle, as I had had such disappointing experiences with the rather inadequate weapons in our kheddas. At that time, we had only an old 8-bore black powder rifle and although I dug out a couple of .577 low-pressure cordite rifles from the Deputy Commissioner's stores, they were not really satisfactory. Eventually I was posted to Goalpara, the crack division of Assam and in those days still a hunter's paradise. Just about this time I managed to get a heavy, high-velocity rifle and, although Milroy was now dead, I felt I had to accede to his wishes and take up elephant control.

There were several crop-raiding elephants in the area, living in the stretch of *sal* forest which had villages all along the edge and tongues of cultivation projecting into it. Only troublesome elephants could be shot, though according to the licence any mature male elephants wandering by themselves in the vicinity of crops were potential victims. I was never very happy about this rule, as it permitted one to follow up the tracks of any solitary or semi-solitary animal near villages and kill him, even though he might not have been really troublesome. It was compulsory to shoot a makhna for each tusker. The scheme was devised by Milroy to supplement the killing of troublesome elephants with the prospect of a reward in the shape of the tusks. On the whole it was a sound scheme, except that in Assam the proportion of tusked to tuskless males is not as much as fifty per cent, so that an elephant shooter is generally hard put to find as many makhnas as tuskers. But Milroy was an astute man and knew that if he did not insist on makhnas being killed, sportsmen would only go after the tuskers. About forty to fifty elephants are killed every year in Assam under proclamation and the control scheme, as well as a few in stockade operations, and this seems to look after the problem of the troublesome male elephant fairly well.

At the time when I first went to Goalpara, I wish someone had suggested that I should dissect elephant skulls, for it would have saved me several unhappy experiences. If one does not know the vital shots, it is impossible to kill elephants cleanly. Looking back, I am a little surprised that the old Doctor Babu did not suggest practical experiments to supplement the quite inadequate drawing of the outline of an elephant's head, with three dots on it to indicate the brain shots, which appeared in the standard reference book on elephants and their diseases by Evans. I did remove the heart from a poor prostrate cow elephant which I had to destroy, but somehow it never struck me to do the same with the brain. I had climbed into a tree in order to shoot downwards at the place where I thought the heart would be, but I was surprised later to find it hidden almost between the forelegs. I was also astonished at its large size – almost as big as a football and so hard with muscle that it was like gutta-percha.

The punch of a heavy bullet fired at close quarters into the temple of an elephant will stun, even if it does not kill immediately. For its perfect execution the elephant must be facing at an angle of forty-five degrees away from the shooter and it is worth holding one's fire to get this position. One sportsman who had shot a number of elephants used to send a man round to attract the elephant's attention and if it was in a paddy field at night, to flash a torch on the animal to make him face in that direction. It is remarkable how long an elephant will lie stunned on occasions and this has misled many a hunter. I learnt by experience that after firing the first shot I must attempt to get up to the fallen elephant immediately in order to be ready for a second shot should the animal not be dead.

A useful shot when an elephant is lying prone is the back-of-the-brain shot, in the spot where the two lobes of the skull fall away to the hollow of the neck. This should be taken with the rifle held parallel to the ground, the bullet being directed downwards into the head. I worked out this shot when studying the sectioned skulls of elephants. The skull is only half an inch thick at the back of the brain, just before the point where the spinal cord begins, and I think one could reach this through the thickness of the top of the neck with a powerful pistol. The shot that I favour least of all is the so-called earhole shot; apart from the difficulty of locating the earhole passage correctly, this has to traverse about eight inches of hard bone before reaching the brain.

I got my first elephant in Goalpara just after I was married. One winter night I was awakened and told that a troublesome tusker that I had been looking out for was feeding in the fields some two miles from the Raimona bungalow. I left my wife still asleep and went out into the pale light of a waning moon. When I reached the field it was about three o'clock in the morning and the elephant was not to be seen. I sat by a fire with the men who were watching the fields and at first light I took up the tracks of the crop raider. They were clearly visible in the dewy grass and led into the jungle. Within a short distance in the forest we saw him leisurely moving away. I had sent for my elephant Mohan Prasad but kept him some distance behind me while I tracked on foot. The forest was open and as I was trying to outflank the wild elephant to get a head shot he heard me and turned, extending his ears in a challenging manner. At that time I had no clear idea as to the position of an elephant's brain but I fired at the frontal bump as he faced me some forty yards away. To my chagrin he merely rocked back on his feet, staggered and then dashed across my right front, going like an express train through the jungle before disappearing into some high grass. It had been impossible to take a second shot.

When I had recovered my breath I called up Mohan Prasad and mounting him, cautiously followed the track of the wild tusker. Standing up on the saddle I could see right over the top of the twelve-foot-high grass. There he was under a tree, facing us and obviously waiting for us. I had read all there was on the subject of following up wounded elephants and I was not going to fall into any trap. My mahout and I remained silent, watching him, and after a minute or two the big tusker turned and moved away towards the river which lay between me and the main forest block. We made a rapid detour and when we reached the river I jumped down and with a couple of villagers who had followed me, went down into the dry sandy bed and began to look for his tracks. While we were scouting about I happened to look up and there was the elephant with his head sticking out of the jungle watching us from the farther bank. We were walking right into him. I threw up my rifle and dropped to my knee, but before I could fire he turned and went off. Then followed a long chase. He moved steadily, but halted now and then to lie in wait for us and though I was eager to finish him, my inexperience was tempered by caution which would not allow me to go up to him in the thick stuff where he invariably paused, which was just as well.

We spent nearly two hours on his tracks until I was longing for breakfast. We stopped in a little open space to dry our dew-drenched clothes and to hold a council of war. It was quite obvious that I had not seriously wounded the elephant and I was very dejected. I had missed the small passage to the brain which is concealed under the frontal bump at the upper end of the elephant's trunk. This is a very misleading shot and if the elephant is not standing perfectly still or if one is not absolutely accurate it is easy to miss the actual opening. Its diameter is no bigger than that of a cigarette tin and it is surrounded by comparatively hard bone. We decided to follow the elephant a little longer and started off again. That we were dealing with a cunning animal was obvious and I did not relax vigilance.

We had hardly gone a couple of hundred yards, the trackers in the lead followed by myself and a man carrying my rifle, when with a trumpeting scream the elephant shot out of some cover straight into our midst. The trackers scattered, the leading man leaving his cloth hanging on a small bush. I sprang to one side, striking my right leg hard against a fallen log and stumbling over it. The tusker stood there squealing with rage and uncertain whom to attack. I turned for my rifle and mercifully my gunbearer was just behind me. I fired into the elephant's temple at about thirty feet and knocked him down like a ninepin with the heavy .475 rifle. I immediately replaced the expended cartridge and shifted my position as he lay stunned, only the tip of his trunk moving a little. I stood over him and was determined not to let him get away this time.

After a while which seemed an eternity to me, the tusker started climbing to his feet unsteadily. I let him get up. It was obvious that all the fight was out of him and he started to turn away like a feeble old man. I raised my rifle and fired into his head once again, at where I thought the brain was. I reloaded and fired again but still he would not go down. It was like a boxer manoeuvring for the kill and repeatedly punching his reeling opponent. He was staggering forward like a drunken man, I within a few yards of him dodging about in the jungle to place my bullets, he intent only on getting away. The rifle was hot in my hands and he was momentarily resting his tusks in the fork of a small tree, when all of a sudden one of the bullets found his brain and he threw up his head with a jerk before crashing to the ground stone-dead. I felt shaken and nauseated then, though strangely enough in those last few moments I had been as cool as ice, although tensed up at the same time. I remembered seeing through the corner of my eye my trackers searching around in the jungle for the cartridge cases as I reloaded and fired, oblivious to the death-drama that was being enacted before them.

The elephant was a menacing-looking animal, with that peculiarly enlarged base of the trunk where the tusks begin which somehow seems particularly formidable in elephants. His tusks were heavy but not symmetrical. I was proud that I had got him after all, though it worried me that I had had to expend as many as seven bullets on him. His head was brought in on a bullock cart and several months later, when the skull was clean, I used a cross-cut saw to cut up the skull in sections, very much like cutting wedges out of a cake. There at last was the brain cavity. Nine to ten inches across and four to five inches deep and set well back in the skull, it resembled nothing so much as a giant clover-shaped bun, the ear holes of the skull draining, as it were, the shallow bottom portion. The correct shot, obviously, was the half-front position between the eye and the ear and just above the cheekbone, into the natural hollow of the elephant's temple. At last I knew where the brain of the elephant was and if in future I made a mistake, the fault would be mine. Years later, when I came to be head of the Forest Department, I ordered that sectioned elephant skulls should be maintained and displayed in places where shooters could learn how to kill an elephant cleanly.

During the five and a half years which I spent in Goalpara I was shooting hard to keep myself busy during my spare time, but I managed to combine work with pleasure. Tracking troublesome elephants took me into out of the way corners of the forests, which proved useful in my supervision of work in the division. I shot only crop-raiding elephants and cattle-lifting tigers, with the exception of one elephant and one tiger which I suspect may have been harmless.

Many a night I went out into the paddy fields at the call of distressed villagers to scare away elephants. Most times a shot over the raider's head would be enough to scare him away, but sometimes only a twelve-bore loaded with small shot would be successful. But if they were really determined crop-raiders, there was nothing to do except kill them.

I shot elephants by daylight in the forest, as well as in the fields at night, but the surest way was by tracking the marauder in the daytime. In this way I shot the Gangia tusker, which gave me my record pair of tusks.

He was a persistent and cunning raider and, on hearing that he had been coming out for several successive nights, I camped in the village specially to get him. One side of a long strip of cultivation was open to the forest and I had a small hut built on the edge of it. It was a night of the full moon in November and he came out early while I was having my dinner – a great mass with two gleaming white tusks, gliding like a ship out of the jungle towards the paddy in the light of the rising moon. He moved like a thief on tiptoe, slowly and very stealthily, and I crouched in the shadow of the trees literally holding my breath. I let him get well into the paddy and start feeding before daring to move. Then I started looking for a line of approach, but there was none. I knew it was useless trying to get up to him directly, so I made my way cautiously to the top end of the cultivation. I was now between him and the jungle. Where the ricefields petered out, I at last found a line of approach through an abandoned house site. My rifle had a large torch light clipped to the barrel and I held it close to my side to avoid the reflection of the moonlight on its bright surface. I crept stealthily towards the feeding elephant but I could no longer see him and I stopped in the shadow of a small mango tree to take a breather.

I was wet with dew and could feel the leeches on my legs, but I concentrated entirely on the elephant. I could locate him by his rhythmic feeding noises – 'swish, swish, swish' as he beat the pulled-up paddy on his knee and then a pause as he put it into his mouth. I listened intently and suddenly the sounds appeared to be coming nearer – he was feeding towards me. It was almost too good to be true. Then I caught sight of him as he cleared the bushes to my left. I thought I noticed a certain peculiarity in the way he fed. He never turned his back on the village and always faced in the same direction. Then I lost sight of him and I waited patiently. Suddenly, from the swishing sounds which were my only guide, I sensed that he was moving away from me. Realizing that I would never get a chance again, I controlled my excited shivering and braced myself for the show-down. On the tips of my toes, placing my feet carefully and avoiding fallen leaves and shrubs, I went forward through the patch of abandoned homestead to get as close as possible to the elephant. My luck was holding, as the cover was just right.

I halted behind the last large bush which was between me and him. He must have been a hundred feet away and once I saw his trunk come up above the cover as he tested the air. Then gradually I began moving to the right and simultaneously raised my rifle. I was almost clear of the bush when suddenly he stopped feeding. I knew at once that he had detected me. 'Now or never!' I thought and stepped to the side for the shot. At the same moment there was a snort and the elephant turned away. I pressed the button of my torch as I pulled the rifle to my shoulder, only to be blinded by the reflection of the light thrown back by a smaller bush which I had not noticed before. Immediately I reversed my movement, running to the left so as to sight the elephant. He was in full stride for the jungle by now and I aimed for his left temple, guided by his eye in the beam of the torchlight. I pulled the trigger once and when he did not go down, a second time. But he hardly faltered in his stride and it seemed as though I had missed him completely. I reloaded my rifle, running after him and shouting to make him turn and charge as I had been taught to do, but with no effect. I had just time for one more long shot somewhere in the direction of the side of his neck and then there was only the splashing as he crossed the stream at the edge of the black enveloping jungle.

I stood there, exhausted and crestfallen to the verge of tears, my clothes damp with sweat and my legs soaked to the knees, while the villagers gathered round. I felt convinced that I had lost the biggest tusker of my life. I explained to them what had happened, going over in pantomime the drama of the last hour or more. They tried to console me but I could sense their disappointment. Mine was worse, because they were my villagers and I had let them down. However, there was nothing to be done and after I had sent off a messenger for my elephant Mohan Prasad to be at the village at the crack of dawn, I went back to my hut. Needless to say I spent a restless and nearly sleepless night, as I went over again and again the events which had ended in my losing the giant tusker. I could only conclude that the elephant had spotted the reflection of the moonlight on the bright metal of the torch on my rifle, though why he had let me get so close to him was a mystery. There was also that strange way of feeding in the paddy field – never turning round and always facing in one direction. I was to know the answers the next day.

Early next morning my faithful Mohan Prasad was there and we took up the tracking from the spot where the raider had splashed across the stream. It was rather difficult at first, following across the grazed land and light grass round the village where there were many old tracks, but once we got into the thicker stuff it was easier. We had not gone very far when the realization dawned on me and my mahout almost simultaneously that there was something unusual in the tracks left by the wounded elephant. They were far too broad to be normal and soon we realized that he was dragging his left leg badly. Immediately my hopes rose sharply. We knew now that he was badly hit and we hoped to catch up with him soon. Sure enough there he was, hobbling along within a mile of the village. He had hardly covered any ground at all during the night.

He was magnificent standing there in the forest facing us with his ears spread forward, full of fight in spite of his crippled shoulder. It was quite obvious that he had a broken bone somewhere and I could not have shot so badly as all that the night before. I could only guess that while attempting to swing the heavy rifle against my natural swing as he ran to the left, I had gone behind and my shot had caught the shoulder, high up in line with the eye at which I had been aiming. I was eager to finish him off, both to save him further agony and because I wanted to have done with it. It was one thing stalking him at night in the bright moonlight, but quite another having him before me in that crippled condition and at my mercy. He went down fighting, trumpeting furiously after the first shot which did not find his brain, but I made sure of things when he struggled to his feet.

When I examined him I found that his right eye was blind.

This then was the explanation of my being able to get up to him so close in the bright moonlight, for I had been on his blind side the whole while. It also explained why he always fed facing in one direction, his blind eye towards the jungle from where he could expect no danger and his sound eye towards the village. I had indeed been lucky, both in my approach and in the shot which had anchored him so close to the village. But night shooting never appealed to me after that – there are too many uncertainties.

The elephant was an enormous animal, as befitting the possessor of such a large pair of tusks. He measured 10 feet 6½ inches from sole to shoulder as he lay and was in fine health, though old. I reckoned he must be nearly a hundred, judging partly by the tips of the tusks which were beginning to show signs of decay. They measured 7 feet 1½ inches and weighed 77 lb. each; the thicker of the two was 18¾ inches in circumference, an inch and a quarter off the world record for the Asian elephant. The longest recorded are a pair of tusks from the Goalpara division of Assam, not very far to the east of where I shot my big tusker; they measure nine feet two inches. The heaviest are from an elephant shot by the Raja of Talcher in Orissa, weighing 120 lb. and 114 lb. respectively. As far as I know, this is a world record for the Asian elephant. The next biggest are also from Assam; a pair from an elephant shot by the late Lord Lytton measured eight feet nine inches and eight feet two inches; while each tusk of another pair which I collected in Goalpara, just north of where I got the Gangia tusker, were eight feet long. I wonder if it is more than a coincidence that the three heaviest pairs recorded from Assam in recent years are all from the Goalpara district, south of the Bhutan Hills, and all within a radius of fifty miles. This region produces the best elephants in Assam and Milroy believed that this is due to the rather dry feeding and unequalled range available for the herds, which move up to the hills during the rains and down to the plains in the cold weather.

Although the Gangia tusker was really blind in one eye, it is extraordinary how short-sighted perfectly normal elephants seem to be at certain distances. I once took my koonki right up to a large wild makhna which was feeding in some high grass on a river bank. We were walking in the dry, sandy river-bed and I was astonished how close he let us come; then suddenly he got our wind and was off in a flash. On another occasion I had a load of young ladies on my elephant when in the distance we saw a makhna, standing near the edge of a swamp and stuffing water hyacinth into its mouth. I approached with some trepidation, but he took absolutely no notice until we were within twenty or thirty yards, when he suddenly went off and was soon lost to sight in the high grass. On another occasion in Kaziranga a party of six or seven persons on two elephants approached a wild tusker feeding in a swamp to within forty or fifty yards across open ground and it was not until the mahouts clapped their hands that the tusker made off. The fact that it was a sanctuary might have accounted for the elephant's lack of fear, but there are other instances which would indicate that the species has very poor sight. On one occasion a friend and his wife were having a picnic lunch on the Diyung river in the North Cachar Hills when an elephant made its appearance on a sand spit about a hundred yards away. Perry, who was the Deputy Commissioner of the district and a person who has had considerable experience with wild elephants, says that he tried approaching him and succeeded in getting to within a remarkably short distance. The tusker took no notice of him until he was close up, although he was right out in the open and there was nothing to obstruct the animal's vision.

What is more, the several remarkably narrow escapes which elephant hunters have had when charged, coupled with my own observations on the behaviour of wild elephants in certain circumstances, makes me inclined to think that they have difficulty in focusing on an object which is not at a certain optimum distance away. Apart from my own narrow escape which I attribute to this weakness, at least two sportsmen say they owe their lives to some unaccountable failure on the elephant's part when by all the tokens they should have been run down in the charge. A tea-planter named Baldwin was once faced by a charging elephant, which he had provoked into turning on him in order to secure the head shot, when his rifle jammed and he was left helpless and convinced that his last moment had come. He could not account for the elephant missing him, as he stood still in its path. Walsh, another tea-planter, described to me how he was following an elephant in thick bush when it suddenly whipped round and charged him; he tripped as he took a step backwards in the act of raising his rifle and sat down at the base of a tree and perhaps this may have made the elephant lose sight of him and charge on and past him. Charlie de la Nougerede had wounded an elephant in thick bamboo jungle in the Garo Hills when it turned on him and brushed past him, knocking him down and walking over his shoulder and arm. Would there be such a high proportion of near misses with any other animal? And could it be accounted for by the setting of the elephant's eyes almost at the outer edges of the wide forehead, rendering it incapable of focusing them on objects outside a certain optimum distance?

Long before I took up elephant control work, of course, I was sometimes forced to shoot elephants because they were too sick and weak to stand a chance; and occasionally it was necessary to shoot them in a stockade because they were uncontrollable. This did not often happen, since it was generally possible to release such animals. Large bulls, in fact, seldom get caught in khedda operations; they usually manage to escape out of the ring of drivers, who will do their best to exclude them from the stockade. Apart from the damage they can do both to the koonkis and to the other captives, particularly the young ones, there is the trouble of disposing of them if it is necessary to shoot them. It is no joke trying to get rid of a four-ton elephant's carcase within the comparatively small area of a stockade. Where there are nearby villages of tribal peoples, some of whom eat elephant meat readily, there is no problem as these people will come down from their hills and cut up and remove a dead elephant in no time. But elsewhere labour must be employed to bury the remains at some distance. The resultant fouling of the stockade may be so great as to spoil the chances of further catching for the rest of the season.

In connection with mela shikar I mentioned the biggest elephant I ever saw captured by this method, a solitary more than nine feet high at the shoulder which took three koonkis to bring him in and three phands to hold him. Normally such an animal would have been left severely alone, but apparently the Phookans had wanted a large elephant for a koonki – although I did not know this at the time – and their phandis had tackled him successfully. In due course I auctioned him, but there were no bidders for what was obviously a handful and I could not sell him. A neighbouring planter, a keen conservationist who had played a large part in the creation of the local sanctuary, came to the depot and when he saw the animal he expressed the desire to purchase him as a shikar elephant. We settled the price, which was double what we were normally getting for such large makhnas, and the deal was closed. When the Phookans learnt that I had parted with the elephant they were very upset, but it was their fault not to have been frank with me from the beginning. Probably they had expected to get him at the customary cheap rate of three hundred rupees.

That evening he was pegged out and tied by his hind-legs to a tree, with the neck rope or phand stretched to another tree in front of him. He struggled violently and I had a suspicion even then that he was stretched out too much, but I was inexperienced and this was my first independent khedda. Next morning, when we untied him to take him down to the river, we found him tottering and weak in the hind-quarters. He had obviously hurt himself severely during his struggles by tugging against the ropes. We got the biggest koonkis in the depot to prop him up and led him gently down to the river. The Doctor Babu and I followed with fear in our hearts, for he was staggering like a drunken man and could hardly move his back legs. When he reached the river edge he lurched forward, with his trunk stretched out and collapsed on the water's edge. We tried to lift him with the biggest tuskers, but failed. We untied all his ropes in the hope that he would try to get up on realizing that he was free. Men brought him titbits of sugar-cane and plaintain leaves, but though we practically put them into his mouth he would not take them.

By this time the whole depot had heard the news and the riverbank was crowded with people, all elephant men and all deeply concerned for the plight of the big makhna. I made them stand away and they remained silently watching. It was possible to go up to him and, provided one kept away from his questing, restless trunk, it was quite safe to touch him. He was a mountain of an elephant and we had the opportunity of examining him closely. The day passed slowly. The Doctor Babu looked up his books and came out with a long name – I think it meant some form of paralysis. He said he could do nothing. I had my own suspicion that it was complete rupture of all the ligaments and muscles in the loins, but I secretly hoped that he would get up during the night and walk away to freedom.

The next morning there he was still lying in the same place and our fears became worse. I began to look up Evans' *Care and Treatment of Elephants*, for the vital shots with which to kill an elephant. The only weapon I had in the camp was an old eight-bore B.P. rifle, a weapon handed down by a succession of khedda officers and seldom used. I did not even know whether the large paper-cased, black-powder cartridges were still fresh. When I broached the question to the Doctor Babu that we might have to destroy the elephant, he would have none of it. He was a Brahmin and hated taking life. I said to him, 'Doctor Babu, we cannot let him lie there starving and it is my duty to destroy him.'

However, we let him remain there a second night and next morning I made my preparations with a heavy heart. Killing an elephant in the upright position is difficult enough, but to kill one cleanly as he is lying on the ground is a task which at that time utterly defeated me. I could only think of the obvious heart shot, as at that time I did not know the shot into the back of the brain. This is the spot which the mahout pokes at with his goad, while he sits on the neck of the elephant a little farther back. A bullet placed here, parallel to the legs and trunk of the elephant as it lies, has to penetrate some ten inches of flesh and muscle of the neck and then there is a thickness of only a quarter of an inch of bone enclosing the brain.

I decided to try the heart shot and I called for a packing case. The silent ring of spectators seemed to be offering up a prayer for the dying makhna. I thought that the heart would be easy to reach,

but all that took place in response to the shot was a spasmodic
and violent twitching of the legs and body and a gush of blood
out of the nostrils, which stained the water red. I fired again and
then again. I was beginning to panic. I went round to the river
edge and lay down in the water for a frontal brain shot. I must
have fired five shots. Finally he lay still, with the blood oozing
out of his trunk and his eye glazing. I staggered to my tent and
was violently sick. Orwell has written a most moving account of
killing an elephant in Burma under similar circumstances.

For the next twenty-four hours I felt ill. I had a great blue
bruise on my right shoulder, the result of the kick of the heavy
rifle. The same rifle came to be known later on as the 'jaw-
breaking' rifle, because it nearly broke the jaw of one of my
assistants and cut his cheek and upper lip badly. He had been
afraid of it. I had also been afraid of it, but only for the elephant's
sake.

This task of destroying a sick or old elephant is a most painful
business. Somehow if the first bullet does not go home – and this
often happens – the situation gets out of control and one generally
has to fire again and again. Milroy and the Director of the veterinary department at the time once had a dreadful ordeal in destroying an old cow elephant which they felt was better put down.
Something went wrong and they could not kill her, try as they
might. Their ammunition ran out and they had to send in thirty-
five miles from Kulsi to Gauhati for more. I think it took over
twenty shots to finish the job and by that time they were both in
a state of near collapse.

I had an equally unnerving experience with Phookan's famous
'sakhni', the name given to a female with tusks. This was a rarity
that not even the oldest elephant men could remember having
seen or heard of before and she was without doubt the most
extraordinary animal I ever saw captured. She sent our biggest
koonkis flying and we had to try and control her by putting in
Joyram Goonda, a powerful makhna which happened to be in full
musth at the time. A young phandi had volunteered to take on
the double job of manoeuvring him and subduing the wild
sakhni. She put up a good fight, but eventually Joyram cowed her,

H

his temper aroused by his musth condition. Even so she required two elephants to bring her out of the stockade. There was such excitement when it was discovered that she was a female with tusks that Phookan made up his mind to keep her for himself and he refused to sell her at any price. The elephant men said she was barren and she was certainly very ugly, with rather stout tusks projecting about a foot from her lip, and she was as savage as she looked.

From the start Phookan had bad luck with her. The next winter he was catching on the north bank and took this elephant with his other koonkis across the Brahmaputra. She gave a lot of trouble when swimming the river and had to be roped to another koonki. It was while she was on the north bank that she killed her first victim, her own grass cutter who apparently had approached her too silently, crouching low in the grass while trying to make out her footprints from among those of other elephants. Three months later she shook off her mahout when she panicked over something that ran across her path and promptly trampled him to death. When Phookan was bringing her back to the south bank in the early part of the winter for my last khedda, she killed a third man. This time it was an umbrella which slipped off her back and which startled her so much that she threw her rider, whom she promptly attacked and crushed to death with her fore-feet. After that the men refused to have anything to do with her and the wretched animal was tied to a tree and abandoned.

There was something definitely wrong with the elephant and Phookan decided to destroy her. This was a most unusual thing for a koonki owner to do, but I suppose he was convinced that the sakhni was an unlucky animal, better dead than alive. He came to me because he had no suitable rifle. We discussed it for a while and when I saw that he had made up his mind I agreed to go out and perform the unpleasant task. I motored out to the Brahmaputra early next morning and had to wait for a ferry to take me across to the Majuli island. It was a cold rainy day in December and I found the dispirited elephant men huddled round a small fire. I asked them to show me where the sakhni was tied and one of the men went with me rather reluctantly. I was shocked at her condition. She was up to her belly in mud and filth and had not been untied for a week. A few plantain stems and leaves were lying about.

The doomed elephant was in a furious temper. She lunged at me when I approached her and would definitely have attacked me if she had not been tied to the tree. It was the first time I had seen her after her capture two years ago and she looked more vicious than ever. For a moment I wondered if there had been some fault or neglect in her training – but then Phookan was very thorough in such matters.

But I had come for another purpose and with the usual tight feeling in my chest I took up my position at an angle and fired at her head. It was difficult, because she kept moving her head sideways trying to face me. It was not surprising that she failed to drop to the shot. I cursed myself and began to get jittery. Next time I tried the heart but here again it was difficult to judge the angle, bogged down as she was in her own filth. She went over sideways and then got up and beat her head in rage and pain against the tree to which she was tied, trying desperately to get at me. Thank God my third shot, which I again directed at her head, succeeded. I got back late that night with a violent attack of shivering, the result of the tiring trip and the unnerving experience, plus my old friend, malaria. I never want to repeat such an elephant execution again. Phookan gave me one of the sakhni's tusks as a souvenir and I had it for several years, until it was stolen from me.

I did not kill very many elephants during my shooting life of about fifteen years. After the first excitement had worn off, I found myself growing careless. So careless, in fact, that I nearly met my end at the hands – or rather tusks – of the tallest elephant I ever encountered and the last one I ever followed.

My mahouts and I had suddenly come upon his tracks high up towards the Bhutan border and the only reason why we decided to follow them was their enormous size. I was always looking out for that eleven-foot elephant and this looked like it. The forest floor was dry and tracking was slow; he had obviously been going fast, not stopping to feed, and we spent the whole afternoon without catching up with him. At the time I was camping at the end of the forest tramway a couple of miles from the Bhutan border; the next day was Sunday and bazaar day and we had to get back to base, I to supervise the payment of labour and the men to do their weekly purchases of foodstuffs. However, we decided to give it another try early the next morning and if we did not catch up with him soon, to abandon the tracking.

Dawn was just breaking as we crossed the stony river-bed where we had left his tracks the previous evening and we spotted a tiger having his early morning drink before retiring for the day to the forest. My men said it was a good omen and that we would come up with the elephant. The tracks led us up to the abandoned Sanfan bungalow and the elephant had walked all around it. Then he had stepped over a large fallen tree lying at such a height that only a very big elephant could have negotiated it. My mahouts whistled softly and whispered that he was a *prokando* (enormous) elephant. I was tremendously keyed up as I visualized a record elephant. Just on the edge of the jungle was the spot where he had lain down, probably in the early hours of the morning, and the earth was moist with the dribble from his mouth. I jumped down to examine the impression of his tusk in the damp earth and my spare mahout, whom I used to bring out as a tracker, did the same. He pointed to the elongated depression, about three inches wide and said in a whisper that the animal was a tusker. I shook my head and whispered back that I thought he was a makhna – the impression was too narrow to have been left by the tusk of such an enormous elephant. There is a difference between the tusks, which are tremendously enlarged incisors, and the tushes, which project directly downwards, unlike tusks which normally turn upwards. This difference in the two types of male Asian elephants is an obscure phenomenon and the pattern is not the same everywhere. In Assam makhnas are very common, while in south India they do not constitute a very high proportion of the males of a herd. In Ceylon strangely enough, almost all the males are tuskless.

In this case there was only one way to settle the argument and

we went on. Shortly afterwards I should have noticed that the
elephant's tracks had begun to zigzag sharply, a sure sign that he
knew he was being followed, but my mind was too full of the
prospect of a record elephant and a makhna too. We passed
through some marshy ground with high grass and as was my
practice, I climbed back on Mohan Prasad and stood up on his
pad to peer over the top. Immediately after we ran into some very
thick jungle matted with thorny creepers and after trying to negotiate it on the elephant, I decided to get down and pressed my
mahout's shoulder to tell him my intentions. By this time we had
become a perfect team – Mohan Prasad, Ontai and I – and they
would go with me anywhere and do anything I wanted them to
do. Handing my rifle to the mahout after pulling the safety catch
back from the firing position, I jumped down as lightly as I could
while the spare mahout slid down the tail of the elephant. Taking
back my rifle, I motioned to Ontai to stay where he was and went
forward with my tracker. Almost simultaneously we came into a
slight clearing with an indistinct sort of path running through it
and the man went forward to try and pick up the trail. There was
an eerie feeling about the place, which was one of the loneliest
and wildest spots I had yet come across in my division, what we
foresters call a 'non-productive blank' given over to rank growth
and climbers and seldom visited by anyone – the perfect hide-out
for solitary elephants.

I was following a little behind with my eyes to the ground
trying to pick out the tracks of the big elephant, when suddenly
I noticed a slight movement in the jungle ahead and before I
could catch my breath out stepped an enormous elephant, his
ears cocked and his trunk questing us. He was surely the biggest
elephant I had ever seen, but his tusks were miserably thin and
not even long for his size. No wonder the impression they had
left in the earth where he had slept was so misleading. In my
surprise and because my mind was bemused with the thought of
this record elephant, which I hoped and half expected was a
makhna so that I could shoot him, I did something which no
elephant shooter should do: I turned to where my mahout Ontai
was on Mohan Prasad and said, in Assamese, 'Hey! It is a tusker

after all!' Hardly were the words out of my mouth and I had turned to face the elephant when he was in full stride, coming at me absolutely silently but with deadly purpose. My voice had been just the indication he had wanted of our location. I had thrown away all the advantage by speaking. 'Now for it', I thought as I raised my rifle to my shoulder, automatically stepping a little to the side to obtain protection from a tree which was standing near me. I sighted on his frontal bump as he came pounding along and when he was about fifty feet away I squeezed the trigger. There was no result. I checked for a fraction of a second and pulled the second trigger, still with no result. Then my mind went blank. I had half lowered my rifle and I am sure my mouth must have been agape. The tusker was almost on me. His head was lowered and he was skidding to a stop. In another second he would have grabbed me. I could look right into his eyes (which I remembered afterwards were light coloured, the sign of a dangerous elephant) when I came to life. Dropping my rifle at his very feet I dived into and under some tangled creepers which draped the tree. Instantaneously I picked myself up and dashed madly forward, up the very track the elephant had made as it charged me. Fear lent wings to my heels. I was wearing light-soled rubber and canvas boots. I had been a sprinter in my youth, with exceedingly good reflexes which never let me down at starts, and I had at one time cherished ambitions ro run for India in the Olympics. It was that long-dormant instinct, that natural talent for a quick start and burst of explosive energy when required, which saved me now.

But as I ran I expected every moment to be grabbed from the rear. It was a forlorn hope I told myself, with a frightening clarity of vision, it was the end! When I reached the wall of jungle from which the tusker had emerged I took an automatic header into it, screwing up my eyes and lowering my head against the cruel thorns. Scrambling to my feet I dashed on, tripping, falling, tearing my way desperately through the cane and thorny climbers. All the while I was unconsciously making a circle towards the high bank which I knew bounded the dead ground into which we had followed the elephant. When I was almost out of breath I heard a shot ring out, and then another. I stopped, only just able to stand for exhaustion, and looked up at a tree under which I found myself thinking 'Can I climb it?' I listened, trying to still the tearing gasps which were forced out of my mouth. Everything was quiet. I ventured a cautious hail to my men. Back came an answering coo-ee. 'What has happened, has the elephant gone?', I shouted and could have laughed with relief at the answering shout – 'Yes, it has gone.' 'Shall we come to you?' called Ontai but I shouted back 'No, stay where you are, I am coming', relief and wonder in my heart.

Judging my position from the direction from which the shouts had come I slowly, for I was in a very exhausted and tremulous state, made my way through the dense jungle, climbing under and pushing down the creepers and thorns with my hands and feet. At last I came to the little opening and there was Mohan Prasad, placidly pulling down creepers and stuffing them into his mouth while Ontai and the other men were perched on his back as usual. I could hardly believe my eyes. They greeted me with grins which turned into sympathetic clickings of the tongue and murmurs as they saw my state. They handed me the rifle and I looked impatiently at it, for all the while I had been fleeing from the elephant I had at the back of my mind the question of what had happened to my rifle, that trusty weapon which up to that moment had never let me down. One glance and I saw the reason why the weapon had failed to function – the safety catch was still on. A momentary aberration had nearly cost me my life, for when I had dismounted from the elephant after slipping the catch to the safety position I had failed to change it to the ready.

We stood in the little clearing going over the incident and they told me what had happened. When I had dived under the creepers, more or less disappearing from sight, the tusker had searched for me practically at his feet, tearing down the jungle and kicking it about, all the while squealing with rage and completely oblivious of the presence of Mohan Prasad at the edge of the clearing. The tracker had run up the path and hidden himself and the elephant had not caught sight of him. It was concentrating entirely on me. Mohan Prasad had shied away instinctively from the sudden charge of the wild elephant and Ontai had found himself momentarily up against a tangle of creepers, but he had managed to hold the elephant with his goad. 'As soon as I saw the elephant come out of the jungle I put a couple of cartridges from your belt into your shotgun', he told me. Wedged as he was against the jungle Ontai had yet managed to turn his body around sufficiently to enable him to discharge first one and then the other barrel into the side of the enraged elephant as he kicked and tore at the jungle looking for me. The effect of the cartridges at such close range and from so unexpected a quarter had the effect of propelling him into the jungle head-first as if ejected from a mighty cannon. Ontai said he could hear him tearing away through the jungle and mercifully in the opposite direction to where I was.

Then we started laughing. It was the natural reaction from tension and I laughed until the tears came to my eyes, while the men laughed with me, occasionally stopping to elaborate on the miraculous escape I had had – we *all* had, for that matter, for if the tusker had spotted our elephant he would certainly have attacked it. My hat was gone somewhere in the jungle, my shirt-back and shoulders were in ribbons and my scalp was full of thorns, while my face and arms were lacerated by the terrible tearing I had undergone in the jungle. Suddenly the narrowness of our escape came upon me and I looked at Ontai. It was he who had saved the situation with his presence of mind and yet there he sat, with a grin on his face as if it was all in the day's work. I was suddenly so moved that tears came into my eyes.

We hurried to get out of that awful jungle and to make our way back to camp. We were in time to catch the forest train with its load of labour and forest staff going back to the base settlement for bazaar day. The story soon spread of our encounter with the 'goonda' – that is what he was really, for he had attacked us in an unprovoked manner, unless you consider tracking him into his lair constitutes unnecessary provocation. I was the subject of much anxious questioning and of respectfully amused wonder as I sat in the guard's van having the thorns picked out of my scalp. And later when I reached the settlement and the doctor got on to my head with a pair of tweezers and attended to my lacerations, my staff and the villagers had to be told the story again and again. As for me, that was my swan-song in the matter of elephant shooting. I was sensible enough to realize that I had really lost interest in what had once seemed an exciting sport. It had been useful in keeping me from brooding over the long separation from my wife and our child whom I had never seen – and whom I never did see, for they were both torpedoed on the way out from England. When an elephant shooter loses interest in a sport that is the dangerous stage, at least according to the books. And so I packed up and stuck to tigers after that.

CHAPTER 13

THE FUTURE

Thirty years ago when I was catching elephants, improved communications were already seriously affecting the elephant trade. The governments had ceased to be large purchasers and the ruling princes and landowners were beginning to look round for the latest thing in automobiles. The pleasant custom of buying a baby elephant, preferably a little she-elephant, to grow up side by side with the youngest member of the household, began to die out among the wealthy families of Bihar and United Provinces. The princes, some of whom had indulged in rivalry as regards the number of elephants they kept, gradually began to reduce their stables.

Timber dragging too was beginning to be done by mechanical means rather than elephants. The great teak companies of Burma had filled their quotas of elephants required for exploitation and the annual replacement of casualties was met largely by calves born in captivity. For these various reasons, and also of course because of the world slump in the thirties, prices remained dull throughout the whole period I was catching elephants – in fact they have never been so low.

Remarkably enough, during the later stages of the Second World War prices showed some signs of revival. Young females which had not yet calved would fetch three thousand rupees (£240) or more, double the price we obtained in the mid thirties. This sudden spurt surprised me and I questioned some of the elephant purchasers from Bihar. Their explanation was that the large amount of money which was in circulation during the war years, and the high prices which were being obtained for agricultural produce, had increased the earnings of the landowners of north-eastern India; and in their traditionally conservative way they were looking out for property in which to invest their surplus money. The rural dweller in India has always preferred to invest his savings in land, livestock or jewellery and if he is a small man his hard cash may be buried under the floor of his house, which is of course the first place that thieves search.

The temporary boom in the elephant trade lasted into the early post-war years, but then there was another slump. The fact is that this trade, like so many others in India, is bound up with the prosperity of the agriculturalist. A general rise in the fortunes of this class may account to some extent for a continued demand for elephants in spite of the abolition of the main patrons of the dealers – the big landowners. A depression, on the other hand, though it results in a decreasing demand, has never yet brought the trade to a complete standstill; happily elephants are still an essential part of religious festivals, marriage ceremonies and other customs in many parts of the country.

In India, elephants were not always protected as they have been since the introduction of the Elephant Preservation Act of 1879. In the south of India and Ceylon rewards were offered at one time for the animal's destruction and even cows and young calves were shot. One resident of the Wynaad in southern India killed three hundred elephants and the practical elimination of the tusker in Ceylon must be attributed to this period of indiscriminate shooting. Between 1845 and 1859, in only a part of that island, rewards were paid for the destruction of no less than 5,194 elephants. During the thirties we ourselves were capturing very large numbers of elephants. In fact by the removal of some nine hundred animals in the years 1934–6 from the forests at the foot of the Naga and Mikri Hills we almost cleaned out the elephants there. In addition, vast areas of forest have been cleared and the Nagas, with large numbers of wartime weapons in their possession, have taken a steady toll of elephants in their hills, even though the animal is protected officially. The inevitable result is that catches have been poor in this area in recent years.

After the war, when I was in charge of the Assam forests, I tried to introduce a system of elephant control with game rangers as in Burma (which had borrowed the idea from East Africa) but with no success. The late Gopinath Bardoloi, then the head of the government and an elephant owner himself, had too great an affection for the animal to expose it to organized destruction and he refused to agree to the scheme. But I wonder if sooner or later some such idea will not have to take the place of the present methods of control, not only in Assam but in other parts of India.

In the days when Milroy's scheme of controlling marauding elephants was first introduced in Assam, there were many sportsmen ready and willing to take on the task of shooting them. But during and after the war there arose a new generation of planters who were more interested in tennis than in the arduous pursuit of dangerous animals. On the other hand, there was an increasing number of Indians wanting to try their hand at the sport; but the close of hostilities brought to a head the acute shortage of ammunition which had manifested itself during the war and there was also a meteoric rise in the price of high-velocity, big bore rifles. This trend has continued and today it is almost impossible for a man of moderate means to equip himself properly for this most exacting form of shikar. If I had kept all the weapons I had bought at insignificant prices during my early days I could have made a packet by selling them now.

The only part of India where elephants have increased in the past twenty-five years is in Uttar Pradesh – the United Provinces of the British period – in the sub-Himalayan forests between Nepal and the Ganges, which is the present western limit of the species. Here, presumably as the result of cessation of catching which was once the monopoly of the Raja of Balrampur, the elephant population has increased from an estimated two hundred and fifty to some six hundred. In places they are becoming a menace to cultivators and the authorities have been seriously considering the

possibilities of reviving elephant catching in some form, though
the real problem will be to find a market for the captured animals.
In Assam, it is the north bank forests with their backs to the
Bhutan and Tibetan foothills, and the isolated Garo Hills, which
hold out the best prospects for elephant herds remaining up to
strength. The same is probably true of the foothills of north
Bengal and of the Chittagong Hill Tracts of East Pakistan. In all
these areas the annual catching will have to be relied upon to keep
the numbers under control.

Very recently, a herd of seventy-nine elephants was spotted
from the air in the North East Frontier Agency. They were coun-
ted as they walked in single file, led by a huge tusker; evidently
they were making their way towards the hills near the Tsangpo
or Dihang (the true Brahmaputra) and it is said that they were un-
disturbed by the low-flying plane.

In the extreme north-eastern corner of the Brahmaputra valley,
elephants have been dispersed by the floods and silting which
destroyed vast areas of forest. In Cachar, elephants are under
pressure from the Lushais who, having cleared all their remaining
forested lands which were the abode of elephants, are now right
up against the edge of the reserved forests at the foot of their
hills. Lushai hunters are killing elephants in great numbers; a
recent letter in the press described elephant trunks drying in front
of fires in the villages and it is rumoured that there is a regular
smuggling route for tusks through the hinterland into Burma.
And yet that very old law, the Elephant Protection Act, was made
to prevent just this sort of thing from happening.

In the south of India the elephant population appears to be
generally under control; but their numbers are bound to decline
with the final opening up of the last remaining forest lands outside
the Government reserved forests. This has been a feature of recent
years following the short-lived Communist régime of 1959 and
the merger of parts of Malabar with Travancore and Cochin to
form what is now known as Kerala. In the plateau country of
Mysore and the adjoining Madras forests, the numbers will
certainly increase if the Mysore kheddas are permanently abandoned as a result of the destruction of the Kakankote site through

submergence by a dam project. In addition, elephants are protected in the famous Bandipur and Mudumalai sanctuaries.

The steady demand for elephants for temple ceremonies and timber dragging in the south-western part of the Indian peninsula will possibly take care of the natural increase of the elephant population of the Western Ghats; but in Mysore it may be necessary to introduce a system of control under licence, as we have had for some years in Assam, in order to supplement the destruction of proclaimed rogues and dangerous elephants. It is interesting that Andhra Pradesh, which includes the greater part of the old Hyderabad State, is contemplating the re-introduction of elephants in the Adilabad forests where they were once found. This scheme offers some small chance for the deployment of the surplus elephants of the Mysore plateau, the nearest source.

In Ceylon the elephant population has dwindled considerably in recent years and the total now does not exceed six hundred, according to recent estimates. The splitting up of large forested areas to provide cultivation for the expanding needs of the people has greatly reduced the range of the elephant and brought it into sharp conflict with the human population. In spite of the law, elephants are being killed in increasing numbers and the authorities have been compelled to issue licences for their capture. Fears are real that the Ceylon elephant is on its way to extinction and Deraniyagala has even suggested that a new home be found for them in the forests of South America.

In Burma twenty years ago the stock of elephants was estimated to be some ten thousand, a figure which was then considered to be excessive. Before the last war, Burma was shooting over a hundred elephants every year, both males and females, in an effort to keep down the numbers. Domestic elephants had increased enormously not only as a result of breeding in captivity (estimated to be some six hundred animals per annum), but also because of the successful introduction of inoculation against anthrax, which formerly took a heavy toll of elephants in Burma. As a consequence, although large herds of working elephants were still maintained by timber companies, there was little demand for elephant catching on a commercial scale. In fact Burma never did capture elephants on a big scale during the British period and many years ago Evans reported that it was only the kings of the country and to some extent the Karens who caught elephants. But the position has now changed considerably. A very large proportion of the six thousand working elephants in Burma before the war was lost during and after the Japanese occupation. After the war, the timber industry suffered as a consequence. It may be expected, therefore, that the demand for elephants will take care of the natural increase in the wild elephant population of Burma, at least for some time. In Malaya the elephant areas have shrunk drastically and in countries farther east the pattern has been the same.

I have written very little about the NEFA (North East Frontier Agency) which has been so much in the news lately, particularly in 1962; in fact, the term did not exist when I was catching elephants and until the independence of India in 1947, the mountainous country adjoining Bhutan and southern Tibet had no particular political designation. There was simply an Inner Line, which ran along the foot of the hills between the plains of Assam and the tribal territory and which is the boundary subsequently claimed by China; and the McMahon Line, far to the north along the watershed of the inner Himalayas, which India and formerly the British, claimed as the boundary between India and Tibet. This tribal belt was administered by the Political Department and access to it was controlled by a series of posts on the main path leading up into the mountains and over the passes into Tibet. No one, not even Government servants like myself belonging to the adjoining state of Assam, could cross the Inner Line and plains people were prevented from going up into the hills. The tribal peoples of the hills – Monpas, Sherdupkens, Daflas, Apa Tanis, Miris, Abors, Mishmis and so on – were thus totally cut off from contact with the people of the plains, except when they came down on their annual cold-weather treks to exchange wool and other produce for salt and tea at the marts of the valley.

This isolation has continued, though to a somewhat reduced

extent, under Indian rule; but a vigorous programme of education, economic improvement, public health services and better communications has been embarked upon through the medium of a greatly expanded frontier administrative service, and large numbers of people from the plains of Assam share in these benefits. Ostensibly, the policy was to protect the simple, tribal mountaineers from 'exploitation' by more advanced elements among the plains people. This policy, naturally, has not been popular with the leaders and people of the Assam plains, who would have liked to see the hills and the plains integrated under one administration. But obviously it has succeeded in securing the loyalty of the hill tribal people, who have remained unaffected by the short occupation of their territory by the Chinese after their rapid invasion and almost as rapid withdrawal. The descent of more than ten thousand tribal evacuees to the plains of Assam, even if their stay is only temporary, will act as a cementing medium between the hills and the plains and there is no doubt that the process of integration of the two peoples will be speeded up.

But while this political boundary has existed as a barrier to humans for more than a hundred years, ever since the annexation of Assam by the British, there has been no barrier to the movements of wild life of the sub-Himalayan zone. Elephants in particular are great travellers and migrate between lower and upper altitudes according to the seasons. The elephants which are captured annually in the plains bordering the foothills of the NEFA and Bhutan belong to the same herds which wander up into the mountains of the NEFA. Stockades are built at the base of the hills near salt-licks and mela shikar is done in the plains. Since the creation of the NEFA, a separate Forest Department has come into existence and they now conduct their own catching inside the line. Thus the elephants are being subjected to double pressure.

Official enforcement of the Elephant Preservation Act in the tribal areas of the Assam hills has never been as strict as it is in the plains and the Act was only extended to the NEFA region in 1962. There troublesome elephants have always been dealt with rapidly and effectively. With virile hunters like the Abors and

Daflas, the killing of an elephant presented no difficulty, even in the days when guns were less plentiful than they are now. These tribes have always used poisoned arrows for fighting and hunting. One of the methods of killing an elephant is to hang a poisoned dart fixed in the end of a heavy log of wood above an elephant path; there is a tripping arrangement and the unsuspecting elephant passing under the booby trap brings it crashing down on to its neck or back, with fatal results. The poison is obtained either from the croton plant or from aconite; Daflas use a mixture of the two. The poisons are collected and prepared in accordance with certain rituals, accompanied by prayers. Fifty years ago the Abor expedition was sent up the Dihang or Tsangpo river to avenge the death of two Britishers, one of them the Political Officer, at the hands of the Abors; they brought back frightening accounts of the deadly poisoned arrows. The effects on human beings were almost instantaneous, the symptoms being convulsions and tetanus.

In 1954, an anthropologist on an official tour of the Siang valley described how an elephant was killed with a single shot from a muzzle-loading gun, the ammunition being a poisoned dart instead of a bullet. When charged by the rogue, an Abor had fired at point-blank range and then turned and ran. After some time he discovered that he was not being pursued and went back with some armed men from his village to find the elephant dead. Naturally there was great jubilation and the whole locality collected to cut up and share the meat. The killer, a very ordinary looking middle-aged man named Ogen Tayeng, was acclaimed for his feat but he modestly gave the credit to 'Gaumen Soin', son of Sedi-Malo (mother earth and father sky), the presiding deity of the village. He had made the poison from roots of the Em plant, brought from the fields of the gods of the northern snowy mountain. The poison had been pounded on the grinding stone in the sacred corner of the village, where it was mixed with the juice of the holy creeper, Talo, which sprouted from the haversack of the great hunter, Kari, after his death. The elephant, who was an intruder, was apparently unaware of all this and paid with his life for daring to attack one who was held in affection by the gods.

This was the explanation of the simple inhabitant of these northern mountains, which were described by a seventeenth-century Indian explorer as 'another world, whose frightful roads are like paths leading to death and whose great forests are full of violence like the hearts of the ignorant'.

But although the tribal people living in the tempo of an outdated civilization have been unable to exterminate the elephant, the forces of modern development and integration are threatening its existence in this last stronghold. The urge to grow more crops, build more roads and generally to spread the benefits of modern life – these inevitably have meant a greater clash between elephants and men in the NEFA. It is significant that there are now demands for the control of elephants. The recent hostilities between China and India, and the prospects of further military operations and development programmes to support them, seem to spell a death knell for the elephants of the eastern Himalayas. There is a price on their heads, but it is not gold.

In spite of the generally decreasing demand for elephants, more than three hundred are still captured every year in eastern India and about twelve hundred were caught in Assam between 1955 and 1960. No wild animal has served man more faithfully through the ages, yet the future of the Indian elephant is as dark as that of his African cousin – if anything it is darker, for the African elephant can be eaten by many sections of the people and might be 'farmed' for its meat, but this is not the case in India. Now that this noble animal is at a crossroads in its history with the introduction of the machine age and the rapid shrinkage of its range through settlement and cultivation, it is useful to pause and reflect on its future.

Stockade catching is not practised so much nowadays because of the heavy capital cost involved; and in any case stockades are generally unsuccessful because of the disappearance of large herds. There is little doubt that the breaking up and scattering of family groups has been caused by continuous and excessive mela shikar, an operation which removes mainly the calves and increases the proportion of large and solitary elephants. According to an experienced catcher, one very rarely nowadays comes across cows with two or three calves at heel, as was common twenty-five years ago. The zoologist can see but one end result of this process: a steady diminution of the stock as a whole.

Where elephant catching is practised by mela shikar or some variant of this method – such as the Balrampur system of the old United Provinces or the pitha shikar method of Nepal – where the attack is made by tame elephants themselves, it should be quite possible to protect crops directly by anchoring koonkis at strategic points. This was one of Milroy's ideas which I developed. The point is not to allow koonkis to wander all over a forest in search of wild elephants, but to fix their base camp so as to give them a five- or six-mile radius of action. This 'anchored' mela shikar works well in keeping off raiding herds and all but the most determined solitaries. But the method is not popular with elephant catchers, who like to be free to roam all over the forest.

It should be possible to subsidize this form of crop protection by charging royalties on elephants so captured. Such crop protection with koonkis was successfully tried out in Mysore by Neelakanta Rao as far back as 1934. In the same way, stockade catching can be subsidized and it is the only method which can cope successfully with large herds of elephants. It is disquieting that stockades are less and less popular in Assam, the main objection being their comparatively greater expense.

There remains the perennial objection to the system of proclaiming troublesome elephants or rogues, which means that anyone however inadequately armed can take a shot at such an animal; and the average hunter feels little obligation to follow up and put an end to a wounded elephant. The best solution would be if a scheme could be worked out whereby the expenditure on a cadre of game wardens would be recovered, even partially, from the value of the tusks recovered. At the same time there would be a considerable saving on rewards offered under proclamation. By these means it might be possible to do away at one stroke with both the systems of proclamation and of elephant control licence, which are found side by side in Asasm. Such a scheme would ensure that only the elephant which is really giving trouble is bumped off, and then only after every effort has first been made to drive it away. It would also give an opportunity for the employment of all those crop-protection methods which one talks and hears so much about but which, if left to the initiative of the local cultivator, remain nothing more than ideas. Finally, the scheme could be tied in with the more general one of protection of crops and farms from other wild animals such as deer and pig, and of livestock from tigers and leopards. This is a matter which is assuming greater importance as the need becomes urgent for general conservation of fauna on the one hand and expansion of cultivation on the other.

If India cannot afford more than token game staffs, even in those regions where the elephant is added to the number of species threatening man's crops and livestock, is it too much to visualize a time when regular shooting licences will be issued on payment of fairly heavy fees and with substantial precautions, as is done in parts of Africa? True the Asian cow elephant does not carry ivory as does its African cousin, nor do all males carry tusks; but in an era of international tourism and professional shikar outfits on the 'white hunter' model, the idea might well work out satisfactorily. There are many people who would rather see an elephant fall to the powerful modern rifle of a sportsman than filled with lead from cultivators' muzzle-loaders, or wounded painfully by inadequately armed local shikaris.

As far as future demands for domesticated elephants are concerned, in the north of India the main market is that part of Bihar south of Nepal where the keeping of elephants is to some extent a necessity owing to the rather sketchy communications and the several turbulent rivers which have to be crossed. Here elephants are still widely used for moving about and in addition, marriages are seldom complete without an elephant to carry the bridegroom. In the south, the trade is based almost entirely on the demand for timber-dragging elephants, but these animals are also kept in the service of temples and by private owners for marriage and religious processions. The supply is based on limited captures obtained by pitting in the west coast forests and from the occasional Mysore kheddas.

Exports to circuses and zoos all over the world also account for a portion of the demand that still exists for elephants in India as a whole. As far as can be foreseen, the shrinking of the forest areas in the Western Ghats will mean a decline in the number of elephants there and the main source is likely to be the forests of Mysore and Madras east of the Nilgiri plateau, in the two large adjoining sanctuaries of Mudumalai and Bandipur.

It would certainly be possible to explore new ways of utilizing this powerful and docile creature other than in the conventional task of timber hauling, its pleasant employment on shikar and tiger hunting, and the traditional customs of using it for processions. There would, for instance, appear to be scope for using the elephant for ploughing and farm work, particularly in areas where conventional ploughs drawn by bullocks cannot be used. There are marginal lands and riverine tracts in the very areas where the elephant is found at present which would respond to the use of disc or mould-board ploughs of suitable design and hauling gear with trained elephants. In one of our big land-reclamation projects a few years ago I initiated such an experiment with promising results, but I could not follow it up. The credit for thoroughly exploring the idea must go to Uttar Pradesh where, as the result of the interest shown by the then Deputy Minister of Forests, various types of ploughs and attachment gear were tried out in the sub-Himalayan terai belt. Eventually a satisfactory arrangement was worked out, although the labour and production figures as compared with tractor ploughing were not very encouraging. But it must be remembered that the experiments were carried out with an ordinary Forest Department elephant unused to dragging loads and I am confident that with practice and training the results would have been much better. The experiments died a natural death with the disappearance of the minister in question through the processes of democracy, but it is essential that they be renewed in the interests of the future of the elephant in that part of India.

Even in a commercial age, when machinery and tractors adapted to working in the mud of a normal paddy field threaten such so-called primitive methods as bullock ploughing, there should be room for the elephant to play his part in the agricultural economy of the country. Perhaps when the problem of thinning out the elephant herds in the UP and the adoption of a suitable type of catching has been solved, the idea of ploughing with elephants in sub-montane country will be revived.

Very recently, elephants have been employed successfully to shunt railway wagons in the Raja Buland sugar mills yards at Rampur. They were made to push the wagons with their foreheads and it was found that a single elephant can move seventy-five tons of rolling stock at a speed of two hundred and fifty to three hundred feet per minute on level track, effecting a considerable annual saving over the use of man power. The animals have proved particularly useful in the monsoon season. As sugar-cane is one of the staple foods of the elephant, there seems no limit to the possibilities in connection with the numerous sugar factories of the Gangetic plain.

Assam has for long had the most humane elephant catching rules in India and a tradition of domestication of the animal which goes back into the dim past. This country is eminently suitable for the employment of the elephant on such tasks as ploughing, hauling and dragging of loads and vehicles; but, except for timber dragging, and in a few places for drawing high-wheeled carts to carry cane in the Majuli, the elephant is used for no work other than the catching and training of its wild fellows. Yet, if we are to believe the traditions and stories handed down through generations, the ancient Assamese even domesticated the rhinoceros and used it for ploughing.

Judging by what has been taking place in the past fifty years, the Asian elephant will eventually be pushed back to the more extensive forested areas and its numbers will gradually fall to the level of the carrying capacity of those areas. But, as it is a fairly prolific breeder and has acquired a taste for the crops and products of man, the problem of its control will always be there. With such a powerful and intelligent animal this will naturally present great difficulties. In fact it is now recognized to be virtually impossible to protect cultivation completely from elephants, though the degree of success achieved is largely a question of how much time and trouble one is prepared to put into the task – which, when translated into economic terms, means how much money.

If the planter of commercial crops like tea or coffee finds it burdensome and expensive to protect his estate effectively from the depredations of elephants, the position of the small farmer or rice cultivator can well be imagined. In areas where herds have been isolated by land-development projects, as in Ceylon, the problems are even worse. When I first came to the country we had one such problem area in Assam, created by the isolation of a forested area adjoining the hills. The situation is not yet completely satisfactory in spite of repeated catching and the destruction of two out of the three bulls that were with the small herd based on the Deroi reserve, from where raids were carried out on the cultivation and tea-gardens all round. In these pockets there is nothing to be done except exterminate the elephants.

To the friend and well-wisher of the elephant it would appear that the onus of responsibility for its future must lie with the authorities and governments concerned. Elephants are a part of the natural wealth of a country in which they are found and if the era of profit from this long-suffering and outstandingly lovable animal has gone never to return, there must be all the more an awakening to the realization that they are now our responsibility. The main hope lies in the fact that in the east the domestication of the elephant is part of the very culture of the people. If this were not the case, the future would look very dim indeed. It is up to man, the elephant's friend throughout the ages, to take decisive steps to ensure its preservation if this animal is not to face intolerable pressure for existence.

In Assam especially, the land of the sage Palakapya who wandered with the wild elephants until he almost became one of them himself, perhaps it is not too much to hope that her people and their leaders will repay the debt of thousands of years of the trade in 'elephant gold' which has been wrung from this noble animal.

GLOSSARY

Ankus: *Hooked goad for driving and controlling elephants.*

Bait, baito: *Sit down.*
Banda: *Figure-of-eight tying of fore-legs of elephant.*
Bandh: *Breed or type of elephant.*
Banji: *Barren.*
Basha: *Grass hut.*
Betoni: *Cane-bearing.*
Bhadralog: *Gentleman.*
Bhang: *Hashish, prepared from the hemp plant.*
Bheel: *Swamp.*
Bihu: *Spring festival of Assam.*
Bor phandi: *Great or head phandi.*

Chota peg: *Small measure of whisky, etc.*

Dak bungalow: *Post stage, traveller's rest-house.*
Dal: *Creeping grass which grows in swamps.*
Dandi: *Elephant path.*
Dao: *Knife for cutting jungle.*
Degi: *Figure-of-eight tying of hind-legs of elephant.*
Dhoti: *Garment worn by Indian men.*
Dhui: *Female elephant which has calved.*

Gaja-mukta: *Elephant 'pearl'.*
Gaja shastra: *Elephant lore.*
Gajali shikar: *Noosing of elephants at the time of the new grass.*
Ghat: *River wharf or crossing; also hilly area.*
Ghee: *Clarified butter.*
Gonesh: *Single-tusked elephant.*
Goonda: *Bad character, rowdy; applied to large male elephants, particularly to makhnas.*
Guddi: *Elephant pad or saddle.*
Gur: *Unrefined sugar, molasses.*

Hal: *Enclosure resembling the ancient stocks in which elephants are trained.*

Hathi, hasthin: *Elephant.*

Hathi jokar: *Elephant shivers, induced by the proximity of wild elephants.*

Hathiputhi: *Ancient book on elephants written on bark of sassi tree (Aquillaria agallocha).*

Howdah: *Platform with seats for riding on elephant-back.*

Jemadar: *Supervising officer.*

Kamla: *Grass cutter.*

Khedda, khedna: *To drive; driving of elephants into a stockade (hence the stockade itself).*

Koomeriah: *Royal or best breed of elephant.*

Koonki: *Tame elephant trained for elephant catching.*

Koonkidar: *Onwer of koonki.*

Kraal: *Name for elephant stockade in Ceylon; elephant training enclosure in south India.*

Kukur singia: *Tracking elephants in khedda operations, literally 'dog tracking'.*

Kumaki: *Name used in south India for koonki.*

Lungi: *Length of cloth worn like a skirt by men.*

Machan: *Platform in tree from which to shoot animals.*

Mahal: *Lease area for elephant catching.*

Mahaldar: *Lease holder of elephant-catching area.*

Mahout: *Elephant driver.*

Maidan shikar: *Catching elephants in open grassy plains.*

Makhna: *Tuskless male elephant.*

Mal jooria: *Association of two or three wild elephant bulls.*

Mela: *Fair connected with religious festival; elephant market.*

Mela shikar: *Noosing wild elephants from backs of tame elephants.*

Mreega: *'Deer' type (weedy type) of elephant.*

Musth: *Psychological disturbance in male elephant, associated with sexual periodicity and accompanied by discharge of fluid from the temporal glands.*

Pagla: *Mad.*

Panthi: *Kraal, enclosure of teak beams for training elephants.*

Peepul: *Ficus religiosa, a tree sacred to the Hindus.*

Phandi: *Professional elephant nooser.*

Pilkhana:	*Place where elephants are tethered, training depot.*
Pitha shikar:	*Form of mela shikar practised in Nepal, literally 'driving and catching'.*
Puja:	*Religious ceremony of a propitiatory nature.*
Raj garh:	*High embankment built by the Ahom kings of Assam and used as road or protection wall.*
Sakhna:	*Male elephant with short, upturning tusks.*
Sakhni:	*Female elephant with tusks.*
Sambhar:	*Large deer,* Cervus unicolor.
Sarin:	*Young female elephant which has not yet calved.*
Satra:	*Hindu Vaishnavite monastery of Assam.*
Shikar:	*Hunting, shooting, catching.*
Sirdar:	*Head man, leader.*
Sodager:	*Elephant trader.*
Terai:	*Swampy area some distance from foothills of Himalayas.*
Than:	*Place where elephants are tethered.*
Topee:	*Sun helmet.*
Tushes:	*Tusk-like development of elephant's incisors, pointing downwards rather than upwards as in the case of tusks.*
Zamindar:	*Large land-owner.*